MARK

MARK

FORTRESS BIBLICAL
PREACHING COMMENTARIES

DAVID SCHNASA JACOBSEN

Fortress Press
Minneapolis

MARK
Fortress Biblical Preaching Commentaries

Cover design: Laurie Ingram

Library of Congress Cataloging-in-Publication Data
Print ISBN: 978-0-8006-9923-9
eBook ISBN: 978-1-4514-3094-3

The paper used in this publication meets the minimum requirements of American National Standard for Information Sciences — Permanence of Paper for Printed Library Materials, ANSI Z329.48-1984.

Manufactured in the U.S.A.

This book was produced using PressBooks.com, and PDF rendering was done by PrinceXML.

CONTENTS

Series Foreword   vii

Acknowledgements   ix

Readings from Mark in the Revised Common Lectionary in   xi
Order of the Liturgical Calendar, Year B

Readings from Mark in the Revised Common Lectionary in   xv
Order of Mark's Narrative

Introduction   1

1. Prologue to Mark's Gospel (1:1-15)   23

2. The Gospel's Promising Beginnings in Galilee (1:16—3:6)   35

3. The Gospel Mystery Deepens— The Word of Promise in   57
   Wider Fields (3:7—6:6a)

4. The Rocky Way— The Word of Promise and The Disciples'   87
   Misunderstanding (6:6b—8:26)

5. Gospel Interlude— Revelation on the Way (8:27—9:13)   117

6. Teaching and More Misunderstanding on The Way   129
   (9:14—10:52)

7. The Gospel in Jerusalem (11:1—12:44)   159

8. An Apocalyptic Farewell Address (13:1-37)   183

9. The Passion of Mark's Gospel (14:1—15:47)   195

10. Epilogue: Mark 16   221

Appendix: Further Preaching Resources on Mark's Gospel   231

Series Foreword

A preacher who seeks to be creative, exegetically up to date, hermeneutically alert, theologically responsible, and in-touch with the moment is always on the hunt for fresh resources. Traditional books on preaching a book of the Bible often look at broad themes of the text with little explicit advice about preaching individual passages. Lectionary resources often offer exegetical and homiletical insights about a pericope with little attention given to broader themes and structures of the book from which the lection is taken. *Fortress Biblical Preaching Commentaries* provide the preacher with resources that draw together the strengths of these two approaches into a single text aid, useful for the moment of preparation halfway between full scale exegesis and a finished sermon.

The authors of this series are biblical scholars who offer expositions of the text rooted in detailed study and expressed in straightforward, readable ways. The commentators take a practical approach by identifying (1) what the text invited people in the ancient world to believe about God and the world and (2) what the text encouraged people to do in response. Along the way, the interpreters make use of such things as historical and cultural reconstruction, literary and rhetorical analysis, word studies, and other methods that help us recover how a text was intended to function in antiquity. At the same time, the commentaries offer help in moving from then to now, from what a text meant (in the past) to what a text means (in the present), by helping a minister identify issues, raise questions, and pose possibilities for preaching while stopping short of placing a complete sermon in the preacher's hands. The preacher, then, should be in a position to set in motion a conversation with the text (and other voices from the past and present) to help the congregation figure out what we today can believe and do.

The commentators in this series seek to help preachers and students make connections between the various lections from a given book throughout the lectionary cycle and liturgical year in their sermons and studies. Readers, preachers, and their parishioners will have a deeper appreciation of the book's unique interpretation of the Christ event and how that influences their approach to living the Christian faith in today's world. The most life-giving preaching is nearly always local in character with a minister rooted in a particular congregation, culture, and context encouraging listeners to think specifically about how the text might relate to the life of the congregation and to the surrounding community and world. *Fortress Biblical Preaching Commentaries* are set forth in the hope that each volume will be a provocative voice in such conversations.

Acknowledgements

In the early twentieth century, a group of artists formed a collective in a small community just north of the German city of Bremen. The town of Worpswede was of no great repute. It sat on the edge of a long, sparsely inhabited swamp-like region known as the *Teufelsmoor*, the Devil's moor. One artist, a painter in the group, crafted a painting he called "the Sower." In the picture, the sower casts his seed on the ground—it is a typical motif and theme in painting from the period. But this artist's sower casts his seed across the strange landscape he came to know in the collective: the Devil's moor. As he does so, the sower casts his seed in the dark, but toward a small dawning light.

I suspect the writer of the first Gospel written would have understood. Mark's Jesus offers the beginning of his apocalyptic gospel and connects it deeply to a parabolic sowing. And it is indeed a seed cast across a dark landscape, a song in the darkness. Yet, amidst the darkness, Mark's Gospel speaks a promise of dawning light.

It was because of this strange apocalyptic promise of Mark that I was so glad to learn that I would be tapped to write a commentary on Mark's Gospel for this series. Mark had long fascinated me. In fact, my first exposure to Koine Greek as a classics minor in my undergraduate work was in Mark. To my mind, this seed had been germinating for some time! For this reason, I want to acknowledge with gratitude the invitation I received from Will Bergkamp, Publisher and Managing Director of Fortress Press, to develop this volume. Its orientation to biblical scholarship and lectionary preaching practice allowed me to see the promise of bringing New Testament studies and homiletical theology into deeper dialogue.

Along the way, I also was reminded of several gifts, old and new, that made it all possible. Two former NT colleagues, Drs. Günter Wasserberg and Tim Hegedus, whom I came to know during my time at Waterloo Lutheran Seminary in Canada, were gracious in providing feedback to early versions of this commentary. Whatever errors remain, of course, are mine. They provided wise and helpful counsel as I developed this work.

Now that I am two years into my new appointment to Boston University School of Theology, however, I need to acknowledge new gifts that helped further cultivate this promising seed. I am grateful to my new colleagues in Boston who have already reinvigorated my scholarship and especially to my new Dean, Mary Elizabeth Moore. She helped make it possible for me to take a sabbatical during my first year in Boston—without which this commentary could not have been written in such a timely fashion. She also has supported me in developing the Homiletical Theology Project (http://www.bu.edu/homiletical-theology-project/), for which I now serve as Director. This project's research agenda has already begun to shape the way I understand my work as a homiletician—and its influence can be seen in the pages that follow. I am grateful to her and the Boston University School of Theology for their support.

I write these words of thanks in the transition from summer to fall, on a liturgical day with an apocalyptic cast tied to the harvest. I cannot help but think that Mark would find it fitting.

With gratitude,

Prof. David Schnasa Jacobsen
Boston University School of Theology
Feast of St. Michael and all Angels, September 29, 2013

Readings from Mark in the Revised Common Lectionary in Order of the Liturgical Calendar, Year B

Liturgical dates are omitted when a Gospel other than Mark is used.

Liturgical Date	Mark	Pericope Title	Page Number
Season of Advent			
Advent 1	13:24–37	The Coming of the Son of the Human, the Lesson of the Fig Tree, and the Necessity for Watchfulness	190
Advent 2	1:1–8	The Preaching of John the Baptist	26
Season of Epiphany (Ordinary Time)			
Baptism of the Lord	1:4–11	The Baptism of Jesus	28
Epiphany 3	1:14–20	Jesus Calls the First Disciples	36
Epiphany 4	1:21–28	The Man with an Unclean Spirit	38
Epiphany 5	1:29–39	Jesus Heals Many at Simon's House and a Preaching Tour in Galilee	40
Epiphany 6	1:40–45	Jesus Cleanses a Leper	42
Epiphany 7	2:1–12	Jesus Heals a Paralytic	45
Epiphany 8	2:13–22	Jesus Calls Levi and the Question about Fasting	48
Epiphany 9/Proper 4	2:23—3:6	Plucking Grain on the Sabbath and the Man with a Withered Hand	51

Transfiguration of the Lord	9:2-9	The Transfiguration [and The Coming of Elijah]	124
Season of Lent			
Lent 1	1:9-15	The Baptism of Jesus, the Temptation of Jesus, and the Beginning of the Galilean Ministry	31
Lent 2	8:31-38	Peter's Declaration about Jesus and Jesus Foretells his Death and Resurrection	118
Lent 2 (alt)	9:2-9	The Transfiguration	124
Palm/Passion: Liturgy of the Palms	11:1-11; and 14:1—15:47	Jesus' Triumphal Entry in to Jerusalem	165, 202
Palm/Passion: Liturgy of the Passion	15:1-39, (40-47) (Alt.)	The Passion of Mark's Gospel	202
Season of Easter			
Easter Vigil	16:1-8	The Resurrection of Jesus	225
Easter Sunday	16:1-8 (Alt.)	The Resurrection of Jesus	225
Season after Pentecost (Ordinary Time)			
Proper 4: 5/29-6/4	2:23—3:6	Plucking Grain on the Sabbath and the Man with a Withered Hand	51
Proper 5: 6/5-11	3:20-35	Jesus and Beelzebul and the True Kindred of Jesus	62
Proper 6: 6/12-18	4:26-34	The Parable of the Growing Seed, the Parable of the Mustard Seed, and the Use of Parables	72
Proper 7: 6/19-25	4:35-41	Jesus Stills a Storm	74
Proper 8: 6/26-7/2	5:21-43	A Girl Restored to Life and a Woman Healed	80
Proper 9: 7/3-9	6:1-13	The Rejection of Jesus at Nazareth and the Mission of the Twelve	83, 93
Proper 10: 7/10-16	6:14-29	The Death of John the Baptist	93
Proper 11: 7/17-23	6:30-34, 53-56	The Twelve Return and Healing the Sick in Genessaret	97

Proper 17: 8/28-9/3	7:1-8, 14-15, 21-23	The Tradition of the Elders	100
Proper 18: 9/4-10	7:24-37	The Syrophoenician Woman's Faith and Jesus Cures a Deaf Man	103
Proper 19: 9/11-17	8:27-38	Peter's Declaration about Jesus and Jesus Foretells his Death and Resurrection	118
Proper 20: 9/18-24	9:30-37	Jesus Again Foretells His Death and Resurrection and Who is the Greatest?	135
Proper 21: 9/25-10/1	9:38-50	Another Exorcist and Temptations to Sin	138
Proper 22: 10/2-8	10:2-16	Teaching about Divorce and Jesus Blesses Little Children	145
Proper 23: 10/9-15	10:17-31	The Rich Man	149
Proper 24: 10/16-22	10:35-45	The Request of James and John	152
Proper 25: 10/23-29	10:46-52	The Healing of Blind Bartimaeus	155
Proper 26: 10/30-11/5	12:28-34	The Great Commandment	177
Proper 27: 11/6-12	12:38-44	The Denouncing of the Scribes and the Widow's Offering	180
Proper 28: 11/13-19	13:1-8	The Destruction of the Temple Foretold	188

Readings from Mark in the Revised Common Lectionary in Order of Mark's Narrative

(Liturgical dates are in Year B unless otherwise indicated.)

Mark	Pericope Title	Liturgical Date	Page Number
Prologue to Mark's Gospel			
1:1-8	The Preaching of John the Baptist	Advent 2	26
1:4-11	The Baptism of Jesus	Baptism of the Lord	28
1:9-15	The Baptism of Jesus, the Temptation of Jesus, and the Beginning of the Galilean Ministry	Lent 1	31
The Gospel's Promising Beginnings in Galilee			
1:14-20	Jesus Calls the First Disciples	Epiphany 3	36
1:21-28	The Man with an Unclean Spirit	Epiphany 4	38
1:29-39	Jesus Heals Many at Simon's House and a Preaching Tour in Galilee	Epiphany 5	40
1:40-45	Jesus Cleanses a Leper	Epiphany 6	42
2:1-12	Jesus Heals a Paralytic	Epiphany 7	45
2:13-22	Jesus Calls Levi and the Question about Fasting	Epiphany 8	48
2:23—3:6	Plucking Grain on the Sabbath and the Man with a Withered Hand	Epiphany 9/Proper 4: 5/29-6/4	51
The Gospel Mystery Deepens—The Word of Promise in Wider Fields			

3:20–35	Jesus and Beelzebul and the True Kindred of Jesus	Proper 5: 6/5–11	62
4:26–34	The Parable of the Growing Seed, the Parable of the Mustard Seed, and the Use of Parables	Proper 6: 6/12–18	72
4:35–41	Jesus Stills a Storm	Proper 7: 6/19–25	74
5:21–43	A Girl Restored to Life and a Woman Healed	Proper 8: 6/26–7/2	80
6:1–13	The Rejection of Jesus at Nazareth and the Mission of the Twelve	Proper 9: 7/3–9	83, 93

The Rocky Way—The Word of Promise and the Disciples' Misunderstanding

6:14–29	The Death of John the Baptist	Proper 10: 7/10–16	93
6:30–34, 53–56	The Twelve Return and Healing the Sick in Genessaret	Proper 11: 7/17–23	97
7:1–8, 14–15, 21–23	The Tradition of the Elders	Proper 17: 8/28–9/3	100
7:24–37	The Syrophoenician Woman's Faith and Jesus Cures a Deaf Man	Proper 18: 9/4–10	103

Gospel Interlude—Revelation on the Way

8:27–38	Peter's Declaration about Jesus and Jesus Foretells his Death and Resurrection	Proper 19: 9/11–17	118
8:31–38 (Alt.)	Peter's Declaration about Jesus and Jesus Foretells his Death and Resurrection	Lent 2	118
9:2–9 (Alt.)	The Transfiguration [and The Coming of Elijah]	Lent 2	124
9:2–9	The Transfiguration [and The Coming of Elijah]	Transfiguration of the Lord	124

Teaching and More Misunderstanding on the Way

9:30–37	Jesus Again Foretells His Death and Resurrection and Who is the Greatest?	Proper 20: 9/18–24	135

9:38–50	Another Exorcist and Temptations to Sin	Proper 21: 9/25–10/1	138
10:2–16	Teaching about Divorce and Jesus Blesses Little Children	Proper 22: 10/2–8	145
10:17–31	The Rich Man	Proper 23: 10/9–15	149
10:35–45	The Request of James and John	Proper 24: 10/16–22	152
10:46–52	The Healing of Blind Bartimaeus	Proper 25: 10/23–29	155
The Gospel in Jerusalem			
11:1–11 (Alt.) (palms)	Jesus' Triumphal Entry in to Jerusalem	Palm/Passion Sunday: Liturgy of the Palms	165
12:28–34	The Great Commandment	Proper 26: 10/30–11/5	177
12:38–44	The Denouncing of the Scribes and the Widow's Offering	Proper 27: 11/6–12	180
An Apocalyptic Farewell Address			
13:1–8	The Destruction of the Temple Foretold	Proper 28: 11/13–19	188
13:24–37	The Coming of the Son of the Human, the Lesson of the Fig Tree, and the Necessity for Watchfulness	Advent 1	190
The Passion of Mark's Gospel			
14:1—15:47 (Alt.)	The Passion of Mark's Gospel	Palm/Passion Sunday: Liturgy of the Passion	202
15:1–39 (40–47) (Alt.)	The Passion of Mark's Gospel	Palm/Passion Sunday: Liturgy of the Passion	202
Epilogue			
16:1–8 (Alt.)	The Resurrection of Jesus	Easter Sunday	225
16:1–8	The Resurrection of Jesus	Easter Vigil	225

Introduction

Week in and week out churches in many North American denominations hear the reading of a Sunday lection from the Gospels. It has become so routine that we may not ever really think how much we owe this to the writer we Christians customarily call Mark. Mark's was the first Gospel with this now common designation. It was in all likelihood the first of the four written in the Bible. It even begins its narrative at 1:1 with a title calling attention to its purpose: "The beginning of the good news (*euaggelion* = gospel) of Jesus Christ, [Son of God]" (parentheses mine). Please notice the lowercase "g" on Mark's first reference to the term *gospel* or *good news*. Mark, it appears, was simply trying to show that his writing was a kind of narrative rendering of what by 70 c.e. or so was known as the basic core of the gospel, theologically understood as the death and resurrection of Christ.[1] With Mark's new narrative interpretation, the word *gospel* includes Jesus' ministry and proclamation of God's kingdom along with his death and resurrection. What is amazing, however, is that this narrative gospel of Jesus' ministry, death, and resurrection eventually becomes a quasi-literary genre in the church, Mark's *Gospel*—hence the capital G. For after Mark writes his "beginning of the gospel," others within a generation seem to take up the literary task along with him. Matthew and Luke evidence clear literary dependence on Mark, and later, in his own quite different way, so does John. We go about today blithely reading aloud a Gospel lection Sunday to Sunday, but it need not have been so. Somehow around 70 c.e. Mark lays a groundwork in the form of what biblical scholar Frances Moloney calls a theologically driven narrative[2] that causes others to write and still many other others to hear and expect a narrative rendering of Jesus' ministry, death, and resurrection.

Of course, we need to be careful about such generic statements. We today can call Mark the first of the Gospel genre all we like, but if we do we may just occlude some important truths. Genre is in actuality a literary term, not a theological one. And in literature there is no such thing as a genre *sui generis*. Whatever Mark is writing, theologically driven or not, is influenced profoundly by the literary and cultural context of his age. Moreover, Mark is also more generally a creature of his time and culture. Since he writes in the common

---

1. James D. G. Dunn, *Jesus, Paul, and the Gospels* (Grand Rapids: Eerdmans, 2011).

2. Francis Moloney, *The Gospel of Mark: A Commentary* (Peabody, MA: Hendrickson, 2002), xvii.

Koine Greek of his day and his text shows he seems to know a little bit about Aramaic (5:41; 7:34) and deals in the occasional Latinism, he must have been the beneficiary of some education. In all likelihood, this meant not only knowing languages, but how to communicate in them. Education in the Greco-Roman world meant some exposure to grammar and rhetoric and with it, practice exercises in imitating epic storytellers like Homer.[3] It is one thing to note that Mark wrote a work that subsequently influenced the ways in which Christians and their lectionary committees later used the word *Gospel*; it is quite another thing to argue that Mark's Gospel somehow emerged *ex nihilo*. It did not.

For that matter, even the limited theological way that we wish to speak of these gospel developments must be qualified somewhat. The irony is that Mark's gospel, Mark's *theology* itself appears "unfinished." His title at 1:1 reads "the *beginning* of the gospel" (emphasis mine). By the time this work ends—and most scholars agree it is at 16:8—Mark's writing seems downright elliptical: "and they said nothing to anyone, for they were afraid." What kind of ending is that? Many readers are left scratching their heads. To underline the point that this is not merely a modern problem, it is also helpful to note that ancient writers were likely no less satisfied with Mark's ending than we. Within a relatively short historical timespan there is an addition to Mark's text (16:9-20) as well as the writing of Matthew and Luke in the latter part of the first century. The latter two authors seem to use Mark's structure, but clearly correct his "unfinished" ending in a much less ambiguous way with very elaborate resurrection appearances. I write this to point out something important about the way we often think of the Bible, especially the New Testament. By virtue of our liturgical practice (some of us likely stand when a Gospel lection is read) and the unique theologies of which we are heirs, we are inclined to think of a writing like Mark's as vested with an authoritative perfection and completeness. Mark's ending bears witness to something different: an unfinished theology. As we shall see, I am convinced it is because Mark invites us to join in his gospel task not so much as indifferent spectators but as disciples who despite the narrative's failure hear also the promise that the risen Jesus is going ahead to Galilee.[4] It may just be Mark's way of helping us so to lay hold of the promise that we theologically begin to put our own oar in the water.

---

3. Mary Ann Tolbert, *Sowing the Gospel: Mark's World in Literary-Historical Perspective* (Minneapolis: Fortress Press, 1989), 36–37.

4. Andrew Lincoln has identified this crucial issue of promise and failure around the ending of Mark as being key for interpreting several parts of the Markan narrative in "The promise and the failure: Mark 16:7,8," *Journal of Biblical Literature* 108.2 (Summer 1989), 283-300.

But if we are to find our way through this unfinished Gospel, and attempt to preach its theologically unfinished gospel, we need to do more than a little homework first. We need to work our way back through the tradition. It is important for us to know the interpretive history in which we stand so we can hear Mark's own voice clearly. That done, then we need to come to some basic understandings about Mark, his historical context, the kind of writing he was producing (genre), its relation to other such writings, and its possible provenance. Once we do so, we will also take some time to consider Mark's characteristic ways of writing—his rhetorical and literary style as well as their relation to his apocalyptic mode and the theological worldview it evokes. These, too, will help us appreciate the unique character of Mark's Gospel before we begin. Along the way we will discover that Mark's Gospel is not just "unfinished," but bears with it a compelling sense of apocalyptic mystery and urgency. While these realities will complicate the preacher's task, they will at the same time also strengthen it.

MARK IN THE HISTORY OF INTERPRETATION

The Revised Common Lectionary has been relatively kind to Mark. Yet with almost no exceptions (Easter Vigil A and C, for example), Mark is confined to Year B of the lectionary. Because of the shortness of Mark's Gospel relative to the others and its nearly exclusive treatment in this one lectionary cycle, the vast majority of the Gospel is in fact covered in Sunday readings. In fact, only 156 verses are not actually read aloud on a Sunday morning in Year B. That means that about 77 percent of the total of Mark will actually be heard at some point during that year. Yet at the same time, it is also important to know what is left out in the remaining unread 23 percent: two of Mark's most important parables (the Sower and the Wicked Tenants), the Gerasene Demoniac, the two great feeding miracles, and half of Jesus' eschatological discourse in chapter 13 among other things. The result of the decision to leave these texts out is that some significant parts of Mark's theological vision have been left out. The preacher will need to work at helping hearers understand this gospel "whole" given the relatively small yet nonetheless significant holes the lectionary has left in even this otherwise well covered Gospel.

It should also be noted that Mark has not always been so beloved in the history of interpretation. Already with Augustine it was assumed that Mark was actually just a Reader's Digest version of Matthew. The upshot of this was that Mark was not typically the object of much concern for preachers and scholars alike for much of its history in the canon. Over the centuries, relatively few commentaries were written on Mark. In fact, it was not until the nineteenth century that scholars turned to Mark because of his seemingly simple, unadorned writing. Their thought was that Mark, in all of its primitive form or framework, was *more* likely to offer information of interest to someone looking for the Jesus of history and with less theological prejudice.[5] The view that Mark was not as theologically invested in his subject matter went somewhat by the wayside with the publication of Wilhelm Wrede's *The Messianic Secret.* Wrede argued that Jesus' command to keep messianic claims quiet showed that Mark's messianic claims about him were a dogmatic invention of the church.[6] Clearly Mark was viewed as having not just an agenda of historical remembrance, but a theological agenda. However, in the eyes of the church, even in this view Mark was seen as wanting compared to the more towering theological perspectives of Matthew, Luke, and John.

Nonetheless, even with the dismissal of Mark's "framework" as a window to the historical Jesus, studies in Mark's Gospel continued to multiply among scholars. One of the first and most prominent developments was the rise of source criticism. While the debate is ongoing, it has been for some time largely a matter of consensus among scholars that Mark, contra Augustine, is no mere abbreviation of Matthew, but is in fact a chief source for both Matthew and Luke. The implication of this, of course, is that Mark is by virtual consensus believed to be the earliest of the Gospels. Later form critics like Rudolf Bultmann and Martin Dibelius then turned to Mark and the other Gospels as a place where oral traditions about Jesus were brought together. It could be that Mark's rough style with its doublets (repeated stories) and occasional non-sequiturs is the result of working with prior traditions that had been preserved orally in Christian communities between Jesus' death on the cross and the writing of Mark's Gospel some thirty to forty years later. Redaction critics like Willi Marxsen continued to work with Mark, but tried to use the findings of the form critics as a way to identify Mark's theology. The idea was that Mark did not simply receive and compile oral traditions, but actually edited them and formed them into the Gospel of Mark.[7]

---

5. The argument is that Mark's Gospel manages to provide us with a basic "framework," a sound and reliable basis for reconstructing the life of Jesus. See H. J. Holtzmann, *Die synoptischen Evangelien: Ihr Ursprung und geschichtlicher Charakter* (Leipzig: Wilhelm Engelmann, 1863).

6. Wilhelm Wrede, *Das Messiasgeheimnis in den Evanglien: Zugleich ein Beitrag zum Verständnis des Markusevangeliums* (Göttingen: Vandenhoeck & Ruprecht, 1901).

7. Willi Marxsen, *Der Evanglist Markus: Studien zur Redaktionsgeschichte des Evangeliums* (Göttingen: Vandenhoeck & Ruprecht, 1956).

In the late twentieth century, Mark saw a resurgence of interest among narrative and literary critics. They found that as they read the Gospel "whole," as a work of literature, they were able to account for more and more of the Gospel. Whereas earlier scholars had seen Mark and other Gospel writers as collectors or editors of traditions who put together, as Martin Kähler put it, "passion narratives with extended introductions,"[8] these literary- and narrative-critics claimed to see something of a unity of the Markan vision. From stars of the literary-critical world like Frank Kermode to biblical scholars equipped with new interpretive approaches like David Rhoads (narrative), Mary Ann Tolbert (literary-historical), Robert Fowler (reader-response), and Tat-siong Benny Liew (postcolonial), Mark was now an important focus of attention.[9] Although many of the old questions remain about history, sources, oral forms, and redaction, this new group's interest in literary-critical questions has helped us peer ever more deeply into Mark's unique Gospel.

HISTORICAL BACKGROUND

At the center of all this, however, is a key set of questions about the production of the Gospel of Mark. These are largely questions of history. Who was Mark? For whom was he writing? What were his sources for writing the Gospel? What is the genre of the Gospel of Mark, that is, how would ancient persons have understood this text? How does Mark's Gospel relate to the others in the New Testament? Some of these questions cannot really be answered at present even as they can be profitably explored. Still, all of these questions are important to consider as we prepare to grasp the Gospel as a whole.

AUTHOR

The authorship of Mark is itself a great mystery. Some of the earliest written traditions offered by a bishop named Papias indicate that Mark helped Peter by writing down his memories of Jesus. Mark, he went on to say, did not write them down in order but in a way that suited him in his telling of the story. This

---

8. Martin Kähler, *The So-called Historical Jesus and the Historic Biblical Christ*, trans. C. Braaten (Philadelphia: Fortress Press, 1964), 80.

9. Frank Kermode, *The Genesis of Secrecy: On the Interpretation of Narrative* (Cambridge, MA: Harvard University Press, 1979); David Rhoads and Donald Michie, *Mark as Story: An Introduction to the Narrative of a Gospel* (Philadelphia: Fortress Press, 1982); Mary Ann Tolbert, *Sowing the Gospel;* Robert Fowler, *Let the Reader Understand: Reader-Response Criticism and the Gospel of Mark* (Minneapolis: Fortress Press, 1991); Tat-siong Benny Liew, *Politics of Parousia: Reading Mark Inter(con)textually* (Leiden: Brill, 1999).

does not tell us a whole lot. In fact, there are even some ancient traditions that relate Mark's Gospel not to Peter but Paul! The upshot is that we cannot say much that is definitive about the author from external evidence.

The internal evidence is not any better. The writing that we now attribute to Mark has no references to a "Mark." The title that we are accustomed to seeing associated with this writing in our Bibles is not in our most ancient manuscripts. The phrase "according to Mark" does not appear until later in the manuscript tradition. In fact, it would not need to appear unless and until there were more "Gospels." This is to say, the need to identify a Gospel as "The Gospel according to Mark" likely emerges only when more than one Gospel is brought together in a collection.

Having said that, we can affirm some of what we have already noted about the author we customarily call "Mark." He wrote in Greek and knew something about Latin and Aramaic as well. As a literate person, he probably had the kind of education that meant he was familiar on some level with basic training and exercises in grammar and rhetoric. The fact that he begins his writing with the title about the good news of Jesus Christ indicates that he is a Christian. At the same time, his knowledge of Judaism and the Jewish Scriptures indicates some familiarity with Jewish traditions. A mistake many contemporary Christians make about the authors and first readers of New Testament texts is the assumption that they were like most of us: gentile Christians. Toward the end of the first century, when Mark and the other Gospels were being written, Christianity was not yet an independent religion. Both the subject matter of the Gospels and their authors or readers should be understood in relation to a Jewish context. As we consider Mark's authorship, it would be wise to remember that we ought not so quickly extract him from the Jewish context of his sources, language, and writing.

PROVENANCE

The place of writing and the community for which Mark wrote are no less easy to discern. There are, in fact, multiple theories. Many have associated the Gospel of Mark with Rome. The traditions from Papias that relate Mark's Gospel to the Petrine tradition would fit with this view. Some commentators argue that the Gospel was written in a time of persecution and that this might have coincided with Nero's treatment of Christians in Rome in the mid to late 60s of the first century.[10] Some relate Mark to a Syrian provenance.[11] Here

10. Ben Witherington III offers an interesting and detailed case for this theory in *The Gospel of Mark: A Socio-Rhetorical Commentary* (Grand Rapids: Eerdmans, 2001), 26–31.

we have a community reasonably close to the turmoil of the Jewish War in the late 60s and a context where gentile and Jewish worlds meet. Another view locates Mark's writing in Galilee itself.[12] The advantage here is that it gives us a meaningful context for many of the distressing events that Mark describes in Jesus' apocalyptic discourse of chapter 13. It naturally links the production of Mark's Gospel with the destruction of the Temple in 70 C.E. More recently, some have argued that the text of Mark was written for a more general audience. In this view, the lack of context has more to do with the dislocation of the Mediterranean world marked by what Mary Ann Tolbert has noted as its characteristic mobility and insecurity—a world in which a travelling, dislocated Messiah would help make sense of dislocated Greco-Roman lives.[13] Others have argued that the circulation of the Gospel itself and its subsequent use by Matthew and Luke and the wider network of Christian communities itself bears witness to a broader audience than we would normally conceive.[14]

Again, however, the evidence in the text does not give us much to go on. In chapter 13 Mark appeals to the reader in an aside, but in no way reveals who he perceives the reader actually is. Mark's text emerges as the first of the Gospels, but without giving us too many cues that help us definitively discern its provenance.

SOURCES

The issue of Mark's sources probably should be understood in light of earlier discussion about the history of interpretation of Mark. The form critics set forth the idea that Mark gathered together oral traditions into his written Gospel, sometime around the 60s or 70s of the first century. Other scholars have posited other sources behind Mark. Helmut Koester, for example, has argued that our present version of Mark relied on pre-Markan traditions and evolved over several stages before developing into what we view as its canonical form in the second century.[15] Other scholars, on the basis of the two-source hypothesis

---

11. Joel Marcus exemplifies this Syrian view in his *Mark 1-8* (New York: Doubleday, 2000), 33–37.

12. Ched Myers, *Binding the Strongman: A Political Reading of Mark's Story of Jesus* (Maryknoll, NY: Orbis Books, 1988), 41–42.

13. Tolbert, *Sowing the Gospel,* 35–40.

14. Richard Bauckham, "For Whom Were Gospels Written?" in *The Gospels for All Christians: Rethinking the Gospel Audiences*, ed. R. Bauckham (Grand Rapids: Eerdmans, 1998), 12.

15. Helmut Koester, "History and Development of Mark's Gospel (From Mark to *Secret Mark* and "Canonical" Mark)" in *Colloquy on New Testament Studies: A Time for Reappraisal and Fresh Approaches*, ed. B. Corley (Macon, GA: Mercer University Press, 1983), 35–57.

of source criticism that we mentioned above, have argued that Mark in some instances may have drawn from "Q" (German for source, *Quelle*), a document that likely stands behind several other places where Matthew and Luke agree against Mark.[16] While redaction criticism in general has built on the notion, at least in Markan studies, that they can see Mark's editorial hand dealing with pre-Markan sources, these arguments have not really had a lot of traction. Mark may well be drawing on prior traditions, but how we determine them and how Mark may have "traditioned" them are not easy questions to sort out.

At the same time, it is clear that in the production of Mark there is a transition at work that must be noted. For whatever reason, the Gospel of Mark seems to represent for the first time a shift from oral to written gospel communication.[17] While we must acknowledge the unique oral reality that lies behind our text, perhaps these reflections on sources should cause us to approach Mark's Gospel with a view to understanding it precisely as a key change in the gospel. How might we become more aware of the ways in which the oral gospel continues to shape the new written Gospel Mark has produced?[18] With this, however, we are already anticipating our concern with Mark's oral and rhetorical force. Perhaps, as Luther said, the New Testament is not so much Scripture but preaching.[19] The oral traditions that stand behind Mark's newly minted written gospel still bear witness in the rhetorical force of Mark's Gospel.

GENRE

This brings us now to the question of the genre of Mark's Gospel. As we pointed out earlier, Mark's writing happens in the context of a Greco-Roman literary world. He writes his Gospel in Greek and in light of that we have to be aware of what kinds of communicative signals Mark's writing is sending. Genre, after all, is not merely a way of pigeonholing a text, a way of assigning

16. Harry Fleddermann, *Mark and Q: A Study of the Overlap Texts* (Leuven: Leuven University Press, 1995).

17. Werner Kelber, *The Oral and the Written Gospel* (Philadelphia: Fortress, 1983), 1–131.

18. Eugene Boring's commentary on Mark pursues this idea in a very consistent way, advising commentary readers to read the Gospel aloud first before approaching the commentary, *Mark: A Commentary* (Louisville: Westminster John Knox, 2006), 1. New Testament scholar David Rhoads has produced a DVD in which he performs the Gospel of Mark from beginning to end, which runs through Mark's sixteen chapters in about the time it takes to view today's average movie. I am persuaded that a performance of Mark helps to explain both what we perceive as the relative crudeness of Mark's "style" relative to the other Gospels as well as its rhetorical and apocalyptic power.

19. Philip Watson, *Let God Be God!: An Interpretation of the Theology of Martin Luther* (London: Epworth, 1947), 149–50.

it a "category." Instead, determining its genre is important because it helps us understand how it might have been read or heard. Thus, if I start with the words "I once knew a man from Nantucket," you would likely not expect me to regale you with a story of a new friend I met in Massachusetts. Instead, you would probably anticipate from the cues of the meter and form that a bawdy limerick would follow where the next line and the final line would so cleverly rhyme with the word "Nantucket" that it would cause you to laugh or groan at the end. Genre is important in that it helps to frame a communication. It will be helpful for us to consider how Markan scholars have understood the genre of his Gospel.

One of the most common and perhaps even consensus ways to understand the Gospel of Mark is as a *bios*, an ancient biography. Ancient biographies clearly differ from modern ones in the ways in which they talk about the person's life. Jesus, in this view, is revealed chiefly by what he says and does in the idealized form of the *bios*. The difficulty, of course, is that the text itself begins and ends in ways that make it hard to reconcile Mark's Gospel with the genre of ancient biography. Mark's Gospel begins by calling itself "The beginning of the *gospel* of Jesus Christ, [Son of God]," but when Jesus appears he does so "proclaiming the good news (gospel) of God, and saying, 'The time is fulfilled, and the kingdom of God has come near; repent, and believe in the good news'" (Mark 1:14b-15, emphasis and parentheses mine). At the end, we have a strange conclusion marked by the failure of the women to tell anyone of the promise he has given to his failed disciples—hardly an ideal conclusion. For this and other reasons, the *bios* remains to my mind a less than compelling choice.

Mark has generated advocates of still other perspectives. Mary Ann Tolbert has compared Mark to a biographical or historiographical variation on the ancient erotic novel, a roughly contemporaneous genre of popular literature that featured divinely guided (by Eros) travels and perils of the main characters along with the occasional crucifixion scene![20] Still others argue Mark is a form of ancient historiography. Here the work of Adela Yarbro Collins stands out, in that she views Mark as form of *eschatological* historiography—a generic variation that allows her to account for Mark's eschatological interest in connection with the genre.[21] This mixed view of Mark's helps her see a connection to

---

20. Tolbert, *Sowing the Gospel*, 59–70.

21. Adela Yarbro Collins, *Mark: A Commentary* (Minneapolis: Fortress Press, 2007), 33–43. In an earlier work, Collins argues that Mark is a kind of historiography "in an apocalyptic mode," *The Beginning of the Gospel: Probings of Mark in Context* (Minneapolis: Fortress Press, 1992), 37–38.

similar kinds of texts in intertestamental Jewish literature prior to and contemporaneous with Mark (e.g., parts of *1 Enoch*).

The struggle, to my mind, is to find a generic designation that accounts for the mixed way in which Mark pursues his writing. Clearly, Mark's work does not represent the high standards of elite literature. His language and his writing style belie this. Mark clearly has a theological agenda, so any generic designation would have to deal with that aspect of Markan subject matter that touches not only on Jesus' person ("The beginning of the gospel of *Jesus Christ, Son of* God," emphasis mine) but also its relation to the purposes of God whom Jesus himself proclaims ("the good news [gospel] of God," brackets mine). That there are biographical and historiographical elements cannot be denied. Yet Mark's apocalyptic mode and the worldview it evokes qualifies radically any such generic designation.

In light of these problems, others have tried to reconcile the unique subject matter of Mark's work with its performative impact. New Testament scholar Norman Perrin once called Mark an "apocalyptic drama."[22] While this mixed view that accounts for Mark's effect is helpful, it is difficult to square with the fact that Mark ultimately *narrates* his Gospel, and doesn't merely dramatize it. Perhaps then it is best to agree with Eugene Boring that Mark's Gospel is a mixed genre whose performative force is a result both of the theological agenda of its author and the oral shape of the traditions that fund it: "a kerygmatic genre, expressed in narrative."[23] To Boring's proposal, I would wish to add that Mark does so in an apocalyptic mode, which borrows something of a worldview through apocalyptic type scenes and motifs in its execution.[24]

---

22. Norman Perrin and Dennis Duling, *The New Testament: An Introduction*, 2nd ed. (New York: Harcourt Brace Jovanovich, 1982), 233–62.

23. Boring, *Mark*, 6–9.

24. Here I am using Alistair Fowler's genre theory, which argues that genres become mixed through the use of "modes," characteristic features of other genres that are incorporated to produce a hybrid variation on a genre. Thus, says Fowler, the heroic novel is a novel by genre, but incorporates elements of the epic (type scenes, motifs, etc.) by use of what he calls the heroic "mode." Two works of Fowler's elaborate on these ideas: "The Life and Death of Literary Forms," *New Literary History* 2 (1971): 199–216 and *Kinds of Literature: An Introduction to the Theory of Genres and Modes* (Cambridge, MA: Harvard University Press, 1982). For a view that questions the value of using "apocalypticism" as a way of reading Mark, see Richard Horsley, *Hearing the Whole Story: The Politics of Plot in Mark's Gospel* (Louisville: Westminster John Knox, 2001), 121–48. I view my project as understanding Mark from a literary-historical perspective, that is, the generic history that can explain the use of the apocalyptic mode in related literature, rather than positing the kind of hypostasized "apocalypticism" that Horsley critiques. Still, his point about how Mark often parodies or subverts the expectations of apocalypses or apocalypticism is a helpful one with which I often find myself in agreement as I read Mark through the

Mark's Narrative Rhetoric

This particular commentary presupposes that Mark, though working with prior oral traditions, is more than merely a collector of those traditions. He is also more than simply a redactor who discloses his theology by working around the edges of the material he redacts. Mark may not quite be beginning from scratch, but like any decent narrator he can decide how he orders his material, what he includes, what he omits, and whether he offers something new as well. One of the best ways to get a feel for this is to consider Mark's "narrative rhetoric," the way in which he tells his story, the perspectives with which he does it, and the style he uses to communicate.[25] Mark is more than a compiler or editor; he seeks to have an "effect" on his readers/hearers. This commentary will take some time to attend to the rhetorical impact of Mark's narration of the gospel of Jesus' ministry, death, and resurrection.

At the same time, it must be acknowledged that Mark does not always do so with the greatest grace and skill. For many reasons, including his occasional bad grammar or misuse of words, one can and probably should assume that Mark was not a likely candidate for the ancient world's equivalent of the Pulitzer Prize in literature. Some ancient traditions described Mark as "stumpy fingered."[26] When reading Mark as narrative art, the description may be apt as well. At the same time, by attending to the *purposes* of Mark's narrative rhetoric and to Mark's apocalyptic theology (below), we may see more than a simple lack of artistry in what Mark has wrought. By the end, we will see that Mark has an effect, a rhetorical force that actually gives his Gospel a unique gravity and power. We twenty-first-century readers and hearers will benefit from Mark's unique, if sometimes awkward, stumpy-fingered narrative-rhetorical theological vision.

apocalyptic mode. For a more detailed treatment of the way I use Fowler's genre theory as a means of reading apocalyptic texts in light of a Jewish literary matrix for the genre, see my *Preaching in the New Creation: The Promise of New Testament Apocalyptic Texts* (Louisville: Westminster John Knox, 1999).

25. Some of the categories and terms I am using in this section come from my reading of Rhoads and Michie's *Mark as Story*, 32–62.

26. The reference is to the Anti-Marcionite Prologue, dated toward the end of the second century, as quoted in C. Clifton Black, *Mark: Images of an Apostolic Interpreter* (Columbia: University of South Carolina Press, 1994), 119.

NARRATOR

One of the most important things to note about the rhetorical force of the Markan narrative is its relationship to the reader. Mark seems to be committed to giving the narratee information that characters in the Gospel do not possess, especially the disciples. From the very beginning of Mark, before the action even begins, Mark discloses something of his purpose to the reader: "the beginning of the gospel of Jesus, [Son of God]." Already with this title at the beginning the reader is being given privileged information: that is, the theological horizon of the narrative itself as the *beginning* of the gospel and something important about the main character, Jesus, whom we readers now know with the narrator to be "Son of God." These crucial early disclosures are no small thing. The horizon of the gospel (*euaggelion*) reemerges at key moments in the story: 1:1, 14; 8:35; 10:29; 13:10; and 14:9. The disclosure that Jesus is Son of God is not perceived by all the characters, at points tragically misunderstood by the disciples, and in the end oddly confessed in the shadow of the cross by the Roman centurion! From the beginning, Mark brings readers and hearers into a privileged position—one that in many ways was even not fully enjoyed by the disciples themselves. This reality will also prove crucial at the point of Mark's mysterious conclusion at 16:8, where the reader then becomes implicated in completing Mark's unfinished gospel theology beyond the failure of the disciples and the otherwise faithful women at the tomb who flee the resurrection scene in silent fear.

On occasions, Mark ratchets up this insider/outsider relationship with readers and characters even more. Readers are privileged to learn information from divine voices that only Jesus himself hears (e.g., Jesus' baptism in chapter 1) and from the omniscient narrator (say, about the hearts of the religious leaders) that help the reader digest the unfolding story and its conflicts. At one point, the narrator in a kind of spoken aside actually addresses the reader in the narrative to ensure that the reader understands a key apocalyptic warning in 13:14.

The overall effect of this is to make the Markan reader something of an insider in the process. This will prove crucial in understanding Mark's overall purpose in communicating his Gospel.

POINT OF VIEW AND STANDARDS OF EVALUATION

Mark's omniscient narrator is crucial for giving readers cues about how to evaluate a character or an action in the story. When, for example, in the baptism scene a heavenly voice discloses to Jesus that, "You are my Son, the Beloved;* with you I am well pleased" (1:11b), the reader is not only privileged to hear information that Jesus knows and the other characters do not, but also is privy to a positive evaluation from God. It is these narrative means by which readers are given a standard for evaluating right or wrong judgments. When another such revelation scene happens in chapter 9 in the transfiguration story, the now repeated divine evaluation on the importance of Jesus as God's Son, the Beloved, is thus not so much for the readers' benefit, but to highlight the difficulty with which characters like the disciples fail to grasp the truth of Jesus. As a result, point of view and standards of evaluation do not only clue the reader into important truths. Indeed sometimes they highlight in Mark's case the obduracy of the disciples or even facilitate as well the ironic power of the words about Jesus uttered by religious authorities and Pilate at his trial. Conversely, the recognition of Jesus by demons in the exorcism stories also prepares the reader for evaluations of other characters. If demons of the old apocalyptic age know who Jesus is, then it is not so farfetched to call Peter "Satan" for not grasping the importance of suffering for Jesus' messiahship in his "old age" thinking at Caesarea Philippi in chapter 8. Just because Peter calls him Christ, does not mean that Peter has faith and will be faithful. Even demons can recognize something of the truth of who Jesus is—as we see in the Galilean ministry of the earlier chapters of Mark.

At other points, the standards of evaluation become important for other characters as well. Since the narrator is omniscient, the reader is given evaluative information about the motives of characters that is not disclosed to other characters in the story, or information that only Jesus and we readers know. Again, these standards of evaluation become important for the privileged role of the Markan reader in the purpose of the story. They represent an important narrative-rhetorical tool.

STYLE

The writer of Mark's Gospel uses a rather strange style to communicate the story. On the surface, the style seems downright primitive. Mark has the occasional grammatical error. He uses the historical present to speak of past events (instead of "Jesus went to X" Mark writes "Jesus *goes* to X"). Many sentences begin with the word *kai*, which means "and." Mark's language is Koine, common street Greek. It is not like the high-flown Attic style that Luke occasionally uses. If one were to read the Gospel without any pious preconceptions about biblical texts, one would probably have to conclude that Mark uses a kind of low-brow writing style more common to popular literature than the elite variety.

While these conclusions are warranted, I think the case can also be made that the style of Mark's writing is also "fitting" for what he writes—and this is in many ways the ultimate test for style. Mark's reliance on conjunctions like *kai* and other connecting phrases or even his frequent use of the word "immediately" give his work the impression of being "on the move." And indeed, Mark's Gospel moves quickly! After some brief introductory material in 1:1-15, Mark's running portrayal of Jesus' Galilean ministry of healings, exorcisms, teaching, and conflict stories leaves a reader downright breathless. The action continues apace as Jesus makes his way from the farthest point, Caesarea Philippi at the edge of the gentile world in chapter 8 to his arrival in Jerusalem in chapter 11. Only there, in Jerusalem, does the pace of the action slow down, giving the reader ample time to absorb all the ironic power of Jesus' final days in the shadow of the cross. It may be that Mark's style also matches his vigorous view of discipleship. Mark's Jesus is "on the way;" his disciples are called to follow in the same, breathless way. As if to underscore the point, the brief resurrection narrative at the end only reintroduces the fast-paced style one last time: "But go, tell his disciples and Peter that he is going ahead of you to Galilee; there you will see him, just as he told you" (16:7). Apparently, even in the resurrection Jesus expects his disciples to be on the move and to keep up with Jesus as he goes ahead.

One other element of Mark's style is important to understand. I mentioned earlier that the genre of Mark is hard to peg in part because of its oral style and feel. Mark, when read aloud, is full of voices speaking, crying, calling out, and confessing. Some theorize that Mark's Gospel was written to be read aloud, to be performed.[27] Even if that is not the case, one can at least agree with Werner Kelber that Mark's Gospel represents a transition from the world of orality to the world of literacy.[28] This may also help to explain why some Markan texts still give evidence of not being remembrances of Jesus from their settings, but rather prophetic oracles or stories of the risen Christ speaking to the church in prophecy. Thus, for example, the story of Jesus walking across the water to his storm-tossed disciples has often been viewed as a post-resurrection story set within a pre-resurrection part of Mark's narrative. Mark's oral style may at points also be a vestige of the more fluid view of revelation that is

27. Important examples of such scholarship are Whitney Shiner, *Proclaiming the Gospel: First-Century Performance of* Mark (Harrisburg, PA: Trinity Press International, 2003); Elizabeth Struthers Malbon, *Hearing Mark: A Listener's Guide* (London: T&T Clark, 2002); and Richard Horsley, *Hearing.*

28. Kelber, *The Oral and the Written Gospel.* While Kelber views Mark as subverting orality for the sake of textuality, I am more intrigued by the notion that the text may have oral vestiges even as it begins a process of writing Gospel.

presupposed when a community gathers expecting to hear the living words of its risen Lord in prophetic speech. This is the stylistic implication of viewing, with Boring, the genre of Mark as a "kerygmatic narrative" in which I see an "apocalyptic mode" as being operative. It means in part that Mark's style intends not only a narrative "overhearing," but occasionally a full-frontal, rhetorical hearing within a living community.

This, to my mind, makes Mark a more thoroughgoing example of what classicist George Kennedy calls radical rhetoric.[29] Mark is not interested in getting his hearers to be reasonably persuaded about this "gospel." Instead, he narrates a story that shows Jesus healing, exorcising, confronting, and, above all, promising. Mark's clumsy, oracular style is at one with this radical rhetoric. It calls the reader into a gospel proclamation that is at once Jesus Christ himself *and* the kingdom he proclaims as the gospel of God. It is not a thoroughgoing reflective piece.

Nonetheless, Mark is more than merely clumsy and insistent with his rhetoric. At points his Gospel reads quite mysteriously. There are sections where there seems to be a non sequitur between what one character says and what Jesus says, or where Jesus makes a prediction that we find ourselves still pondering. Mark may be more action than reflection, but his urgent kingdom rhetoric pushes the reader to the edge of apocalyptic mystery nonetheless—and that is also part of Mark's appeal.

NARRATIVE PATTERNS

Mark's narrative rhetoric also features the use of certain patterns that are helpful for a reader to grasp—especially insofar as they help reveal something of Mark's purpose. Two narrative patterns are especially noteworthy with respect to their rhetorical effects. The first is Mark's way of using doublets, or repeated stories, to make a point. Mark has two feeding stories, one where five thousand are fed and another with four thousand. Viewed independently, it appears once again Mark is an inept narrator. When one considers the repetition, however, in light of the disciples' inability to understand Jesus and his ministry, the meaning becomes clearer. The reader senses that Jesus is making a rather clear point (and allies him or herself with the narrator and Jesus). The disciples, through this use of narrative rhetoric, seem to be becoming more and more "hard-hearted," unable to see the truth that is dawning on us readers. Another narrative pattern

---

29. George Kennedy, *New Testament Interpretation through Rhetorical Criticism* (Chapel Hill: University of North Carolina Press, 1984), 7.

typical for Mark is intercalation. Here, two stories are told in such a way as to be mutually interpretive. One important example in the Markan narrative is the contrast between the story of Jesus' hearing before the officials that is happening as Peter's predicted denial is unfolding. Both inside and outside a kind of hearing is taking place—Jesus is faithful; Peter falls short. Through the use of intercalation, Mark invites the reader to engage in such acts of comparison and contrast in light of the unfolding action. We will make note when Mark is using this narrative-rhetorical tool to help us explore his purpose for telling his Gospel about the gospel.

BEGINNINGS AND ENDINGS

Finally, it is important to understand the roles of beginnings and endings in narrative rhetoric. Somehow our reading of Mark's Gospel must make sense of the whole. We cannot "lose the forest for the trees"—especially since our goal is to help preachers move beyond the day's lection in antiseptic isolation so that Mark's whole gospel can, to paraphrase Donald Juel, be set "on the loose" once more in our midst. Being aware of beginnings and endings helps us do just that. Mark's Gospel, as we have noted, begins with a title about the beginning of the gospel and a kind of prologue that set the terms for what follows. While the theme of the gospel (*euaggelion*) returns from time to time, it receives special emphasis in the end when the women receive the good news of Jesus' resurrection and his going ahead to Galilee, the very site where his own gospel ministry began. Mark uses the beginning and ending of his Gospel, and sometimes even the beginning and ending of the episodes that make it up in such a way as to signal shifts, markers of opening and closure. In ancient rhetoric this was known as an *inclusio*. These oral markers of beginnings and endings help to orient the text for us and help us continually to hear Mark's Gospel whole. They are elements of Mark's narrative rhetoric that aid us in discerning Mark's gospel purpose from 1:1 to 16:8. This will help us read Mark's Gospel not just as one thing after another, but as a focused, meaningful discourse.

MARK'S APOCALYPTIC MODE

We would be mistaken, however, if we viewed Mark's Gospel as if it were just another clearly ordered piece of Hellenistic rhetoric, let alone a lucid example of high literature. While Mark is a somewhat educated writer with a purpose, he is telling his kerygmatic narrative *in the apocalyptic mode*. The Bible features only a couple of true apocalypses: Daniel 7–12 in the Hebrew Bible and Revelation in the New Testament. While there are many other texts with apocalyptic themes, motifs, and forms, these two texts are our best canonical examples of what full-blown apocalypses look like. Neither of these texts reads like an everyday, realistic narrative. Moreover, when we twenty-first-century people try to read them, we do not find it easy to relate to the world we know. If Mark is indeed writing his kerygmatic narrative in an apocalyptic mode, we will need to do a bit of apocalyptic homework to understand why he writes as he does. In order to do this in way that connects clearly with Mark's Gospel, we will highlight ways in which the modal version of an apocalyptic genre becomes manifest in Mark's narrative world.

AS REVEALED IN MINOR CHARACTERS

One of the most consistent ways in which Mark summons the apocalyptic mode is with his use of characters. There are frequent stories about people, for example, whose lives are distorted by demons. The first few chapters of Mark feature several exorcisms, and if it is not the demoniacs who bear witness to Mark's apocalyptic worldview, it is the demons themselves who recognize Jesus for who he is. Mark's Jesus announces God's kingdom in 1:14, but his kingdom preaching and ministry are not the onward and upward vision of nineteenth-century liberalism as we sing in our twentieth-century Fosdick hymns; rather, it is about a battle between God's reign and Satan, who holds people and even their institutions in his grasp. Apocalypses are full of such demonic and angelic characters. Jesus through his preaching is on the front line in an apocalyptic battle. The question is how. That is where Jesus' story, for all its exorcisms and confrontations, takes a surprising and nonetheless apocalyptic turn at the end.

AS REVEALED IN FINAL SETTINGS

Mark's narrator wishes us to see much of the Jerusalem setting of the end of his Gospel in thoroughly apocalyptic terms: his cross and resurrection. Mark 13 is an important part of this setting. Here Jesus speaks before his death, in a form related to the genre apocalypse called a "testament," where he looks ahead and sees the apocalyptic difficulties that are to come.[30] Here Jesus not only

---

30. For some good examples of this in Jewish apocalyptic literature, see the *Testaments of the Twelve Patriarchs*, which were likely written before or roughly contemporaneous with Mark's Gospel.

predicts the coming destruction of the temple, a topic of no doubt lively interest in Mark's own time between 65–75 ce, but also other apocalyptic concerns: persecutions, false messiahs, earthquakes, wars, famines, cosmic birth pangs, family division, the desolating sacrilege, darkened sun and moon, falling stars, the coming of the Son of the human (or "Son of Man") in the clouds, and the gathering of the elect.[31] In typical apocalyptic fashion, Jesus asks his hearers to stay awake and to hold fast.

What is remarkable about this standard apocalyptic, testament-like speech, however, is the way that it continues to shape the unfolding narrative in Jerusalem. Jesus warns about being handed over by loved ones and delivered up to councils, when this is precisely what happens to him in the subsequent chapters. When Jesus is praying in the dark in Gethsemane, the disciples fail to stay awake despite Jesus' warnings at the end of chapter 13. When Jesus dies on the cross, the afternoon sun grows dark and darkness falls on the land. At the end, at a tomb of all places, an angel appears to announce apocalyptic resurrection news. In Jesus' trials, in his death, and in his resurrection, the apocalyptic world is dawning even now: for those with eyes to "watch" and "stay awake." Jesus undergoes these apocalyptic events already in his trial, crucifixion, and resurrection because of his gospel and knowing that these events will continue until that gospel is first preached to all nations (13:10). In this sense, the gospel of Jesus Christ "begins" already in his life, crucifixion, and resurrection.

Earlier in Mark's Gospel, other settings help us in seeing traces of Mark's apocalyptic mode. Jesus struggles with Satan in the wilderness during his temptation. When the cosmic forces of wind and wave seem arrayed against his disciples, Jesus walks out on the water and in another place even silences the wind as if it were a demon. In these settings, and programmatically in Jerusalem, the great cosmic apocalyptic battle is being fought against the forces that hold humanity and earth in a kind of slavery, from which Jesus has come to ransom humanity.

AS REVEALED IN THE IDENTIFICATIONS OF JESUS

Scholars have long wrestled with the various titles given to Jesus in Mark's Gospel. While it may be impossible to find a clear, consistent, propositionally

---

31. Here I use the term *Son of the human* in lieu of the traditional *Son of Man*. Because of the nuances of the phrase where it sometimes refers to humanity and other to a transcendent figure, as well as the greater inclusiveness of this translation, I am opting for the phrasing *Son of the human* for this commentary going forward.

oriented Christology of Mark's Gospel that makes sense of all those titles in a systematic way, a consideration of them in light of the apocalyptic worldview in its time can shed some light on how they hang together for Mark.[32] One way we can deepen our reading is to see how Mark's interpretation of Jesus emerges in particular out of a Jewish context, one in which apocalyptic formulations of messiah, Son of the human, prophet, and teacher held meanings that are key for understanding Mark's apocalyptic gospel. While many of these terms will need to be explained as the commentary unfolds, some of the more apocalyptic influences can shed some useful light.

First, it must be said that the language around Christ or messiah is especially fluid in this period. Christians often talk about "the Jewish conception of messiah" as if it were merely a foil. Judaism is a very diverse phenomenon at this time—it is in fact big enough to include Christian movements within it, many of which are still within Jewish communities even toward the end of the first century. As an example of this diversity, one might consider the way the language of messiah is used in Qumran. There the term is used to speak not only of a royal messiah, but also a priestly messiah. In some apocalyptic literature of the time, there is also an emphasis on how these messianic conceptions also relate to teaching—in the case of the royal messiah this means in particular a connection with the revelation of secrets and wisdom (e.g., *1 Enoch*'s Book of Similitudes).[33] This does not mean that other messianic conceptions are not in play, but it does help to broaden the way we typically use that language, especially as we deal with his apocalyptic Gospel as one marked by revelation and the disclosure of mysteries.

The language of the *Son of Man* or what I am calling *Son of the human* is also quite interesting in this period. While it is true that there are significant traditions about this that can be traced back to Daniel 7–12, the figure was something of an ongoing concern in intertestamental apocalyptic literature. In fact, as Adela Yarbro Collins points out, one can find an especially helpful development in the Similitudes of Enoch that provides a meaningful context for the use of the term in Mark: the "hidden Son of Man."[34] Since in apocalyptic

---

32. Scholars have long sought to develop a Christology from Mark. The problem is that Mark doesn't think systematically about Jesus' identity in any way remotely propositional. Some recent writers have tried to find a way of developing a "narrative Christology" that accounts for the fact that what Mark offers us is a narrative, not a propositional treatise. For a recent example of this, see Elizabeth Struthers Malbon, *Mark's Jesus: Characterization as Narrative Christology* (Waco, TX: Baylor University Press, 2009). For our purposes it is sufficient to see how traditions of interpreting Jesus in Mark help underline the Gospel's apocalyptic character.

33. Collins, *Mark*, 48, 66.

literature there is often a fusion of messianic language and this tradition, what we have in Mark is representative of some broader tendencies in Jewish apocalyptic writing in the period. Collins puts it this way:

> A certain analogy between Mark and the Similitudes of Enoch suggests the theme of the secret identity of Jesus should be seen as the literary adaptation of an apocalyptic motif. . . . In any case the analogy is striking. The author of Mark seems to have adapted the tradition of the hidden Son of Man in composing an account of the earthly Jesus. Rather than being hidden in the presence of the Lord in heaven, Jesus, the secret Son of Man, walked the earth and revealed his identity to a chosen few.[35]

Here we see how even the portrayal and identification of Jesus in Mark's Gospel takes on an apocalyptic hue. Jesus' hiddenness as Messiah and Son of the human is not about being coy, but is part of an important emphasis on hiddenness and revelation in the Jewish apocalyptic tradition.

AS REVEALED IN DIVINE ACTS OF REVELATION (BAPTISM, TRANSFIGURATION, CROSS)

Ched Myers has offered an interesting thesis that has value both as an apocalyptic grid for reading Mark as well as providing clarity. In Myers's view, Mark has three "pillar stories" portrayed in an apocalyptic light. He sets them up with the following parallel elements:[36]

BAPTISM	TRANSFIGURATION	CRUCIFIXION
heavens rent	garments turn white	sanctuary veil rent
dove descends	cloud descends	darkness spreads
voice from heaven	voice from cloud	Jesus' great voice
"You are my son, beloved"	"This is my son, beloved"	"Truly this man was son of God"
John the Baptist as Elijah	John appears with Elijah	"Is he calling Elijah?"

With Myers's structure, we can begin to see more deeply how the apocalyptic mode influences and even shapes Mark's Gospel. What makes his Gospel so

34. Ibid., 60.

35. Ibid., 70.

36. Myers, *Binding the Strongman*, 391.

interesting is precisely this apocalyptic take. For our purposes, its connection with the reader, who from the beginning is party to these limited revelations or disclosures, is really the key. The reader is there from the "beginning of the gospel of Jesus Christ" through the cross and the dawning apocalyptic news of Jesus' resurrection. It is precisely this that makes it for us readers a beginning as well.

PROSPECT: HE HAS GONE AHEAD TO GALILEE

Mark's Gospel ends with a beginning as well. This is true on more than one level for the preacher. Within the text, the young man in his apocalyptic white robe tells the utterly frightened women the good news for Jesus' failed disciples: "But go, tell his disciples and Peter that he is going ahead of you to Galilee; there you will see him, just as he told you" (16:7). He mentions Peter by name among all those failed disciples and offers them a promise. Then the narrative ends. Unlike Matthew, Luke, and John's Gospels, we do not get to witness resurrection scenes and a commissioning by the risen Lord. We are only given an empty tomb and a promise in the midst of failure. It leaves us readers a bit at our wit's end—except for one thing: the substance of the promise itself. Jesus goes ahead to Galilee—the place where it all *began* and thus invites readers and disciples to begin at the beginning of the gospel again. Mark gives us enough of a promise to keep us going with his Gospel of the gospel, but does so with an *unfinished narrative*.

He also gives us who preach these texts something of his unfinished theology. And this is where the preacher's work really begins. Again, one thing we can surmise is that many of Mark's first readers thought it unfinished as well. Matthew and Luke used Mark's structure, but added some much more definitive resurrection endings. They also tried to clean up Mark's occasional bad grammar and stumpy-fingered style. Luke postponed Mark's eschatological edginess. Matthew rolled back some of the more categorical statements Mark made about torah. Whatever it was, his readers felt compelled to "finish" Mark's theology, or at least to rework it. We preachers may need to do so as well from time to time. We live in an age where it is quite difficult to envision bodies of water inhabited by storm demons and where we are more likely to refer troubled persons to psychologists than to defer to exorcists. Yet, do we not sense in a very powerful way the intransigence of evil, and the way even our institutions seem to hold our humanity in their sway? On an ethical level, we too are painfully aware of our Christian church's long history of anti-Semitism. Does this mean that we need to revisit some of Mark's anti-Jewish sentiments—especially since Christianity no longer is a minority sect in Judaism, but is in fact now so much more powerful? These, to my mind, are just a couple of ways in which we might ourselves take up Mark's unfinished theological task when we preach. It means that understanding Mark on his terms is just the beginning. It means that we, too, take up the work as preachers and begin in startling and mysterious ways to name God into the world again.[37] Mark announced the good news of Jesus who himself came preaching good news of God. Perhaps Mark in all his apocalyptic edginess can nudge us out of our own closed systems to preach the gospel trusting in the promise that the risen crucified One has already gone ahead.

---

37. This phrase I got from my teacher, David G. Buttrick, who uses the idea of naming God into the world again in his landmark *Homiletic: Moves and Structures* (Philadelphia: Fortress Press, 1987). After all these years, I still find it a persuasive and compelling way of thinking about the unique task of preachers as homiletical theologians.

1

Prologue to Mark's Gospel (1:1–15)

With his Gospel in the apocalyptic mode (see Introduction), Mark wants to shake up the reader's world before the story even starts. The prologue does just that, setting the stage for the coming apocalyptic drama. Instead of beginning with a narrated story, Mark's Gospel begins in v. 1 with a title that announces "the beginning of the gospel of Jesus Christ." It quickly moves from the title to the sounding of a series of scriptural voices culminating with the appearance of John the Baptist who proclaims the coming of a stronger one in vv. 2–8. This latter announcement serves among other things as an introduction to the theme of Jesus' strength and ability relative to others, an issue that recurs in Mark's Gospel (3:27; 5:4; 9:18; 14:37). The narrative then shifts surprisingly in vv. 9–11 to Jesus' baptismal appearance marked by a divine voice that from the "ripped open" heavens reveals Jesus as "my son, the beloved." This same divine, verbal revelation will be echoed on the Mount of Transfiguration in 9:7 and in the presence of Jesus' eschatologically sun-darkened cross and "ripped open" temple curtain by the centurion's human voice in 15:39. Jesus subsequently overcomes Satan's wilderness testing in vv. 12–13 and finally appears in Galilee, preaching the gospel good news of God concerning the apocalyptic fulfilling of God's coming reign in vv. 14–15. The fast-paced prologue unit is marked by clear signs of opening and closure by a threefold repetition of the word for gospel or good news (*euaggelion*) at 1:1, 14, and 15.

The fact that this prologue is more thematic and impressionistic than straightforward narrative helps us to understand its role relative to the story about to unfold. Think of the witches' scene at the beginning of *Macbeth*, or Goethe's *Faust* and its "prologue in heaven." We hearers of this announcement are being supplied with information from the start and are given an apocalyptic insider's view of what is about to happen. The focus is the gospel from beginning (1:1) to the end of the unit (1:14, 15). When John the Baptist and Jesus show up, their appearances are marked with the biblical Greek word for "it came to pass" (*egeneto*, 1:4, 9). Before there are any disciples, religious leaders, demons, or Romans to narrate, we are given access to the apocalyptic-like revelation in several ways. All of these help to frame the narrative about to begin.

First, the heavens are ripped open (*schizomenous*) and we readers are made privy to the divine information that otherwise only Jesus hears: "You are my Son, the Beloved; with you I am well pleased." The idea of the opening of heaven as a way of signaling apocalyptic revelation is commonplace in apocalypses and related literature (Rev. 4:1, 11:19, 19:11, *T. Levi* 2:6, 18:6, 2 *Bar.* 22:1, *Apoc. Ab.* 19:4). Second, although Jesus is driven out into the wilderness by the Spirit to face temptation, Jesus *defeats* Satan after forty days. Satan will continue to be an adversary throughout Mark's Gospel, but even here Jesus is enough to defeat him and cope with wild beasts, a pairing that shows up in contemporaneous literature related to apocalypses (*T. Naph.* 8:4, *T. Benj.* 5:2, and *T. Iss.* 7:7). Again, the narrator gives us privileged information about Jesus' power relative to Satan. Third, Jesus proclaims in direct speech God's apocalyptic gospel good news of the kingdom. Part of his announcement is to let it be known that the time has been fulfilled.

The apocalyptic character of the prologue is furthered by its connection with Isaiah, whose later tradents in deutero- and trito-Isaiah have been tellingly described as proto-apocalyptic by Hebrew Bible scholar Paul Hanson.[1] New Testament scholar Joel Marcus points out that Deutero-Isaiah seems to prophesy many of the themes that Mark's prologue announces here:[2] Isaiah speaks of good news (Isa. 40:9, 41:27, 52:7, 60:6, 61:1), calls for the heavens to be opened (63:19), and announces the reign of God (40:10, 52:7). The fact that the text begins with the "beginning of the gospel of Jesus Christ" may also be a marker for one of Deutero-Isaiah's favorite themes: that the new eschatological thing God is doing surpasses even the beginning. All these deutero- and trito-Isaianic themes have impacted Mark's take on the apocalyptic tradition and perhaps therefore color from the beginning of Mark an understanding of the gospel that also includes Satanic testing and demonic exorcisms, healings and eschatological announcements of the "forgiveness of sins," foretastes of heavenly banquets, resurrections from the dead, and cosmic portents of evil and destruction. This may explain also the strange way in which Mark uses Scripture to introduce the appearance of John in 1:2. First, we must notice that the actual Scriptures quoted are not solely from Isaiah but conflated from Mal.

---

1. Paul Hanson, *The Dawn of Apocalyptic* (Philadelphia: Fortress Press, 1975), 27.

2. Joel Marcus, *Mark 1-8* (New York: Doubleday, 2000), 139.

3:1 and the Septuagint's version of Exod. 23:20. The actual quote from Isa. 40:3 appears only in Mark 1:3! Having said that, we need to note theologically that the first conflated scripture text is a promise. The "beginning of the gospel" begins with a promise from God. Second, the reference to Isaiah helps underline Marcus's point that Isaiah provides a crucial intertext for the apocalyptic mode of the prologue itself. Finally, the use of both texts sets up the dynamic of the arrival of John the Baptist (Mark 1:4-8) and in turn the way he introduces Jesus relative to the gospel of God's apocalyptic kingdom purposes (1:9-15)—for the kingdom itself is an announcement also deeply rooted in Jewish apocalypses and related writings (1 En. [The Parable of Enoch] 25:3-5; [Similitudes] 62–63; As. Mos. 10:1-3a).

Preachers should note two key terms in the title of 1:1. First, the verse ends with a disputed textual reading "the Son of God." In all likelihood, the phrase has been added here. If it actually belongs there, it is confirmed already in Jesus' baptism by the private heavenly voice. In this way "Son of God" becomes a key to the reader who overhears it for grasping the subsequent story and creating distance between the reader and the disciples and others, who do not know this. Second, Mark characterizes what follows as the "beginning" of the gospel. When a preacher preaches, there is a little potential of a new theological naming of the gospel for this time and place commencing. If Mark conceives the story of Jesus life, ministry, death and resurrection as the beginning of the gospel, perhaps we are also invited as theologians of the gospel to take it up going forward, in this way completing the theologically-driven narrative that Mark leaves incomplete at the strange ending of 16:8. Yet whatever that gospel entails, it needs to be at least as expansive as our Biblical text. The gospel here is not just Jesus (1:1), but also the gospel-of-God kingdom that Jesus himself proclaims (1:14-15) and its resultant faith/repentance, too. This text gives preachers a wonderful opportunity to go deep as homiletical theologians.

LECTIONS

This prologue to the Gospel of Mark is entirely covered in the lectionary, albeit piecemeal and in different seasons of the liturgical calendar. In fact, the lections for three very different days of the church year actually overlap amidst the scant fifteen verses of Mark's opening section. This means that the problem with preaching with the lectionary any of these days is the way the lections threaten to separate what Mark is trying to hold together. Preachers will want to resist reading these lections in overly isolated ways and be sure to keep Mark's larger narrative agenda in view.

Lection: The Preaching of John the Baptist
1:1-8; Advent 2

The same title that brackets the prologue as a whole, serves to frame even this brief lection for Advent 2. Preachers will find this helpful, for an understanding of the scriptural voices in 1:2-3 and the picture of the prophet Elijah in 1:4-8 will make the most sense when the whole Gospel of the gospel is kept in view: a concern for Jesus' identity (1:1) and for God's reign (1:14, 15) are both part of that gospel frame for Advent 2.

In Mark 1:2-3, the prophet Isaiah is invoked from the very start. We have noted above why this is significant for an apocalyptic Gospel that picks up proto-apocalyptic themes from the later Isaianic corpus: gospel/good news, "ripping open" the heavens, and so on. The connection with v. 2 is a bit problematic because of the conflated nature of the quote, combining as it does elements of Mal. 3:1 and Exod. 23:20. The notion of the way is linked to the wilderness, even though Mark's use of Isaiah 40 as we have it relates it to the voice. Still, the connection with Isaiah is important to Mark's agenda—and not just because it introduces the character of John the Baptist.

John the Baptist indeed appears in vv. 4-8. It is important to begin by noting that he appears "in the wilderness." Clearly this is significant for Mark as an opening setting for the prologue generally. The wilderness is a place of temptation, but also divine redemption. The river Jordan, the site of John's baptizing, is itself connected with important transitions in the Hebrew Bible. The description of John is also evocative, namely of a whole cluster of Hebrew Bible expectations about prophets that Mark plays on allusively, especially Elijah in 2 Kings 1-2. For now, the point is that the Isaiah conflation of prophecy is quoted in 1:2-3, and John "appears" in 1:4. The narrator is therefore already intending that we be persuaded about the reliability of such prophecy—a theme that will recur in Mark's Gospel. At the same time, the narrator also has some surprises in store. John may be described as the prophet *par excellence* associated with the wilderness as a place of return and repentance—a message to which people massively respond. Yet, as great as these moments are, they point ahead in the narrative. In v. 7 John himself announces that one "stronger" than he is coming. The text quite quickly returns us to *Jesus' identity*. At the same time, the narrator likes to keep people guessing. Both John's and Jesus' identities prove somewhat pliable in the unfolding story: they are confused with one another even as late as 8:28! We shall note that Mark as a narrator is fond of such complexity and seems to inject a sense of apocalyptic mystery around Jesus' identity and his parabolic teachings as well.

Yet that is not all. Mark's agenda goes beyond the gospel of Jesus (1:1) to include the gospel of God's reign that he preaches (1:14, 15). Mark's material in 1:1-8 accomplishes this inclusion by focusing on "the way" (1:2, 3). Again, given the context of Isaiah, the language of "the way" is already freighted intertextually. Eugene Boring points out that the way cited from Isa. 40:3 in Mark 1:3 refers to God's way back to Zion through the wilderness—it is not an ethical term, but a theologically redemptive one.[3] This notion of "the way" becomes programmatic for Jesus and his actions from here in the prologue all the way through his ministry, suffering, death, and resurrection. The upshot is that the theme of the way in Mark, which is so important for following Jesus, will nonetheless have this theological meaning in view. God is up to something in Jesus' way—even when disciples are the ones called to follow in it.

All of this then is eventually tied to the promise that John the Baptist offers. As the classic prophet, he only points to Jesus—and the Jesus to whom he points is the focus of an important promise in vv. 7-8: "The one who is more powerful than I is coming after me; I am not worthy to stoop down and untie the thong of his sandals. I have baptized you with[*] water; but he will baptize you with[*] the Holy Spirit." We have already touched on the theme of the "stronger one" in the apocalyptic description above. The promise of the Holy Spirit invokes language of the new age, an apocalyptic allusion that begins to take shape already in the subsequent text of Jesus' heaven-ripping baptism in 1:9-11. Yet there is also the element of surprise here. John says he is "unworthy" to untie his sandals. Still, John—in situational irony—will baptize Jesus himself in 1:9! This Jesus is the object of prophetic prediction and longing, though he does not conform to *every* voiced expectation. The narrator signals early on that Jesus will be something like the new wine that bursts the old wineskins (2:22). Even scriptural promises may need to be reinterpreted as this Gospel about Jesus and the kingdom unfolds.

---

3. Eugene Boring, *Mark: A Commentary*, New Testament Library (Louisville: Westminster John Knox, 2006), 37.

The Advent 2 reading comprises the section that focuses on the gospel of Jesus' person and the announcement language from the Hebrew Bible. Shrewd preachers will notice that the language of God's reign in the left out material of 1:15 is present in the Isaianic intertext we mentioned above, so perhaps this case can be remedied. It means, however, that our Advent practice will have to live more deeply into the twofold sense of Advent that is its true power: we wait for (baby) Jesus, but we also wait for the fullness of divine promise of God's reign to dawn as well. One way to deal with this is to jump ahead to v. 15 when preaching this text. If the point of Mark's Gospel is a gospel that includes both Jesus' person (1:1) and the reign of God (1:14-15), any Advent 2 preaching would be enhanced by drawing that in as well. The intertext from Isaiah could then serve as a bridge for preachers wanting to place Advent hope in connection not just to Jesus' person but to his announcement of the coming kingdom.

Good Advent preaching will also be enhanced by understanding the notion of "the way" consistent with the Isaianic prophecy in which it is embedded and in the Markan narrative that it grounds. Here the structure of the lectionary is a friend to discerning preaching as Isa. 40:1-11 is the Hebrew Bible lection for the day. The important takeaway here for Advent 2 is that the "way" is not just an ethical concern—as in, "Jesus is coming soon so get your stuff together." Rather, the way is about God's *advent*; preparing for it means getting ready for the new thing God is doing on the "way" from the wilderness to Zion, redeeming God's people. In Jesus' case, the way subsequently means through suffering, death, and resurrection—the way to Jerusalem, the cross, and beyond. We may be called to follow, but the "way" is first God's in Jesus Christ. That may be the best advent good news of all.

Lection: The Baptism of Jesus
1:4-11; Baptism of the Lord

With this lection we begin by taking a step back to the previous section. We incorporate the material about the appearance of John baptizing in 1:4-8 described in the paragraphs above and bring it into close relation to the apocalyptic ripping of the heavens at Jesus' baptism in 1:9-11. Doing this juxtaposes John and Jesus, and precisely around the issue of Jesus' baptism. Again, the important issue is to make sure that all is not reduced to the gospel of Jesus' mysterious identity (1:1), but also includes a vision of the kingdom that Jesus also later proclaims (1:14, 15).

To summarize, John's baptizing connects to the scriptural voice in vv. 2-3 that announces God's *purposes* in sending a messenger to prepare the way.

The way evokes God's redemptive purposes analogous to God's return of God's people through the wilderness to Zion in Isaiah 40. John in proclaiming baptism (not repentance in order to be baptized!) bears witness to God's "redemptive" way unfolding in the one who is coming.

Jesus, therefore, like John "appears" (*egeneto*) in v. 9 "in those days," that is, in eschatological time. Ironically, in the latter half of that verse he is baptized by the very one who thought himself unworthy to untie his sandal, thus subverting at least one expectation—the first of many in the Gospel! In short order, the apocalyptic scene unfolds. It happens "immediately," a favorite Markan word here and going forward. Jesus is coming up from the water in v. 10 and sees a vision of the heavens "ripped" open (see above) and the Spirit as a dove descending into (*eis*) him. The presence of the Spirit adds an eschatological element of the new age to our already apocalyptic scene of the open heaven. The idea that the Spirit broods over the waters at creation may allude to an eschatological act of God in remaking creation here. The role of the Spirit in the subsequent struggle with demonic spirits in the narrative going forward will point to God's decisive engagement. The heavens were ripped open for a reason! As Donald Juel puts it, God is now "on the loose."[4] To that NT scholar Brian Blount adds that God is committed here to Jesus' boundary-breaking ministry to come.[5]

In v. 11, a heavenly voice spells out the meaning of the event in a private word to Jesus that we readers are privileged to hear: "You are my Son, the Beloved;[*] with you I am well pleased." With these words from heaven, Jesus' identity is indeed decisively invoked. The fact that it is done so that Jesus alone hears it among any narrated characters, while we readers also overhear it, gives us crucial information going forward. Jesus' identity, already slightly blurred by the confusion around the voices of Scripture and John's baptizing, is now set forth for the benefit of Jesus and the reader. Jesus is God's Son, the Beloved, and the object of God's pleasure. It is tricky, of course, to try to explain all this from extant titles. Because we are operating narratively here, it is best to see how Mark narrates the unfolding of Jesus' identity. Suffice it to say, at this early point, the *meaning* of Jesus' status as God's Son is contested and spelled out over sixteen chapters of Mark's Gospel. However, the evaluative stance offered by the divine voice is designed to clue the reader in on its importance

4. Donald Juel, *Mark*, Augsburg Commentary on the New Testament (Minneapolis: Augsburg Fortress Press, 1990), 34.

5. Brian Blount and Gary Charles, *Preaching Mark in Two Voices* (Louisville: Westminster John Knox, 2002), 22.

here and in the narrative going forward. The key here is that the revelation of Jesus' identity by means of the heavenly voice represents an apocalyptic mystery through the "ripped" heavens, one also disclosed to us readers at the beginning of Mark's Gospel. Still, we can and should speak more broadly of the language's context here. The scriptural intertext from Ps. 2:7 speaks of royal anointing. *Son of God* does not mean some full-fledged view of the Father/Son relationship in later Christological or Trinitarian reflection—those come to fruition centuries later in Chalcedon and Nicaea, not in first-century Mark. Instead, this refers chiefly to God's role relative to kingship, thus implying some royal, messianic entailments. The language of Son of God is also common for speaking broadly of agency. Jesus as God's Son does what God intends and purposes as God's agent. The language of being "well pleased" comes from Isa. 42:1, which links this scene to the servant who brings justice to the nations in Isaiah. The language of "beloved" may also point to the binding of Isaac in Gen. 22. Again, the implications of this are not spelled out here, but evocative of the unique sense of Jesus' mysterious identity that will unfold over sixteen chapters. For now, we have this mysterious, boundary-breaking apocalyptic revelation, which both discloses and prompts questions. For the sake of the narrative going forward, this barebones yet evocative description of Jesus' role is important.

Preachers therefore need to read this snippet of text in light of the whole of the prologue and knowing that so much more is to come in Mark's unfolding narrative Gospel of the gospel. In its present truncated state, Mark 1:4-11 does lift up the identity of Jesus in his baptism, but the prologue of 1:1-15 does not do that only. Again, the Isaianic language points to something more than Jesus' person, as does the ripped-open heavens of this baptismal scene. Something is at stake for the apocalyptically split cosmos with Jesus' baptism, beyond his identity alone. It is also about the gospel of God's reign that Jesus will announce (1:14, 15) and embody (1:16ff) in astounding ways. On the Baptism of the Lord, it will be important to make that connection and to underline the unique understanding of baptism here as a profound locus of divine, boundary-breaking engagement through Jesus' messianic and yet servant-like identity. Those preachers who can reach back to the Advent 2 reading will find help in providing a context for doing so. Preachers who can look forward to Jesus' coming reign-of-God ministry in Epiphany will help to name the divine purpose in this baptismal boundary breaking more profoundly. It is not just about Jesus' identity here; it is also about a God who is "on the loose" and whose purposes cannot be contained in the otherwise safe boundary between heaven and earth. Thus, new creation may also be coming into view in Jesus' unusual baptismal scene. And that is worth preaching about this Sunday!

Lection: The Baptism of Jesus, The Temptation of Jesus, and The Beginning of the Galilean Ministry
1:9-15; Lent 1 (and Epiphany 3 Part I)

Of the three lections from this section (1:1-15), this third split of the prologue (vv. 9-15) is most likely to carry the full freight of the whole. Here the disclosure of Jesus' identity, his struggle in the wilderness with Satan, and his proclamation of God's reign help to hold much of the text's breadth together and show why the split heaven of Jesus' baptism is important. In all three lections, the force of these events is to disrupt overly personalistic readings of Advent, Baptism of our Lord, and Lent. There is in fact a cosmos in play and the struggle includes a Jesus who points beyond himself to God's kingdom purposes. Our sermons should do no less.

The previous section explores the significance of the Jesus' baptism in detail (see above). Here it is probably enough to summarize thusly. The apocalyptic revelation of Jesus' identity through the ripped-open heavens sets the stage by disclosing to Jesus and to the reader the preliminary structure of his identity: the royal, messianic Son of God and Isaianic servant operating under the power of the Spirit. The fact that it is a "ripping open" points to the cosmic, eschatological purposes of God. Both parts are crucial for understanding the action that follows vv. 9-11 in vv. 12-15: Jesus' testing in the wilderness and his proclamation of the gospel of God's reign.

Mark's Spirit is not exactly a cosmic chum nor some cozy "comforter." In v. 11, Mark points out that the Spirit "immediately drove him out into the wilderness." The Greek verb Mark uses here is the same for driving out or casting out demons. It is as if Jesus, having received the Spirit in 1:10 through the ripped-open heavens, is now thrust out into the heart of the struggle. The wilderness becomes once again a paradigmatic place of testing. The word "testing" is one chosen here with care. The other gospels go into the substance of Jesus' *temptations*. Mark is not interested in the almost psychological conflict that Matthew or Luke portrays. Instead, Jesus is tested (*peirazomenos*) in the sense of our "time of trial" by Satan for forty days. The mention of wild beasts underlines the kind of eschatological danger he faces that sometimes shows up in apocalyptic literature and related types (see above)—although the mention of "with" the wild beasts may also imply a kind of eschatological healing of creation. And yet, Jesus manages to overcome this with the help of angels, God's intervening agents, who actually serve him. The upshot is that Jesus' ministry begins with a Satanic struggle. When the desert dust clears, he appears to have won his skirmish in the wilderness. This is no cozy gospel story; it has neither cooing baby Jesus nor bath-robed shepherds. This Gospel begins in an apocalyptic vision of Jesus' identity that pushes him immediately into the fray with Satan in vv. 12-13.

In light of this, Jesus' proclamation in vv. 14-15 makes even more sense. Having come through the time of trial, Jesus, who as the narrator and God have informed us is himself the gospel of God's Son, now preaches back in Jewish/gentile mixed Galilee his own gospel, *the gospel of God*, which Jesus as God's agent mediates. It begins with a somber note in v. 14. John has been handed over (the root verb in Greek is *paradidōmi*, the word for Jesus' handing over and betrayal in the coming Gospel narrative), which here reminds the reader of the cost of such proclamation as John and now Jesus embody. In narrating it this way, John now passes from view and Jesus comes renewed front and center in the narrative. His first words then proclaim this odd gospel of God. What is the gospel of God? Jesus immediately fills in the blank in v. 15: "The time is fulfilled, and the kingdom of God has come near;* repent, and believe in the good news." Jesus himself may be the gospel (1:1) and we readers know that he is Son of God (1:11), but Jesus himself points to God's ultimate purposes that are about to be fulfilled: God's coming reign, which is coming near. Such coming near eventuates in repentance and belief—again it is God's action of bringing the reign close that sets human response in motion. The proclamation confirms some of the earlier intertext from Isaiah that we mentioned in the prologue material above. The language of God's reign and gospel/good news is material that comes from the proto-apocalyptic materials in 2 and 3 Isaiah. Here Jesus places that "gospel" at the center of his own proclamation, and its connection to the immediately preceding struggle with Satan in the wilderness only underlines its meaning. Jesus can proclaim this coming reign of God because in him Satan is already being overcome and eventually even bound and tied up (2:27). The stage is set for Jesus' ministry in Galilee.

Since this text appears in full in Lent 1, it can become a helpful occasion for the preacher to remind hearers after the Epiphany season what was at stake in Jesus' ministry in Galilee. Because it includes elements of the messianic and servant motifs of Jesus' baptism and the ripped-open heavens, it also points forward to elements of the narrative that will be important in Jesus' Jerusalem ministry and passion on Palm/Passion Sunday and Easter. The text sums up important themes that will guide hearers in grasping the unique shape of Mark's Gospel and the gospel it proclaims. Some of this lection also appears in Epiphany 3, in that case joined to some of Jesus' initial calls in 1:16-20. This has the advantage of providing a crucial context for those calls and helps explain some of the immediacy of their response. When Jesus proclaims the kingdom, he is not offering some timeless message, but a timely one (*kairos*) that provokes such immediacy and struggle as these texts even now at this early stage portray. In this sense, the treatment of the text in Lent is actually enriched—so long as preachers and hearers see the cosmic horizon of the testing and struggle in light of both the gospel of Jesus' identity *and* the gospel Jesus preaches: the gospel of God and God's coming reign.

2

The Gospel's Promising Beginnings in Galilee (1:16—3:6)

With this first major section of Mark, we see Jesus in his "Galilean spring." His gospel ministry has begun and meets with impressive results. Yet because his gospel has an apocalyptic tinge, even the springtime is not all blossoms and blooms. Jesus meets up with an unclean spirit, sickness, and yes, a stretch of controversy, too. In fact, by the end of this opening section Jesus' opponents will begin to coalesce into an early conspiracy against him. As we shall see in Mark's unfolding Gospel, the gospel is not proclaimed without opposition either. In that respect, even this Galilean spring includes some early storm clouds on the horizon.

THE GOSPEL'S PROMISING BEGINNING IN GALILEE: THE GOSPEL PROCLAMATION (1:16-45)

INTRODUCTION

This is an exciting moment in Jesus' gospel ministry. He calls and people just follow. He teaches and his hearers are amazed at his authority. Jesus casts out demons and heals and the crowds throng to him. The only shadows cast in this section are due to the realization that comes from the demons who encounter Jesus. The demons recognize what Jesus represents: an apocalyptic incursion of the divine kingdom into the realm of Satan.

LECTIONS

All of the texts in this subsection are covered in Year B of the lectionary during Epiphany 3–6 over four consecutive Sundays. The lections also move successively, thus giving the preacher the opportunity to build from week to week. As this represents the first moments in Jesus' reign-of-God ministry, they offer an excellent opportunity for these four weeks after the Epiphany. The texts help to reveal Jesus for who he is and demonstrate the kingdom to which Jesus himself points in his proclamation.

LECTION: JESUS CALLS THE FIRST DISCIPLES
1:14–20; EPIPHANY 3

Here the action begins. The prologue has set the stage for what Norman Perrin has called Mark's "apocalyptic drama."[1] The key for considering what follows with our text's twofold call narrative of the first four disciples is the section immediately prior that rounded out the prologue: 1:14-15 (for extra details, see the final lection in chapter 1). Jesus has announced the "gospel of God," which is the kingdom. It is near and the time for fulfillment is here. In these summary verses of 1:14-15 of Jesus' gospel proclamation, Jesus is mentioned as coming into Galilee. As startling as the call narratives are in vv. 16-20, it is necessary to see them in relation to the beginning of Jesus' ministry of the gospel of God in vv. 14-15. It is the announcement of the good news, the report after the mysterious apocalyptic struggle with Satan in the wilderness, which helps frame the suddenness and radicality of the new disciples' response in 1:16-20.

The apocalyptic tendency is also intimated through the description of Galilee's lake as a "sea." An inland body of water of such size would likely be named a lake (cf. Luke 5:1), both in our time and in Jesus'. Here, however, the geographical naming may have more symbolic import. The sea is the setting of the forces of chaos. Mark will return to this designation later for similar apocalyptic purposes. The calls in our text take place in this apocalyptic geography of Mark.

---

1. Norman Perrin and Dennis Duling, *The New Testament: An Introduction*, 2nd ed. (New York: Harcourt, Brace, Jovanovich, 1982), 233–62.

With v. 18 we hear already for the third time in Mark the Greek word for "immediately" in his narration (1:10, 12). This word is a characteristically Markan one that emphasizes the moment as significant. Other Gospels may be more elegantly written. Mark's use of terms like "immediately" reflects the urgency of his apocalyptic gospel. The gospel presses forward, for the time is short. Readers need to understand the reasons for Mark's urgency in order to grasp the unfolding action.

The calls themselves are analogous. They focus on Jesus' action in calling and show surprisingly little interest in elaborating the disciples' response. We postmoderns might want to know what makes someone drop their nets and leave dad and the family business in a boat, but not Mark. The text follows a stereotypical structure of calling (1:16-18 = 1:19-20). Jesus moves, Jesus sees the two potential disciples at work, Jesus summons them, and the disciples let everything go to follow. Notice how Jesus is the subject of almost all of the action. When the disciples do respond, we do not get spiritual exercises or explorations of the disciples' inwardness. They just let go and follow. The only differences between the two sets of stories viewed structurally are the names of the disciples involved and the details of their work. For emphasis' sake, the second set has James and John leaving Father Zebedee in the boat with *hired hands!* Apparently the Zebedees were middle class.

The action makes little sense to us, in part because we may be inclined to confuse discipleship with a lifestyle choice. When we frame these Galilean calls with Jesus' Galilean proclamation of the kingdom, it begins to make more sense. Jesus brings good news that God is entering the fray with an apocalyptic gospel of the reign of God. Their response is no more and no less a heeding of that gospel call. It is not so much an act of their voluntaristic wills as a response to an eschatological promise of gathering and judgment (Mark 1:14-15 and perhaps the fishing reference of Jer. 16:16-18). As Jesus himself puts it promisingly, "Follow me *and I will make you* fish for people" (emphasis mine). The call is part of an apocalyptic drama because it offers the gospel of God's reign and a promise that pries people loose for discipleship.

The stereotypical response to this gospel call is important here, but also for understanding later failure in the narrative, especially the rich man of Mark 10:17-22. When the seed of the gospel is sown, mystery still attends it.

Promise is not a guarantee. Promise is fragile and must reckon also with failure.

For contemporary preachers in the season after Epiphany this means finding some way to connect the way we think about a call to discipleship with God's eschatological purposes. We tend to come at these issues from a decision perspective. This text, by contrast, places God's eschatological purposes as both context (1:14-15) and heart of the call. Preachers today will want to remember this as they plot sermons on this text. The disciples are not decisive heroes, really—certainly not in Mark's portrayal where the disciples eventually flee and fail miserably. Right now they hear the trumpet call and discern the meaning for tomorrow. It flows not from their internal resources, but from the naming of the kairos moment. Theological work on the part of preachers in days of crisis like ours may still find ways to discern how God's purposes shape and enable our discipleship today. Sometimes even we act in the present empowered by a dawning future. Such realities will help us to name and understand the disciples' calls more fully.

The choice here of this text for the season after the Epiphany is apt. These texts, especially early on, focus on the honeymoon period of Jesus' reign-of-God gospel ministry in Galilee. These early sprouts of the gospel promise help to show us how it takes root, even as it helps us make sense of the resistance and rejection that it eventually faces in Mark's apocalyptic drama.

Lection: The Man with an Unclean Spirit
1:21-28; Epiphany 4

With this text, Mark's apocalyptic gospel of God's reign encounters its own first skirmish with the demonic opposition. The fact that this skirmish takes place once Jesus has been teaching authoritatively in a holy place (synagogue) and at a holy time (Sabbath) only underlines the conflict. Jesus' gospel meets with unqualified success in the call of the first four disciples in 1:16-20; but here the opposition begins to reveal itself and, in the process, it also reveals Jesus.

Christians who read about an event in Jesus' lifetime as taking place in a synagogue need to understand what that means historically. The religious significance of a synagogue is something that intensifies after the temple's destruction in 70 c.e. Prior to this time, a synagogue was likely something more akin to a community center. This may not have excluded religious activities like the reading and interpreting of Scripture on the Sabbath, but it does not mean that the synagogue was an exclusively religious location either. Still, Mark clearly wants to narrate something unusual in this setting. In this early, programmatic scene in Jesus' gospel ministry, he appears in a synagogue, teaches, and then *heals an unclean person*. The location of this action makes an important point for the story going forward.

The first part of the text concerns Jesus' teaching. It prompts amazement among his hearers, not so much for its content as for its effect. Jesus' teaching is not derivative but with authority. It may well be that the contrast here is between the scribes' role in interpreting given tradition over against Jesus' prophetic role, which both preceding pericopes have underlined in various ways.

Just at this point, however, a man shows up with an unclean spirit—in that holy space and at that holy time. With a kind of demonic recognition, he senses the threat that Jesus represents in his very presence: "what is there between us and you, Jesus of Nazareth? Have you come to destroy us?" (translation mine) Here is the apocalyptic element in this story. It is no longer just an exorcism, because the spirit senses that Jesus has "come" and with an eschatological purpose that is inimical to evil. In such stories of exorcism, naming implies power: "I know who you are, the Holy One of God." By naming Jesus, does the unclean spirit seek to gain power? The narrator has none of it. He describes Jesus rebuking the spirit, telling him in Greek to "shut up," and commanding it to come out. The unclean spirit obeys, but not without convulsing and crying in a loud voice. The scene concludes with yet another description of amazement and an elision of Jesus' authority of exorcism and his authority of teaching. Its powerful conflated newness is a recognition of the world-altering reality that Jesus represents in the synagogue that day. Immediately his fame spreads.

Here we may have the first whiff of the so-called "messianic secret" motif. While Wilhelm Wrede's theory (see Introduction) no longer meets with wide agreement, there does seem to be an ironic distance set up with respect to Jesus' identity. Please note here that the unclean spirit recognizes Jesus, yet the crowd's reaction focuses instead on Jesus' authority, not his demonically disclosed identity! Through this "secret" readers are brought in on an insight that characters in the story fail to notice. The upshot is that neither the miraculous exorcism, nor even authoritative teaching, is sufficient for faith. This also underlines the fragility of the gospel promise that Jesus embodies.

In this first chapter, these events reveal the surprising power of Jesus' gospel ministry. Yet here, in this first skirmish with the demonic, we recognize what is at stake. The gospel of God's reign surfaces demonic opposition, too. In the process, Jesus is revealed for who he is, of all things, in the confession of the unclean spirit! The beginnings of the gospel in Galilee may well be promising, but they are also a struggle. Whatever following Jesus means, it is even in Galilee by no means all sweetness and light.

For preaching on Epiphany 4, this portends a wider horizon. We usually think of stories of demons as belonging to the realm of the personal and use a psychological hermeneutic to keep it contained: "Deep down, we all have problems." This text, however, pries loose our captive middle-class religiosity. The struggle over the man with an unclean spirit has a broader scope. The fact that this is caught up with Jesus' *teaching* is also significant. The struggle over evil is where the gospel of God's reign meets world. Where the demonic shows up is a local or personal manifestation of a wider skirmish between the old age and the new. Preachers thinking theologically about this story should keep this view at the center of their theological reflections. Struggle in the church is not new—especially among mainline Protestants! Here Mark may give us a way to rename our struggles and see their intransigence in light of a dawning sense of the gospel.

LECTION: JESUS HEALS MANY AT SIMON'S HOUSE
AND A PREACHING TOUR IN GALILEE
1:29-39; EPIPHANY 5

Our text contains some of the same things we have been dealing with in chapter 1: this mysterious apocalyptic Jesus, his ministry of healing and exorcism as the frontline of the apocalyptic struggle, and what all this "reveals." What is different here is that we no longer just have stories of healing (1:19-31), but summaries of healings (1:32-34) along with the prospect of something new (1:35-39) with a change of place. They seem to cap off Jesus' busy day in Galilee so as to leave a strong impression of his beginning ministry in Galilee and the mysterious force that drives it onward.

The healing story in 1:29-31 features Peter's mother-in-law and is classic in terms of form. Her sickness is described and the healer is told of her need. Jesus acts by grasping her hand and raising her. She is healed and now empowered to serve just as the angels served in 1:13. Interesting here is the verb of Jesus' action. Peter's mother-in-law is "raised." Is this a harbinger of resurrection? Sometimes healings are given this eschatological sense and it would fit into the apocalyptic context of Jesus' reign-of-God ministry. Please note that we learn along the way not just the promise of healing but the cost of what Simon Peter has given up since 1:16-18 to follow: a job, a house, a mother-in-law, and presumably a spouse (anticipating 10:28-31).

After this, however, references to healings and exorcisms are not so much narrated as summarized in 1:32-34. That all this summary is described in connection with Sabbath sundown demonstrates a sense of piety and Jewishness. The fact that so many healings and exorcisms are mentioned underlines Jesus' strange power and apocalyptic impact. The elusive language of v. 34 only emphasizes this all the more: Jesus did not let the demons speak. We readers know who Jesus is from 1:1 and his baptism in 1:9-11. Opposing demons recognized him in the synagogue earlier (1:21-28). Here Jesus keeps silencing them because they "know him." Other characters are not party to the secret revelation, for it is not yet time to be revealed. Still, we readers understand.

Yet Mark's Gospel refuses to let Jesus rest on his laurels. This Jesus is no crowd pleaser, but some mysterious person on a mission. Before sunrise, he heads off to a deserted place to pray to God. How useless this prayer might seem given the context! His disciples hunt him down and let him know that everyone is looking for him, implying he should stop praying and go back to Capernaum. Jesus, however, will not be managed—even by his disciple handlers. Jesus announces that the reign-of-God ministry now moves ahead to neighboring towns. This would sound more like an itinerary issue, except that in 1:38 Jesus may be using I-disclosive language about preaching: "that is what I came out to do." His leaving is about purpose, a mission of proclamation and demon exorcism. The otherness of God comes with healing and exorcism; the same also drives Jesus beyond the cheering crowds of Capernaum.

For preaching purposes, the miracles, exorcisms, and summaries point beyond themselves. Nowhere is this more clearly manifested but in Jesus' mysterious disappearance to pray. Jesus has a sense of purpose related to prayer, yes, but also to the next task: proclaiming the message there also. All of these events keep reminding us of God's overarching purpose and coming realm. For preachers, the stories of Jesus in his early ministry also point ahead.

Although this pericope is a bit of a hodgepodge of narrative and summary, it fits nicely into the framework of Epiphany 5 readings. We see Jesus' kingdom action, even while we remember its epiphanic purpose. Preaching that takes Jesus' apocalyptic mission seriously will want to connect healings not to mere miracle, but to a divine revelatory purpose in the midst of human need and inadequate perception. Jesus has come for this purpose. Mysteriously, and beyond our control, Jesus also goes elsewhere for this purpose . . . to other horizons beyond our own.

Lection: Jesus Cleanses a Leper
1:40–45; Epiphany 6/Proper 1

Jesus' reign-of-God ministry of preaching with healing and exorcisms seems to reach its apotheosis here. According to Joel Marcus, this text, in the way the story is narrated, all but turns a healing *into* an exorcism.[2] In recognizing this, the reader can plausibly connect Jesus' improbable response and words to the person with leprosy in vv. 41, 43 to what would otherwise seem to be just another healing.

We have our own associations with the word *leprosy*. We are likely inclined to think of the malady we call today Hansen's disease. Leprosy is in this biblical sense a skin disease sufficient to render one unclean in terms of torah. This explains also why the text is so important. What is described here is not so much a physical healing, but a social cleansing. Jesus' action renders the man clean and able to return to normal human social relations. Our feelings about Hansen's disease or miracles of healing may obscure the powerful legal and social implications of the person's disease and his or her relation to the community in the time. We can be grateful that we are moving away from labeling persons by the name of a disease (the leper), yet the text's present language painfully reminds us of the power of such naming to ostracize and so the text offers hope in a boundary-breaking Jesus who is not bound by it.

2. Joel Marcus, *Mark 1–8* (New York: Doubleday, 2000), 207–11.

Once again, the afflicted person appears before Jesus in typical healing story fashion. The story moves through all parts of the healing form with the concluding demonstration of a healed state. What makes this healing story unusual is two things: Jesus' response after touching the man and the very different results for the once leprous man and for Jesus. Jesus' response is a little difficult to pick up through the NRSV translation. The phrase "moved with pity," represents a variant in the Greek, whose more likely counterpart would be translated "grew incensed" or "angry." Also, when in v. 43 Jesus is "sternly warning him," the text translates the next verb as "sent him away." Yet his latter word is in actuality the same Greek verb used in exorcisms, "cast him out." When Jesus fights disease it is not altogether different from his fight with the demonic. Yet this exchange may be causing the once leprous man and Jesus to exchange roles. Now the afflicted one has been cleansed—that is, restored to community—while Jesus must go off alone in desert places and is not able to go into any city openly. The confrontation with demonic evil in Mark's apocalyptic gospel is indeed a struggle and discloses unlikely reversals to the healed *and to the healer.* The healing/exorcism causes the reader to pause in the presence of mystery.

Lest we miss the point, Jesus does not heal and discard torah in the rush to cleansing. He charges the cleansed man to keep quiet and show himself to the priest as a testimony to them (Lev. 14). The fact that he does not keep quiet means the narrative moves ahead. The question about torah, even for a healer who charges following it, can be troublesome for someone willing to touch person with leprosy as subsequent chapters show. Yet sometimes news is so good, it just cannot be hidden but must be revealed even in its mystery.

For preachers, it is important to remember that this text seems to breach the wall between healing and exorcism. The upshot is that preaching the reign of God addresses us even in that busy intersection where illness, evil, and human sociality meet. Kingdom language sometimes sounds like a leftover from nineteenth-century liberalism. Here, Kingdom language locates divine action in the space between us: perhaps where we are even most vulnerable and susceptible to evil's intractable power. This story gives preachers the opportunity to explore in our world what the good news looks like in relation not just to human interiority nor as a remote human historical project, but in the midst of the connections of our lives and the price we pay for such solidarity. This text offers an unusual homiletical-theological invitation to the preacher who wishes to name the reign of God today in the midst of such busy, ambiguous intersections.

The text fits the profile of an Epiphany text, but requires some theological recalibration. The strangeness of Jesus' response to the leper pushes our compassion more deeply to the inscrutable passion of God. Jesus is no bandaid; he does not heal lightly. He is revealed in this story as struggling with the demonic and its intransigence. He does so even at great cost, taking on as his own the deserted isolation that until now was the lot of the leprous man himself. Thus it makes for an unusual, painful, and yet mysterious Epiphany 6.

Preaching the Gospel but Not without Opposition (2:1—3:6)

Introduction

The promising ministry in Galilee continues, but storm clouds are gathering over the Galilean landscape in the form of this, the first of five consecutive controversy stories to follow. Jesus still heals and exorcises with powerful signs of God's coming reign, yet now the opposition to Jesus comes closer to the surface. Both here and in subsequent pericopes in Mark 2:1—3:6, objections to Jesus and his work are becoming more public. By the end of this controversy story subsection, Herodians are already plotting against Jesus in 3:6. Joanna Dewey argues that the subsection that begins here and runs through 3:6 has a concentric shape converging on 2:18-22—the disciples' feasting and the bridegroom's removal.[3] This center text highlights an eschatological newness to Jesus that points simultaneously to God's coming reign *and* to Jesus' death. Mark portrays this part of the Galilean ministry as a continuation of gospel good news (1:15), but invites us to consider an emerging theological mystery of Jesus' identity in controversies.

Lections

The pericopes of this section do a nice job of connecting with the calendar's frame for Epiphany 7–9. Where Jesus' ministry and identity are manifested, the theological mystery of his life, death, and resurrection are all invoked.

With this subsection in particular, where the conflict between Jesus and Jewish religious leaders seems to sharpen with every story, preachers need to stay mindful of turning this intra-Jewish conflict into Christian anti-Judaism. The Jewish leaders make good points: God is indeed one and usurping divine

---

3. Joanna Dewey, *Markan Public Debate: Literary Technique, Concentric Structure, and Theology in Mark 2:1-3:6* (Chico, CA: Scholars, 1980).

prerogatives makes for a theological problem. Somehow Christian preachers will need to preach such texts in ways that do not perpetuate stereotypes.

But there is also something here to watch out for with respect to the miracles that occasion the controversies. Able preachers will need to move behind miraculous pyrotechnics to see the difficult, legitimate theological issues lurking here, even now in the face of questioning opposition. In the process, however, preachers can recast faith as more than just the opposite of some imagined Jewish foil, but a "roof-raising" (e.g., 2:1-12), boundary-breaking, living, trusting relationship with the God of promise in Jesus Christ.

Lection: Jesus Heals a Paralytic
2:1-12; Epiphany 7/Proper 2

At the beginning of this episode, Jesus returns from deserted places to Capernaum, the site of his busy day of reign-of-God ministry in Mark 1. The language of "home" in 2:1 probably refers to Simon's house viewed as a kind of home base of operations. The locals remember Jesus' first day of ministry in Capernaum and crowd the door while Jesus teaches "the word," perhaps reminding readers of Jesus' gospel of God in 1:14b-15. The crowd is also important narratively in that when some friends carrying a paralyzed person (on the labeling of persons with diseases, see the text box in Mark 1:40-45 above) try to bring him to Jesus for healing, the great crowds themselves block the way! The paralyzed person and the four friends, however, are not dissuaded and begin to de-roof the roof of this house, commonly described as made up of wooden beams, mud, and thatch. A healing narrative that spends so much time drawing our attention to the efforts of this stretcher crew is trying to score a rhetorical point—a fact lost not on Jesus, nor on the contemporary reader. So Jesus responds to the scene by saying something rather unexpected, "Son, your sins are forgiven."

The strange switch of subject here, from a standard healing story to a focus on Jesus' capacity to forgive sins, is a first example of a common Markan narrative practice called "intercalation." Intercalation is Mark's way of placing something between a story sandwich—in this case, a controversy about forgiveness in the middle of a healing narrative. For us, this intercalation seems like a non sequitur. Although in our culture we sometimes are inclined to think of some forms of sickness as a moral failing (alcoholism, or the connection of smoking to lung cancer), the idea that someone may be paralyzed in connection with sin may be for us a bit of a stretch. However, the connection with sin here does not necessarily mean either that Jesus or anyone else is assuming sin *caused* the paralysis. Sickness can be simply a mysterious manifestation of evil all tied up with sin. What is assumed here, however, is that Jesus' reign-of-God ministry of forgiveness *is* connected with the healing in that both are connected with God's new age. The narrator wants us to realize that this story is not just another healing miracle, but a sign of the eschatological reign of God, which Jesus teaches, proclaims, and manifests. Preachers would be wise to point out the difference between a backward-looking sin/causation model and a forward-looking forgiveness/kingdom model of healing. Mark's intercalation of story and reign-of-God theology may be his way of making an important point for faith.

So here, in the middle of a healing story, we shift into an unexpected debate about forgiveness and who has a right to pronounce it. Scribes, men learned in the law, were apparently questioning this in their hearts as blasphemy, that is, a human usurpation of a divine prerogative of forgiveness. Apocalyptic Jesus, a discerner in spirit and thus bearing a kind of divine ability to search hearts, grasps this and brings it out into the open with a series of questions in 2:8-9. The questions go to the heart of discerning this theological relationship between forgiving sins, healing, and Jesus' identity. In the midst of it comes Jesus' first self-designation as the Son of the human (Son of Man; see Introduction). He asks which is easier to do: to say words of forgiveness or healing—a question grounded more anthropologically than theologically. For a human, it is indeed easier to say "you are forgiven" than "you are healed." In the divine economy, however, the problem of offering divine forgiveness is indeed more problematic! Still, the argument goes from the lesser to the greater—or here from the easier to the harder—thus the healing itself is *confirmation* of the truth of Jesus' claim. Jesus, having put his confirmation on the line, then enacts it in direct speech in 2:11 to the paralyzed man: "I say to you, stand up, take your mat and go to your home." The response is the confirmation of his claim that he is indeed authorized as Son of the human and a sign of the new age of God's kingdom.

This is the first time the Markan Jesus refers to himself as Son of the human. The designation is historically a problematic one for exegesis. Sometimes, Son of the human is just an indirect way of saying "human being." In intertestamental Judaism, the Son of the human becomes a more ambiguous figure as a kind of semi-divine agent beginning in Dan. 7 and continuing through noncanonical apocalyptic literature of the time. Here the Son of the human seems to appear in an ambiguous, mysterious way. He is authorized to do new-age sorts of things, like forgiving sins. When he does so, however, the agency of those actions is still considered to be God's. Thus, the initial references to verbs of forgiveness seem to be in the passive, implying divine agency (2:5, 9). Moreover, when the once paralyzed man "rises" in 2:12, he does so in an ambiguous divine passive verb, "raised." Could this be another harbinger of connecting healing with God's resurrection reign? It is still hard to say—the Greek grammar here is so convoluted it is difficult to tell whether the Son of the human language is in Jesus' own words or an editorial comment by Mark inserted in the narrative. But that may just be Mark's limited narrative point in introducing Son of the human language here: Jesus' identity is an apocalyptic one marked by theological mystery . . . and now scribal opposition.

The connection of this strange turn to Son of the human language in Mark 2:1-12 is no accident from the narrator's perspective. This healing story is more than just restoring limbs; it is also even more so about trusting Jesus' word, his proclamation of God's reign. The text dwells on faith in that word, in that gospel, by showing the paralyzed man and his four friends going through the roof in their trust of Jesus. The fact that all were amazed and glorified *God* (contrary to the charge of blasphemy earlier!) and never saw anything like it underlines the newness of Jesus' kingdom proclamation in word and deed. This is faith in Jesus, better also to add, faith in the new way of God that this Jesus is announcing. Yet such moments also prompt crisis: the scribes "question" in living contrast to such new-age faith. There is no good news, no reign-of-God promises without also bumping into opposition and struggle—even in Epiphany. Yet faith, faith in the God of that promise, goes through the roof. This tension offers a beautiful opportunity to Epiphany 7 preachers to name the gospel this day in light of the trenches in which we struggle and yet are animated by dawning faith.

LECTION: JESUS CALLS LEVI AND THE QUESTION ABOUT FASTING
2:13-22; EPIPHANY 8/PROPER 3

This lectionary reading has two halves: vv. 13-17 and 18-22. The second half of the lectionary reading is significant not just for itself, but as the center point for the whole controversy subsection that runs from 2:1—3:6, so it is especially important for lectionary preachers to keep that in mind.

What makes this particular first-half pericope in vv. 13-17 unique is that like 2:1-12 it relates a controversy story to another form, in this case the call narrative. Mark 2:13 begins a lot like 1:16-20. Jesus walks along, sees persons at work, and calls them; they, in turn, leave it all and go to follow. These elements are all present in 2:13-14. The chief differences are twofold. First, there is no specific reference to what Levi son of Alphaeus gave up after he leaves his tax collector's booth. There is here no talk of nets, or mending, or hired help, or dads bobbing sonless in a fishing boat on the sea (1:19-20). Second, what Levi leaves is not some prosperous, respected employment, but a despised, ritually unclean job: running the local tax office. It is this reality, this *difference* from the call along the sea, that drives the controversy in 2:15-17 to follow.

Consequently, we cannot understand the call and its relation to the controversy without grasping Levi's identity. Mark does not list Levi as one of the Twelve, although other gospel writers, like Matthew, give a different name for a tax collector who follows and list him among the official disciples. The name Levi may involve some literary license. Joel Marcus points out that the name Levi in that period was not infrequently associated with sons who had Levitical pedigree.[4] Thus hearing of a Levi named as "tax collector" might have been sufficient to make any pious person roll their eyes. It is important to know that not every tax collector was as rich, for example, as Luke's Zacchaeus. Some tax collectors would have been underlings in the system and not the kind of rapacious wealthy person we imagine. The life of collecting taxes, however, would have been in relative terms financially comfortable. Still, it would have likely brought a person like Levi in contact with unclean foreigners, Roman collaborators and lackeys, and not a few coins with idolatrous images on them. Furthermore, what makes tax collectors so problematic is that they thus sin "professionally," that is, habitually. That is the problem with Levi.

So when Jesus begins reclining at table with Levi in 2:15ff, and other tax collectors and sinners (again, think *habitual*) join in the dinner party, a problem ensues. Jesus may call and Levi may follow in service of Jesus' reign-of-God gospel, but the Pharisees see Jesus' eating practices as eating away at the very

---

4. Marcus, *Mark 1–8*, 225.

foundations of Jewish life. This is the first significant reference to the Pharisees, and in a section where controversies with Jesus' opponents are highlighted. We need to get this situation right. The Pharisees are not black-hatted bad guys. They represent a lay movement within Judaism that takes the people's gracious election to holiness so seriously they are willing to apply torah to all of life—even sections of the Levitical code for priests are applied carefully and faithfully to ordinary living. The esteem with which the Pharisees are held in the period is great. Unlike some other parties, they believed in written *and* oral torah—and, please take note, they believed in resurrection! They test and challenge Jesus perhaps in part because they see him not as an enemy, but a fellow traveler with dicey travel companions. When Christians jump too quickly to anti-Jewish stereotypes, we miss the truth of the matter. If Jesus and the Pharisees did not share some common concerns and causes, they would have not taken interest in anything he or his disciples did.

Nonetheless, Jesus is breaking with certain understandings of purity as it relates to the divine purposes. In good Jewish fashion, Jesus will elsewhere in this section cite biblical examples, precedents, even folk wisdom to make his case. Something new is emerging here—and the newness is God's through Jesus and the kingdom Jesus proclaims. While in this case Pharisees keep boundaries for the good of God's people under serious Roman and gentile threat for the sake of honoring God's sovereignty and the order of a good creation, Jesus is breaking boundaries and arguing that God's purposes are tied intimately to a coming, divine kingdom. God, consistent with God's promises, is like a good physician. Thus, God is seeking to cure the creation of the sickness it really suffers from. So the controversy ends by recapitulating the call of 2:13-14. Jesus, as eschatological agent of God has "come" not to call righteous types, but sinners, like these ones, around his reign-of-God table.

This first half of Epiphany 8 in vv. 13-17 gives us important information about Jesus, his disciple retinue, and the emerging conflicts of this promising Galilean reign-of-God inauguration. However, the center of gravity lies in what follows in the next pericope: the relationship of old wine and new in vv. 18-22. This subsequent section helps makes sense of the conflict with the Pharisees that we have just witnessed. More importantly, it will help us understand this whole conflict of 2:1—3:6 as tied up with the apocalyptic moment in time.

With this second half of the pericope in vv. 18-22, we come to the center point of our five-part series of conflict stories in 2:1—3:6. In this case, however, the controversy is not so much with Jesus, but his disciples. The fasting practices of John the Baptist and the Pharisees' disciples are contrasted with the non-fasting behavior of Jesus' disciples.

Jesus' response in v. 19 and for the balance of this text, which combines a controversy now with a saying from Jesus, places the practice of fasting within an eschatological framework. Through his use of the bridegroom metaphor, Jesus highlights the incongruity of fasting during such a joyful time as a wedding. Two things are highlighted by Jesus' eschatological take on the problem.

First, others fail to recognize the presence of the bridegroom right now. Just as the presence of the bridegroom indicates the time of wedding celebration, so also Jesus' presence betokens a unique timeframe. Fasting now would be tantamount to not knowing "what time it is." Jesus makes his point with a rhetorical question in v. 19 to which no one can really respond otherwise.

Second, Jesus anticipates something odd that fits neither the celebratory wedding frame nor run-of-the-mill apocalyptic expectation. The presence of the bridegroom should indicate a new state of affairs, but Jesus speaks of the bridegroom being "taken away" in v. 20. This is no ordinary wedding, nor is it an ordinary eschatological sequence. The saying, here at the center of this five-controversy section of Mark 2, highlights Jesus' *death* as an eschatological turning point, reinforced by the language of "on that day," language that is itself eschatological. While this will become quite clear in Mark 15:33-38, where Jesus' death is portrayed as an apocalyptic, sun-darkening, sacred-cosmos-splitting, centurion-confessing turning of the ages, the reference here is early and startling. Here at the heart of controversies is a claim about Jesus himself and the strange mix of joy and loss that accompanies his untraditional wedding celebration metaphor.

This very tension then connects with the saying that follows in vv. 21-22. What we have are metaphors of incompatibility. The comparisons with cloaks and wine are commonplace and would be consistent with the concerns of persons of small means. Sewing un-shrunk cloth to patch an old cloak makes no more sense than pouring new, fermenting wine into old wineskins. The old just cannot contain the new and something catastrophic results. Part of this disruption is manifested in the choice of words. The word for "putting" the wine into wineskins actually means "casts" or "throws" and is the same Greek root word used to describe Jesus being driven out (1:12) and demons being "cast out" (1:39) earlier in Mark. The word likewise for "tear" in v. 18 is the same root word used to describe the splitting of the heavens in Mark 1:10. The language evokes in a sideways fashion the apocalyptic crisis that Jesus and his gospel represent. The thought is capped off with a final statement: "but one puts new wine into fresh wineskins." What is at stake in 2:18-22 is this incompatible tension that Jesus represents. While it does not mean that Judaism is repudiated (matters of torah do in fact matter), it does mean that Jesus emerges as something new that cannot be contained either. There is, in short, no point to losing either old wineskins or new wine! The old is indeed worth preserving, whether cloak or wineskin. Yet Jesus' incompatible newness is what is at issue here. This point will only become clearer in Jesus' disputes with others in the unfolding Markan narrative. Viewed in light of the tear and the ferment of Christianity in its Jewish context decades after Jesus' crucifixion when this text is committed to writing, it may also speak to the tensions of community relations at a time of profound loss and change.

These consecutive texts (2:13-17 and 2:18-22) belong together in the lectionary for Epiphany 8, but represent only two subsections of Mark's larger argument. Nonetheless, late Epiphany preachers can still benefit from them. The subsection from 2:18-22 is the real center point of this controversy chiasm. The second half of our Ephipany 8 text gives us an important frame for the first half of the lection in 2:13-17. It may be tricky to think of the call of Levi and the challenge posed to the law in that call story as controversy narrative. Fortunately, 2:18-22 gives us a way of framing this discussion. The newness Jesus represents is tied up with his person, and his person with his death. For a community itself dealing with its own tensions at the time of writing, it makes it possible to reflect on call in a new way, in a strangely *incompatible* way, which corresponds to their own experience at a time of profound loss and change. The homiletical theologian for Epiphany 8 might profitably view such a frame as an opportunity to think out loud about call—especially for those who serve in now disestablished mainline churches. While we face nothing like the marginalization of some persons and groups, this disestablishment gives us a window, perhaps again for the very first time, on the way such language functions to illumine common life in struggle over the old and the new—and point a way forward, too. Perhaps a text like this can help us be honest about our own crisis and the promise as well.

LECTION: PLUCKING GRAIN ON THE SABBATH AND THE MAN
WITH A WITHERED HAND
2:23—3:6; EPIPHANY 9/PROPER 4

Again, the lectionary combines texts in Mark that are carefully designed to integrate individual controversy narratives into a communicative whole:

2:23-28 and 3:1-6. With this lectionary text, we encounter the first of our final two controversies of the five in Mark 2:1—3:6. Following the incompatible metaphors of vv. 18-22, the text is a good example of how Jesus still cares about torah and its interpretation, too.

Mark begins in the first half of our lection, 2:23-28, by describing a scene where Jesus and his disciples are moving through a field. As they do so, the disciples are plucking grain on the Sabbath. The Pharisees in v. 24 raise an objection about its conformity with law. The implication is that what they are doing constitutes harvest work and thus contravenes the Sabbath. Although the disciples are doing the plucking, Jesus, as their teacher, is in their view responsible for their actions. The importance of that is that Jesus' authority is brought into question. In the following verses, Jesus then offers two responses to their statement, both of which, in different ways, interpret Sabbath and its meaning.

Sabbath is a good and wonderful thing. It is mentioned not only in the Ten Commandments, but first of all in the narrative of creation in Genesis. It has a special meaning in Jewish identity not just because God commands it as a remembrance of Exodus liberation, but because God also gives it as the crown of creation's seventh day. In an age where we human beings sometimes define ourselves by work, Sabbath is a reminder of the divine order that refuses to participate in the reduction of humanity to what we produce. Christians today need to understand that Sabbath, and disputes about it, cannot be reduced to matters of picayune legalism. Sabbath matters to the Pharisees, to Jesus, and yes, to Mark, too. As a countercultural act in our time, we would do well to attend to its value here as well.

Jesus' first response in 2:25-26 initially takes the form of a rhetorical question. Jesus refers the Pharisees to a Scripture text about David and his companions and what happened with the bread of the Presence in the time of Abiathar the high priest. Joel Marcus raises some questions about this interpretation and what it means—the fit of Jesus' response to the Pharisees' question about *work* on the Sabbath is a little off.[5] Nonetheless, the phrase for the companions in Greek, "those who were with him," does capture the shape of the argument Jesus wishes to make. The argument concerns David and those

---

5. Ibid., 244.

in relation to David and a seeming violation of law. The point is, at least in part, that law can be suspended for human need—a principle that interpretations of Jewish law have also observed in various ways.

The second response in vv. 27-28 is indirectly scriptural and directly Christological. It is the former because the place of Sabbath and relation to humanity in God's primal act of creation is invoked. It is Christological because the general principle applied to human beings is now specifically related to the Son of the human title in Mark that here, as Adela Yarbro Collins notes, is likely linked to the apocalyptic revelation of Daniel 7.[6] Here, as something said within the narrative world, it makes little sense. However, from the standpoint of the reader, who has already been cued in on Jesus' identity in specific ways over the first two chapters, the mysterious apocalyptic claim seems to riddle Jesus' authority to interpret torah.

This fourth controversy story is important precisely because it follows the center point of the concentric stories in 2:18-22, the text about fasting, the old and the new, and their incompatibility. It is important to note that Jesus here is not abrogating torah; he is not repudiating Judaism. At the same time, he is taking an interpretation of Jewish law and relating it to some Christological claims that would be startling to his textual audience, the Pharisees. Christian interpreters need to see this crux of chapter 2 clearly. Jesus is a Jew. The interpretation of torah that he gives is within the Jewish orbit. But the Christological twist he gives it in the end is a startling claim that is not easily "contained." Christians should preach such texts in light of that tension and not prematurely resolve it by turning the Pharisees into legalistic foils. The Markan community a few decades after Jesus' crucifixion is in a different place and must have been struggling to figure out where it stood relative to the Jewish tradition in which Jesus and their common life arose. Contemporary preachers have the opportunity here to think about traditions, identities, and differences in a way that is productive and respectful of others. Whatever Epiphany is, it is not an excuse for language that hides or occludes the Judaism from which Jesus springs and in light of which Jesus' arguments actually make sense. The fact that it is an apocalyptic claim of Jesus as Son of the human should temper any perspective that is too easily resolved: the story riddles Jesus identity and locates it in apocalyptic mystery, playing on Dan. 7. Anything that reduces that claim and stifles the mystery is of a different order altogether.

6. Adela Yarbro Collins, *Mark: A Commentary* (Minneapolis: Fortress Press, 2007), 205. Collins also points out that this connection of David in the first response in vv. 25-26 is thus underlined by the messianic claim about the Son of Man in vv. 27-28, making the two responses related as a kind of riddle in Mark.

In this final part of our Epiphany 9 lection, Mark 3:1-6, we consider yet another Sabbath event: the healing of the man with a withered hand. In this story, however, the objection in this fifth controversy story is not about the disciples, but about Jesus himself. By the end of the story, the emerging conflict of chapter 2 takes an especially dark turn. Jesus' opponents may once have merely reasoned in their hearts. Now, however, Jesus pronounces their hearts hardened and the Pharisees seek an alliance with Herodians to destroy Jesus, in a kind of human inversion of the demon's perceived threat in Jesus from 1:21-28. What started off as promising beginnings has taken a fateful turn that will eventually lead to a Roman cross.

Jesus is reported as entering the synagogue yet again in 3:1. The narrator reminds readers in the subsequent verse that this too happens on the Sabbath. This reminds us of other conflicts in Mark 1:21-28, but also the immediately preceding text concerning his disciples' Sabbath behavior in the grain field. Here, however, it is Jesus himself who is taken to task. The Pharisees are described as "watching" him with the idea "that they might accuse him." The narrator signals to us that the conflicted relationship has indeed sharpened. The Pharisees are portrayed as not happy with Jesus.

In vv. 3-5, Jesus clearly acts with some awareness of their feelings and intentions. He begins by telling the man with the withered hand to come forward, the Greek term meaning literally "rise up to the middle." The verb is reminiscent of resurrection language; the man is brought from the edge to the center. In v. 4, however, Jesus no longer addresses the man with the withered hand, but poses a question to the Pharisees about the law. His rhetorical question allows no negative answer. Any decent interpreter of Jewish law would have to agree that Sabbath is indeed about saving and not killing. Most commentators note that the question is a bit out of place. There is no immediate indication that the man is in mortal danger, so the exchange is not quite apt. Their silence seems to provoke powerful emotions from Jesus in v. 5: first anger and then grief at their hardness of heart. The term, of course, is intertextually freighted. Hardness of heart is for Pharaohs, not Pharisees. It also bespeaks a strange mystery. God seems to harden hearts in some cases; yet human beings also do things that lead to such cardiosclerosis, too. Sometimes it is hard to tell where human culpability leaves off and the mystery of the divine will begins. With this tragic state of affairs revealed by Jesus' apparent apocalyptic prescience in discerning their hardened hearts, Jesus proceeds with the healing. Jesus' word suffices. Eugene Boring points out that, without touch, no "work" was really done on that Sabbath in the synagogue![7] Nonetheless, the point of the healing is the controversy and the narrative it sets into motion. Now Pharisees, the representatives of faithfulness and purity, are working with Herodians, who probably represent some Jewish party willing to collaborate with Romans. They begin even here at the conclusion of Jesus' promising beginnings in Galilee to find a way to destroy him and the gospel he proclaims in word and deed. At the end of these five controversy stories here at Mark 3:6, it is good to remember once again from our concentric controversy texts' midpoint in 2:18-22 that new wine and old wineskins may just be incompatible (see Epiphany 8).

A text like this may just be pressing homiletical theologians to go someplace new. We stand at the other end of a long history of Jewish/Christian relations. This text begins with a Christian movement within Judaism experiencing tensions, yes, tensions of the new and the old. We contemporaries, by contrast, stand far away beyond the point of the parting of the ways—the point where Judaism and Christianity represent truly distinguishable religions. The question is how we Christians, as people of the promise, honor the relations we have in light of the struggle that once was intra-Jewish but now is something else. Perhaps the task here is not to replicate Mark's narrative-theological decisions but to take them up again in our own time and place as a way of working through an unfinished theology.[8] The fact that Jesus' death is foreshadowed in this text makes such a move helpful and perhaps necessary. At the very least, Christian preachers are obligated to distinguish between then and now, just as they need to distinguish Herodians from other Jewish parties. When we preach, we do so in the presence of others. What will we say with Mark this day? Is there a gospel to preach that embraces newness, names its incompatibility and otherness, and yet refrains from turning an "other" into a foil? If the gospel truly is something truly new, I do believe it must be possible. Perhaps even now God is placing it on the tips of our tongues.

7. Eugene Boring, *Mark: A Commentary*, New Testament Library (Louisville: Westminster John Knox, 2006), 95.

8. This notion I take up and elaborate on in my article, "Preaching as the Unfinished Task of Theology: Grief, Trauma, and Early Christian Texts in Homiletical Interpretation," *Theology Today* 70, no. 4 (2014): 407–16.

3

The Gospel Mystery Deepens—
The Word of Promise in Wider Fields
(3:7—6:6a)

In this next major section of Mark, the scope of Jesus' ministry, the gospel that is himself (1:1) and the reign of God (1:14-15) is sown across wider fields. The promising beginnings of that gospel ministry in Galilee set the stage, both for a powerful apocalyptic pushing back against anti-divine forces and a revelation of the growing opposition to Jesus. Yet with this extension of Jesus' gospel reach, the apocalyptic mystery of the promise goes deeper, too. The problems with which this gospel meets poses questions: why does this gospel embody God's apocalyptic power, but also meet with failure? Jesus continues his gospel proclamation, but joins it now to mysterious parables and revelatory acts that meet repeatedly with a lack of understanding and incomprehension on the part of those closest to Jesus. The gospel promise is an apocalyptic mystery that does not escape human failure—even if its disclosure does open up deeper understanding for those who, like the reader, seem to stand on the outside. This emerging mystery of revelation and incomprehension will carry us across the region just short of Caesarea Philippi in the subsequent chapter, the Markan narrative's farthest point from Jerusalem.

The Gospel Mystery Deepens:
The People Thronging Jesus (3:7-19)

INTRODUCTION

This brief section does not appear to be a highpoint in the Markan narrative. It is, however, important for setting up what follows. In these two texts we see summaries both of what Jesus does and who is ultimately close to him as followers. Both texts set off the mystery of who Jesus is. He is thronged by the crowds. Later we will see his own disciples, here carefully named and appointed as "the Twelve" in 3:13-19, struggling to understand him for most of the unfolding narrative. Moreover, one of these very Twelve will hand him over by story's end.

PASSAGES OMITTED FROM THE LECTIONARY

Both of the texts in this brief subsection are absent from the lectionary. They orient the reader by giving a summary of Jesus' typical activity and by naming names of the insider's circle of those who follow Jesus: the Twelve. Both help to frame the odd mystery that is Jesus' gospel ministry.

A MULTITUDE AT THE LAKESIDE (3:7-12): OMITTED FROM THE LECTIONARY

This text, which does not appear in the lectionary, has an important history in Markan scholarship. K. L. Schmidt made it famous by designating it as one of Mark's "summary statements."[1] Indeed, it seems to bear that quality as a narrative pivot point. Here, however, I wish to view this summary pivot as a kind of preview of Mark's next major section. There is old here to be summarized: crowds, healings, exorcisms, and charges to keep it all secret. What makes this text interesting, however, is the way it brings in new material to frame what follows. If the previous chapter was about Jesus' promising gospel success in Galilee, with emerging opposition, here the apocalyptic mystery deepens. The language sets the tone: Jesus "withdraws." Jesus needs a boat to avoid being crushed (the Greek word is the verb form of the apocalyptic term for tribulation: *thlipsis*). The crowds "fall upon him." The demons call him the title that only readers (1:1) and God (1:11) know, namely "Son of God" (3:11), even though Jesus mysteriously does not want any of this revealed (*phaneron*, 3:12). The fact that Jesus' draw is now well beyond Galilee also sets the stage. The text reads like a geography lesson. But in this section, geography

---

1. K. L. Schmidt, *Der Rahmen der Geschichte Jesu : literarkritische Untersuchungen zur ältesten Jesusüberlieferung* (reprint of the 1919 Berlin edition; Darmstadt: Wissenschaftliche Buchgesellschaft, 1964), 104-08.

is narratively significant. Jesus' word spreads abroad and cannot be contained. Yet this sown word is also a deepening word, bringing with it both threat and tragic incomprehension. In the widening struggle, the gospel is revealed in its full apocalyptic mystery from here to Caesarea Philippi in Mark 8, where the strange yet growing truth will set Jesus on the road to Jerusalem and a cross.

It is no accident that this summary statement has so many crucial geographic references. Narratives often use space as a way to define and frame the action. The fact that Jesus withdraws toward the sea to do his healing and demon-exorcising ministry is worth noting The sea is place of concentrated demonic power where Jesus can demonstrate his authority, as later water-walking episodes will demonstrate! More important here, however, are the place names associated with the people coming to Jesus. The places represent essentially the four directions and even include gentile locations. The shift of place marks a shift in the narrative and these many geographical references help the summary to be a preview of Jesus' spreading gospel and deepening, troubling apocalyptic mystery.

Nonetheless, this mysterious, apocalyptic gospel that is Jesus himself (1:1) and God's reign (1:14-15) does need people to proclaim it. The mystery of the word is not esoteric. It is a promise that must be spoken. So now Jesus turns to his disciples in order to establish their role in the coming chapters. The summary section of 3:7-12 has now set the stage for Jesus' gospel to spread and the apocalyptic mystery to deepen.

Since the text is not part of the lectionary, it is wise to note what a close reader of Mark's Gospel will miss proclaiming or teaching. Too often we speak of revelation theologically in unambigious terms. The light is either on or off; there is either disclosure or darkness. Mark, however, loves apocalyptic mystery. Here disclosure does not bring kumbaya moments. Instead, the gospel itself brings opposition. Moreover, even where it is received as healing or freedom from demons, there is the ever-present threat that it will overwhelm Jesus—hence the needed boat in 3:9 as a waterborne escape hatch. Summary texts like this seem about as interesting to preaching as biblical "begats" or lists of long-forgotten persons. But with Mark, apocalyptic mystery is always lurking in the gospel and encouraging preachers to think deeply, *theologically*, about what that gospel means today in the midst of our places, our conflicts, our threats, and our promise.

JESUS APPOINTS THE TWELVE (3:13-19):
OMITTED FROM THE LECTIONARY

This text is likewise not part of the lectionary. It reads, like the summary statement above, rather woodenly: a kind of list that merely goes through the motions. Still it does merit close reading. For while the list is important enough, it is the frame of the names that sets it off properly (vv. 13-15, 19).

The frame begins with a shift in location. Jesus goes up the mountain. The mountain is a place of revelation, poised somewhere between heaven and earth. If the first part of Mark was focused on Jesus' promising Galilean gospel ministry in relation to himself and God's kingdom purposes, in this major section this ministry of gospel promise is shared with others to deepen and widen its work. Therefore, on the mountain Jesus sovereignly calls to himself (1:16-20) those "whom he wanted." Their only response is to come away or "depart" to him. Jesus in v. 14 then appoints the Twelve, evoking in this place of revelation eschatological Israel renewed, but with a special calling: that they be "with him." This revelatory, solemn calling and appointing seems predicated on Jesus' person—and to such a degree that this being "with Jesus" grounds their twofold commission to preach and have authority to cast out demons. What the mountain reveals, then, is this special relationship that Jesus gives to the Twelve from here on out as the ground for their being sent. They are to preach and embody his twofold gospel mission that is intimately tied to his person ("the gospel of Jesus Christ" in 1:1) and equally tied to the announcement of God's reign (the gospel of God" in 1:14b-15) , an apocalyptic overcoming of demonic forces. The preaching ministry in particular is also tied to the future, missional gospel ministry in 13:10, and thus sets this revelatory moment also in relationship to the Markan community and the reader.

The tying of this revelatory gospel commissioning to the Twelve is repeated in v. 16 and underlined further by the listing of the Twelve, and the unique added naming of three of them to Jesus' inner circle. At the same time, something may be afoot from a narrative perspective. The references to the Twelve happen from here on out in Mark's Gospel. They are an insider's subset of disciples. We readers are privileged to see this revelatory moment and to share in the meaning of it. As the narrative proceeds, this insider, mountaintop revelatory knowledge that we readers share will be crucial for understanding both the heights and depths of this moment of revelation. We readers are here, as in the beginning (1:1 and 1:9), given the role of insiders, too.

As for the Twelve themselves, however, Peter is given pride of place and a nickname, the rock. Please note that Mark is unlike Matthew here in refusing to go ecclesiastical on the naming—there are no promises here about building the church on him nor prevailing against the "gates of Hades" (cf. Matt 16:17-19). As critical readers of this Gospel, we must let Mark be Mark. Peter's role in this Gospel is indeed foundational, but it is also ambiguous, as the subsequent failure of the Twelve and the disciples as a whole will painfully illustrate in the Markan passion narrative in chapters 14–15.

Two others of the Twelve receive added nicknames from Jesus, although the "Sons of Thunder" reference is a bit puzzling. It may be that they receive this nickname not because they are temperamental, but because they will be exposed to a kind of eschatological storm.[2] Beyond this, the list of names continues. Discerning readers will notice that the names do not always agree with those of other Gospel writers. Two other nicknames, though not given by Jesus here, are worth mentioning. In v. 18, another Simon has the nickname Cananaean. Most scholars seem to think it a translation of the word for "zealot."

This leaves us finally, now that the gospel is poised to be proclaimed wider with a called and appointed Twelve, for the gospel to go *deeper*. For the twelfth apostle named is Judas. The mystery begins with Judas's extra name, Iscariot. While there are various theories, it may well be that the name identifies him with a revolutionary party that did its business with daggers. Enough other theories about the name Iscariot exist to keep even this shrouded in mystery.

Yet while this extra name provides Judas the character with a little intrigue, the subsequent phrase with which v. 19 ends is the most important of all: "who betrayed him." With this first explicit mention, the mechanism by which Jesus will meet his demise is introduced—and precisely on the mountain of revelation. The gospel widens here by designating those who will share in Jesus' gospel ministry; but the gospel also deepens here in apocalyptic mystery. For the first time, we can foresee that Jesus will be betrayed—better, "handed over" (*paradidōmi*)—and that this gospel of Jesus' person and God's kingdom purposes will meet with *failure*. Please recall that this same "handed over" verb appeared in 1:14 to describe John the Baptist's fate! The implication is also startling when we think about the mountain as a place of revelation and Jesus' vocational sovereignty: from the reader's perspective both things are held in tension. God through Jesus calls, appoints, and in cases even renames apostles. But in the wider sowing of the gospel, the seed of its failure in betrayal and death is also now germinating here at 3:19. Mark's style of language and narration may in his Gospel be clumsy and crude, but his theology of the gospel goes deep—deep into the soil of the earth. Here on the mountaintop, more is revealed than Jesus'

2. Joel Marcus, *Mark 1-8* (New York: Doubleday, 2000), 264.

soaring vision. It also includes the depths of its power, which will pass through failure: a failure set in motion by a member of his chosen circle of the Twelve.

Again, this text is not part of the RCL readings. Nonetheless, it offers something significant to preachers who venture beyond its textual boundaries. As a symbolic narrative, Mark 3:13-19 helps preachers to think theologically about Jesus' sovereign call and gospel commission. Yet all of this rests on both the grace of Jesus' action, and the mysterious quality of revelation on the mountain. For on this mountain is revealed two important things to those called: the grace that is a call to mission *and* the "handing over" that it entails. While Jesus' fate is not the same as ours—we are not messiahs, thank God!—nonetheless, those called to be "with him" will know in their bodies what his fate means for them as well. Such is the mysterious apocalyptic revelation on the mountain for those whom Jesus summons to be "with him."

LECTIONS

This final pericope in the subsection here of Mark 3 is the only one in the lectionary. Fortunately, its juxtaposition of families in relation to the gospel and doing the divine will sets up a beautiful tension for grasping Mark's mysterious gospel message.

LECTION: JESUS AND BEELZEBUL AND THE TRUE KINDRED OF JESUS 3:20-35; PROPER 5

The lectionary committee's choice of vv. 20-35 as a pericope is a wise one. It is an example of Markan intercalation: a kind of sandwiching of story and teaching material that works together to produce a crucial, unified meaning. The intercalated material here follows naturally from the previous unit. In 3:13-19, Jesus summons his disciples and calls and appoints the Twelve to be with him. We, who have witnessed this mysterious revelation on the mountain, are ourselves made insiders in the process. In 3:20-35, the mystery of insiders and outsiders is explored more explicitly. The story on the edges of the sandwiched intercalation, 3:20-21 and 31-35, is about Jesus' family and their concern that his behavior might mean he is crazy. In the middle of the sandwich, vv. 22-30, is a series of statements and teachings that explain how Jesus is no demonic crazy person, but Satan's stronger enemy. As a result of this reversal in teaching in 3:22-30, family insiders are now seen as outside the will of God while those who do God's will are the true insiders, family. The story of Jesus' family has undergone an inside-out, reign-of-God reversal.

Mark 3:20-21 starts by setting the story frame. Jesus comes home and the crowds are so great that he and they cannot eat. Then Jesus' family hears of what is happening. The term here for family is those "around him," thus setting up the contrast with the phrase from the last pericope, in which the disciples were called to be "*with* him." His family arrives to seize him because people were saying Jesus was beside himself. The notion here is that he was insane—an idea perhaps connected to the demonic in Jesus' time.

The transition to the sandwiched middle material is now set. In 3:22, the scribes come down from Jerusalem and add to the conflict. While the family diagnosis is insanity, the scribes escalate the situation by describing Jesus as having "Beelzebul." The implication is that Jesus thus casts out demons by the power of the chief demon. This is not just idle language here. Such a claim is deadly business in Jesus' day.

This scribal accusation, now more explicitly theological in its claim, thus sets Jesus' teaching in motion. In v. 23, he summons them all to himself and teaches them in parables.

Jesus' teaching in parables is an important part of his ministry, especially in Mark. The only problem is that Jesus does not seem to know contemporary parable research. In Mark's Gospel, the definition of parable is somewhat broader than the modern designation. C. H. Dodd famously defined a parable as "a metaphor or simile drawn from nature or common life, arresting the hearer by its vividness or strangeness, and leaving the mind in sufficient doubt about its precise application to tease it into active thought."[3] Here in Mark, however, the parable is a bit more far-ranging. It is sometimes a metaphor or simile, but it can also be an allegory or even a saying, perhaps showing more commonality with the broader notion of the Hebrew *mašal*. Rather than get caught up in formal characteristics, it is best to see it as a kind of comparison that can take many forms. Within the Markan narrative, however, parables have a further function. They often help to separate insiders from outsiders, thus deepening the apocalyptic mystery that is Jesus in Mark.

---

3. C. H. Dodd, *The Parables of the Kingdom*, rev. ed. (London: Nisbet, 1961), 5.

In a series of parables or comparisons Jesus then tries to show that the scribes' accusation is untenable. The form here is a series of comparisons spawned by a rhetorical question. Assuming the scribes are correct, that Satan is casting out Satan, then what we have is chaos in the kingdom of Satan! Satan's *house* would be divided (3:24-25)—here the divided houses and political intrigue of Herodian life and imperial households may be being invoked. With one last question, Jesus broaches his point. If Satan is so divided, he is done (3:26b). Stick a pitchfork in him. Yet clearly Satan is not yet finished. So now, having rendered the metaphoric frame of the scribes untenable, Jesus offers his own (3:27). Satan's house is not so much divided; rather Satan as the owner of that house has been bound and his goods are now being plundered by the "stronger one." Jesus is that stronger one (1:7) and the plunder has only begun. The beauty of Jesus' metaphoric frame is that it also invokes some important apocalyptic motifs: the binding of Satan and the activity of God as divine warrior.[4] It is not Satan, but God who is busy, acting in the stronger one.

Clarity about this series of comparisons helps to explain the long troubling verses about blasphemy of the Holy Spirit in 3:28-30. Over the years, Christians have fretted about this statement. The more scrupulous among us, not understanding Jesus here in Mark, are too quick to be sure that they must have somehow so blasphemed and stand under its sentence. The history of interpretation would seem to indicate that guilt is not just a Protestant thing or a Catholic thing, but a Christian thing. Lord, have mercy!

The good news here is that we can clear up those over-scrupulous worries by reading the text closely. Why? The rhetorical strategy is not guilt inducement, but paradox. The first statement in v. 28 is a blanket one that is startling in its scope: all will be forgiven the sons of humanity, even blasphemy! Using eschatological statements, Jesus announces the divine fire sale on mercy. The first word is cosmic-wide forgiveness. The second part of the statement, v. 29, needs to be read therefore in relation to the first. Blasphemy of the Holy Spirit is not a matter of casuistry, but paradoxical refusal and loss. It is not that Jesus teaches scrupulosity here, but rather points out that a misnaming of the divine in mercy (that is, falsely calling it demonic) is paradoxically the only thing that can exclude someone from the blanket promise of v. 28. Why would anyone do so? Only because their point of view has become so stilted that they cannot see God's liberative mercy when it stares them in the face. The statement, in other words, exposes the obstinacy of Jesus' opponents in calling his exorcistic work "demonic." The bar for blasphemy of the Holy Spirit is thus

---

4. Adela Yarbro Collins, *Mark: A Commentary* (Minneapolis: Fortress Press, 2007), 233–34.

exceedingly high. In such moments they are failing to discern rightly God's will and Holy Spirit work of freeing from the demonic and missing out on God's wildly gracious Holy Spirit.

With that, we return to the outer slice of bread on Mark's intercalated sandwich in vv. 31-35. We have wrestled theologically with houses, Satan, and Holy Spirit mercy only to come back to the question of insiders and outsiders in relation to family. Now mothers and brothers stand *outside* sending and calling just as Jesus himself did in 3:13-19. The crowd even pipes up and asks him to behold them outside, seeking for Jesus. But Jesus has turned the relationship of outsiders and insiders inside-out. With a rhetorical question he reframes their perspective as well. Family is made up of those who do God's will, not those who treat Jesus as demonically crazy, or worse, are doing the work of the leader of demons. And those who do God's will are those gathered in the crowd—they are the ones Jesus beholds as mothers, brothers, and sisters. Two extra notes deepen this statement. Jesus' statement omits fathers. That is God's job, as 14:36 points out in relation to the divine will. But, equally important, sisters are included. The vision here is of a new, eschatological family, a new group of insiders, now revealed in light of Jesus' own plundering of the demonic house.

Preachers who treat this text need to understand it in light of its context in this new section of Mark. This is not a family values sermon—not just because it seems to refute conservative North American norms, but because it relates its reframing of "family" to God's redemptive purposes in Jesus' reign-of-God ministry. Hearers will find it strange to hear of family life spoken of so cavalierly. Family life *is* good, otherwise Jesus himself would not make it a reframed figure for the community that does the divine will in 3:35. Instead of turning this to a referendum on family values, preachers should take the discussion in a theological direction that places all our lives into the arc of God's kingdom purposes. Treating this text as an isolated pericope would make this less likely. Good exegesis and good homiletical theology requires us to go deeper.

THE GOSPEL MYSTERY DEEPENS: THE PARABOLIC GOOD NEWS (4:1-34)

INTRODUCTION

This chapter of Mark represents one of the longest sustained sections of teaching in the entire Gospel, surpassed only by Mark 13. Its significance as a subunit of the Gospel of Mark is often highlighted. A literary-critical treatment like Mary Ann Tolbert's in *Sowing the Gospel* makes the case for this parable as being programmatic for large parts of Mark' Gospel, along with the parable of the Vineyard Tenants.[5] Still other commentators, like Joel Marcus and C. Clifton Black, point to the elaborate chiastic structure of the whole chapter and note the sower's connection to the ending of Mark on chapter 16 where again much failure meets up with the articulation of a gospel promise. The chiastic structure they identify centers on the explanation of the parable in 4:13-20:

A	Narrative introduction (4:1-2)	
B	Seed parable (4:3-9)	
C		General statement (4:10-12)
D		Explanation of the parable (4:13-20)
C'		General statements (4:21-25)
B'	Seed parables (4:26-32)	
A'	Narrative conclusion (4:33-34)[6]	

The placement of the parable's explanation as the center point of this chiasm emphasizes its importance for understanding Mark's key parable here. The importance of this text is not just its content about the mystery of the kingdom, but its apocalyptic way of mediating it. Modern parable theory might be tempted to discard this explanation in 4:13-20. Some would argue emphatically that parables are not allegories. Yet Mark's Jesus has a different agenda here. As we shall see below, the parable of the sower is itself a mysterious "revealing" in a kind of apocalyptic mode. It is there to make sense of the preaching of the word in light of Satan's crumbling reign and God's emerging reign. It is a mystery to be understood that God's purposes can be worked out when the gospel is preached (1:1, 1:14b-15) even though there are all too many signs of its failure. Below we will learn that the image of sowing and harvest is an apocalyptic commonplace, especially as a great harvest is a kind of eschatological fullness.

Yet when the gospel meets with opposition, persecution, and apostasy, how can we say that God is still God? This parabolically layered chiastic text, nested like Russian dolls with one inside the other, presses behind narrations of the word's sowing to get at the divine mystery of its failure and promise. It

---

5. Mary Ann Tolbert, *Sowing the Gospel: Mark's World in Literary-Historical Perspective* (Minneapolis: Fortress Press, 1989), 164–65.

6. I have followed fairly closely the division in Marcus, *Mark 1-8*, 289. Very similar chiastic structures can be found in Francis Moloney, *The Gospel of Mark: A Commentary* (Peabody, MA: Hendrickson, 2002), 85–86 and C. Clifton Black, *Mark* (Nashville: Abingdon, 2011), 117.

ventures a theological interpretation of the word's success and its abject failure in the present. It is an apocalyptic mystery not because it is incomprehensible, but because it is still in the process of being revealed. In fact, it is the promise of extravagant harvest that keeps the text pointed toward an extravagant God whose reign is brought near by the sowing of the gospel word.

PASSAGES OMITTED FROM THE LECTIONARY

Most of Mark 4 is omitted from the Revised Common Lectionary. The final two parts of the chiasm, however, are included as a lection for Proper 6. By considering each of the elements of the chiasm in succession, we will have a better context for preaching the few verses of this programmatic text for Mark's Gospel in an apocalyptic mode.

THE PARABLE OF THE SOWER, THE PURPOSE OF THE PARABLES, AND A LAMP UNDER A BUSHEL BASKET (4:1-25): OMITTED FROM THE LECTIONARY

4:1-2 (A)

The parable begins with the first part of the chiasm described above. This first element in the chiasm in vv. 1-2 (A) sets the scene. Here the emphasis once again is on Jesus' teaching. In this setting, however, the teaching is developed. The setting by the sea (2:13), the necessity of the boat (3:9), and the size of the crowds are now commonplace (2:2, 13, 3:9, 20, 32). With this introductory material, however, Mark frames what follows by highlighting the fact that Jesus was teaching many things "in parables" (4:2).

4:3-9 (B)

With this second element of the chiasm in vv. 3-9 (B) we now hear the parable of the sower itself. Its importance is attested right away with a double command to pay attention: "Listen! Look!" in 4:3. The scene appears to be a familiar one—a scene involving practices around the sowing of a field.

> The biblical scholar Joachim Jeremias was well known for describing practices of sowing in ways quite consistent with this parable.[7] First, a

sower sowed the seed; afterward, tilling turned the soil over the seed. On first reading, the agricultural practices in the parable might strike us as unusual and haphazard. For the time, however, they may well have been plausible. However—and this is where Mark is truly parabolic here—what is exceedingly surprising is the yield. If the parable describes a failure with about three quarters of the sowing surfaces, those places where the seed does indeed thrive are responsible for yields that strain credulity. Through this hyperbolic result, we can sense that we have pressed beyond the everyday world to the eschatological harvest.

The figure of seed and harvest was a common one in apocalyptic literature of the time. One can find similar kinds of references in apocalyptic literature from the period, for example, in *2 Bar.* 70:2; *1 En.* 62:7-8; *4 Ezra* 4:26-29; 8:37-41; and 9:30-31. What makes Mark's parable unique is the strong emphasis on failure juxtaposed with the uncommon surprise of the fourth soil's yield. Mark's Gospel in the telling of the parable of the sower seems bent on disclosing a strange reality. Sowing the seed meets again and again with failure—and yet it is done in light of an extravagant eschatological promise of yields in the range of thirty-, sixty-, and hundredfold.

The final command of 4:9 separates out what has been described. Hearers are exhorted to hear. This parabolic mystery with which Jesus teaches presupposes a capacity to hear that not all possess. Again, the mystery has to do with explaining both the failure and the promise of the gospel word. It is tied together with the mysterious sower's sowing of the word; its apparent thwarting in fields full of demonic birds (*1 En.* 90:8-13, *Apoc. Ab.* 13:2-14), shallowness, and thorns; and its ultimate eschatological fruitful results. We will see in the next section that it is a strange mystery, but not one forever unknowable. It is rather a mystery that is being revealed.

4:10-12 (C)

In this third chiastic element, C, the mystery goes deeper. Please notice that it is the Twelve who ask questions. These Twelve and those "around them" are presumably insiders, even as they hope for an explanation. Jesus speaks to them using the divine passive: "To you has been given the secret of the kingdom of God, but for those outside, everything is in parables." The secret or

---

7. Joachim Jeremias, *The Parables of Jesus*, 2nd ed. (New York: Scribner's, 1972), 11–12.

mystery of the kingdom becomes the key for interpreting the parable. It is *given*, presumably by God. To those on the outside, however, the parable alone will have to suffice. What follows in the final verse of this part of the chiasm is one of the most troubling verses in Mark. In the Greek, the grammar is such that God becomes the author of the outsiders' inability to see and understand. Mark is quoting for the Christian community a familiar text from Isa. 6:9-10 that links a prophecy of judgment to God's intention to harden hearts. While many attempt to explain away this grammar or point to problems with his quoted material, Mark is adamant. The mystery of incomprehension of the sown word is not about human decisions, but a divine, sovereign intention to harden hearts.

Again, this is where preachers must do their theological homework. Mark's Gospel is written at a time of troubled relationships. If scholars are correct in dating this text to around the Jewish War and the destruction of the temple, Mark's community would seem to be in crisis. In such moments, how can you explain the Jewish rejection of the gospel, or the burgeoning gentile response in its favor? This reality is troubling to Mark and forces the Gospel writer to think deeply about the purposes of God. Add to that important, unresolved, and unfinished theological task of the Markan Gospel one that is unique to our time. In recent historical memory, six million Jews were killed in a Holocaust that happened with some Christian resistance, but mostly Christian compliance, whether actively or passively. Is Mark's theological option open to us any more? Christian preachers going forward may need to take up Mark's theological task anew. We can honor Mark for seeing it indeed as a mystery: God's purposes amidst failure and promise are indeed hard to discern. However, after so many deaths in the twentieth century, do we need to find new language beyond a divine hardening of Jewish hearts whether ancient or modern?

Nonetheless, it is important to remember two things about where this subsection ends. First, it precedes a section in chapter 4 where the disciples—the insiders—have to ask for a parabolic explanation! Apparently the lines between insiders and outsiders are not as hard and fast as Mark's use of the Isaiah quote would indicate. Second, even the hardening of hearts and the mysterious revelation are not forever. Rejection is not destiny. The point of the promise is to point to a harvest beyond the present futility. Yet, as Joel Marcus points out, Mark himself identifies this revelatory promise elsewhere, especially 4:21-22.[8]

---

8. Marcus, *Mark 1-8*, 307.

Indeed, this odd paradox may be precisely the important connection between this text and Mark's strange ending with the failure of the disciples *and* the women (cf. Matthew and Luke!) juxtaposed with the resurrection promise in 16:1–8. Even this text begins to point beyond its own hard dualisms toward a ripening promise of harvest.

4:13-20 (D)

With this part of the chiasm, D, we enter the center of the parabolic figure. In these verses Jesus goes beyond explaining the parables generally to the Twelve and those with them. Now Jesus unpacks the parable of the sower in particular. The question Jesus asks in 4:13 deepens the mystery. It is asked for rhetorical reasons but underlines the need for divine action to enable their understanding of Jesus' teaching. The comparison identifies the seed as the word and then proceeds to describe different kinds of soil. In v. 15, Satan is explicitly linked to the bird's action in the parable itself. The connection in v. 16 to rocky soil uses a word that connects playfully with Peter's name in Greek and elaborates on the word's reception initially with joy and later under duress. The connection with the cares of "this age" underlines the two-age apocalyptic thinking in v. 18. Only with the final good soil does the seed bear fruit, and again, with eschatological extravagance.

Mark's Jesus uses the phrase "the word" with some ambiguity here. At various points in the text even "the seed" is likened not so much to the word as to the different soils' qualities of reception to it. At the same time, there is a strong divine determinism working through it. There is no sense that one must somehow become "better soil." This is not about self-improvement. Instead, it is an attempt to reflect on the apocalyptic mystery of gospel reception. The connection to persecution in particular points us ahead to difficulties in preaching the gospel in chapter 13, the other long speech in Mark's Gospel. Theologically, it tends to underline not only *God's* activity but also Satan's so that the soils are a "field" of apocalyptic struggle to which Jesus' own kingdom proclamation and teaching have pointed repeatedly until now. In Jesus' sowing of the gospel, that reign is already arriving even if the evidence for it is itself mysterious and ambiguous.

At the same time, this particular parable is more than just one among many. This is a paradigm for interpreting a large part of Mark. This is true not just because of the connection of the seed to the word of the gospel. It is also true because Jesus himself must explain it. The pattern of story (B), request for explanation (C, specifically 4:10), and interpretation (D) is common to apocalyptic writings. In apocalypses, it is often a narrated dream or vision that causes a seer to ask questions of an angel, who in turn interprets the narration for the seer. The parable of the sower portrays the apocalyptic mystery of the gospel, but the gospel itself is tied deeply to who Jesus is as the interpreter of the parable.

4:21-25 (C')

Within the chiastic structure of the chapter as a whole, this section C', like its C counterpart in Mark 4:10-12, is concerned with the theological problem of interpretation itself. The earlier text did so with reference to the deepening apocalyptic mystery of parables themselves and appealing to a text from Isaiah to justify its confounding nature of speaking parables to *keep* persons from understanding. This text, by contrast, sets that strange mystery of concealment within a wider eschatological frame of reference that points toward an unveiling. It begins with a two-part rhetorical question about the placement of a lamp. The first part begs a "no" response; the second part, an affirmation. The purpose of anything being concealed is its ultimate revelation. Mark also uses the same language of "in order to" to make the point with Jesus' words. It is a necessity, a *divine* necessity, that conditions the concealment of the parables themselves and views it as a temporary measure.

The second part of our pericope, vv. 24-25, reinforces this by use of several divine passives in the future tense: ". . . still more will be given you," "more will be given," and "even what they have will be taken away." The divine passive implies that God is the subject. Because these passive constructions are in the future tense, they point to God's eschatological purposes. All of these help the reader deal with the odd, perplexing parables. To some, to outsiders, they conceal, but only for a time. Concealment must give way, in God's good time, to ultimate revelation. In the meantime, we hearers are to pay attention and measure well.

This is, as Joel Marcus points out, the nature of "the hidden action of God in the world."[9] These apocalyptic parables embody typical ways of viewing the world from an apocalyptic framework: light, revelation, and a critical moment of judgment, too.

---

9. Ibid., 320–21.

LECTIONS

With this section (B') and the next one in vv. 33-34 (A'), we not only round out the chiasm that we described in the introduction to Mark 4 but rejoin the lectionary reading cycle. This particular section gives us two more seed parables along with the concluding material in vv. 33-34. The context of the chapter as a whole helps to make these seed parables make sense in light of the apocalyptic mode that underlies the whole unit.

LECTION: THE PARABLE OF THE GROWING SEED, THE PARABLE OF THE MUSTARD SEED, AND THE USE OF PARABLES
4:26-34; PROPER 6

4:26-32 (B')

The first of the two seed parables is vv. 26-29, often known as "the seed growing by itself." The clustered imagery of seed, earth, sprouting and harvesting continues. The apocalyptic frame for such imagery is also continued—and this becomes important if we read this text apart from its immediate context in Mark. This growth is compared to the reign of God. The odd part of the comparison is the passiveness of the sower who keeps sleeping and rising. Eventually, the seed itself sprouts and grows up. The word "all by itself" helps to underline the claim: it is the root for our term "automatic" in English. The determined sequence of events that the growth involves also points to its apocalyptic origins in v. 28: "first the stalk, then the head, then the full grain in the head." The sequence of growth has its own pattern. Even harvest is signaled by the readiness of the fruit's yield—when it is ripe, harvest is here, with all of its eschatological connections (Joel 3:13). The use of the figure of seed growth and harvest as representative of the division of times is a commonplace of apocalyptic literature.[10] Theologically, it points to the hiddenness of that reign in connection with its ultimate inevitability as something that God has determined.

In the second seed parable, the parable of the mustard seed in vv. 30-32, the same image cluster continues. With this apocalyptic parable, however, the comparison points to the nature of God's reign itself. This reign of God is not

---

10. Marcus offers an incredibly detailed listing of such precedents in Jewish apocalyptic literature in *Mark 1-8*, p. 328.

like the kinds of seeds and growth we normally think of. NT scholar Bernard Brandon Scott argues that Jesus' use of this image is a kind of burlesque on the tree of Lebanon image that was common in the period.[11] God's reign will be like those impressive cedars of Lebanon that are huge and powerful. Jesus takes a different tack, using the mustard seed to underline both the smallness and hiddenness of God's kingdom purposes at the outset, but while showing its verdant growth as a cosmic shrub as a kind of parody of the powerful cedar of Lebanon image. The connection of the two is made particularly clear by the imagistic appeal in v. 32—especially the mention of "large branches," "birds of the air," and lodging "in its shadow." These images show up frequently, if piecemeal, in other parables with a more triumphalistic orientation: especially Dan. 4:12, 21 as well as Ezek. 17:23 and 31:6. Here the apocalyptic mystery is given a kind of ironic hope. The seed is hidden, though the kingdom will emerge. When it does, it will be something verdant and sheltering, even if it will *not* be of the triumphant vision we would expect of a "reign of God."

4:33-34 (A')

With these concluding verses of the parables section, A', the chiasm is given closure. The same phrase about teaching them in parables is nearly repeated from the opening section, A. One key difference is the phrase "as they were able to hear it." With this addition, Mark reminds the readers of the concealment/revelation mystery at its apocalyptic heart. Since this itself also brings in the distinction between insiders and outsiders, v. 34 continues apace. Parables are central to Jesus' speaking in all their confounding nature. However, Jesus explains everything to his insider disciples. The apocalyptic mystery is not dispelled, but continues. In fact, beginning with the next session, the mystery of the kingdom becomes more tightly connected with Jesus' own person.

It is important to see Mark's seed vision as a whole when using these texts for preaching from the lectionary for Proper 6. Our culture tends to view seeds, growth, and harvest not as some mysterious, hidden miracle, but something that we can manage. If we read the parable of the mustard seed, for example, in light of our own Horatio Alger and human potential stories (small seed, *big future!*), we will miss the unusual theological depth of Mark's vision. The seed is one thing when it goes into the ground. There is also no absolute guarantee that it will grow up. Somehow, however, deep in the soil, it germinates, sprouts

---

11. Bernard Brandon Scott, *Hear Then the Parable: A Commentary on the Parables of Jesus* (Minneapolis: Fortress Press, 1989), 386.

and becomes something different. It is not a manageable phenomenon, but a mysterious, discontinuous miracle. Mark's Jesus builds on these expectations in his use of the imagery, and especially in contrasting his vision of God's reign with the usual "cedars of Lebanon" gambit. Whatever concealment and revelation are, they happen in Mark's gospel on God's terms and for God's purposes. The two parables here as featured in the lectionary should invite to similar theological depth for a church that struggles with the hiddenness of God and God's strange purposes, which both shatter our own expectations and transcend them in God's good time.

Lection: Jesus Stills a Storm
4:35–41; Proper 7

This story of Jesus and the storm is a narrative coda to Jesus' teaching in the balance of chapter 4. If Jesus teaches in parables with a succession of sowing metaphors and parabolic reflections, this narrative text shows Jesus himself in the midst of apocalyptic tumult. The setting is important in this regard. Jesus asks the disciples to set out in their boat around evening to go to the other side. The details in v. 36 are a bit puzzling—especially the mention of other boats. These "other boats" are not mentioned again within this short narrative. With the great windstorm, however, and this setting on the sea, we are in apocalyptic territory once again. The danger with the swamping of the boat in v. 37, thus, is not just a maritime disaster, but a cosmic one. The apocalyptic emergency ends up being underlined by Jesus' own sleeping in the stern and the contrast with the disciples' cry. In the midst of apocalyptic turmoil, the faithful cry out, "how long?" Yet the focus of their concern is really about Jesus' identity: do you not care if we die? The urgency of their concern is embodied both in their waking of the sleeping Jesus and their assertion that he must not care about their death. Jesus reacts not by appealing to meteorological forecasts or with wisdom about the changing weather. Instead, Jesus responds by "rebuking" the wind and saying to the sea, essentially, "shut up." Jesus handles the storm in ways we in a non-apocalyptic context struggle with: he treats the storm and sea like demonic forces. The point of this, however, is not to persuade anyone of a certain antiquated cosmology, but to invite readers to see Jesus for who he is: as one whose word can silence and thwart demonic forces. Jesus' own questions to the disciples in v. 40 about their cowardly nature and not having faith "yet" underscore the point. The apocalyptic hiddenness of the parables continues to struggle to register with Jesus' disciples, but now they are focused on his person. Their fear in v. 41 along with their question highlight how Jesus is the parable of his parables here: "Who then is this, that even the wind and the sea obey him?" For all the parables of the kingdom and its hidden, mysterious nature and God's steadfast commitment to revealing everything, Jesus himself is still something of an almost parabolic mystery to his own disciples.

One of the great temptations in biblical narrative for Western, middle-class readers is the psychologizing of biblical texts. This particular narrative has been the subject of some misunderstanding along these lines. We often will interpret this text in psychological terms: "We all fear. But Jesus calms our fears." For many reasons, this psychologizing hermeneutic is inadequate here. The claims of Mark's apocalyptic Jesus go far beyond our fears. First, the disciples as a group are all in a boat together with Jesus. More importantly, the urgency of the storm is far more than a personal problem; it is a cosmic one. The whole world seems to be going to hell in a hand basket. This apocalyptic reading invites us to a greater depth than the usual psychological bromides that our culture offers. The disciples pose questions that go far beyond an overcoming of one's own personal fears: the question as to whether Jesus even cares in the midst of cosmic threat, and the wonderment over who he is in his ability to hold cosmic, demonic threats at bay. We owe this text, and many others, a more adequate hermeneutic than a breezy personalizing and psychologizing one.

Again, it will be important to keep the context of Mark 4 in mind when interpreting this text for Proper 7. Its force invites careful theological reflection and hard-won depth in light of cosmic, demonic threat. We are products of a recent history where we imagine ourselves masters of our world by virtue of reason and technology. Yet here in our time, we are also aware after the Holocaust and genocides that evil is indeed more intractable than our modern, rational minds would like to admit. Therefore, while this text is very familiar, its power may just be found by pursuing its mythic insights *and* its questions about a Jesus who does not seem to care, together with his unfathomable identity at the end. Preachers comfortable with the apocalyptic mystery at the heart of the Markan vision will be able to preach such a lectionary pericope with greater insight.

The Gospel Mystery Deepens—
The Word of Promise in Wider Fields:
The Good News on Different Shores (5:1—6:6a)

INTRODUCTION

In this subsection, the gospel that is Jesus and the reign of God that he proclaims moves back and forth across the sea of Galilee. While the NRSV translates *thalassēs* as a lake—and rightly so in this case—the meaning of the word normally understood as "sea" carries part of the symbolic freight, as an earlier lection showed. Here in these pericopes, Jesus is revealed for who he is since his identity is so closely connected with the gospel (1:1). Yet because his gospel ministry involves healings—and here they sometimes occur in marginal places—such healings point to not just Jesus' identity but also the shape of the apocalyptic kingdom he announces. Within little more than a chapter we see the Gerasene demoniac, a woman, and a young girl healed. And yet, the gospel mystery still deepens. In Nazareth, this astounding reign-of-God ministry seems reined in. The locals do not accept Jesus, nor does his ministry have much effect. Such is the parabolic nature of his mysterious, unfolding apocalyptic gospel.

PASSAGES OMITTED FROM THE LECTIONARY

With this subsection of Mark we have once again departed from the lectionary. This classic story of the healing of the Gerasene demoniac is left out of the lections for Year B. Its absence is regrettable, in part because this exorcism story embodies so much of how Mark understands this apocalyptic gospel in the shadow of empire. The Gerasene demoniac reminds us contemporary interpreters that it is important to remember that miracles and exorcisms are more than magical thinking. Because they are deeply connected with Jesus' proclamation of God's reign (1:15), they also touch on the political. Preachers who see the value of this would be wise to find a way to work this pericope into some Sunday in Ordinary Time just to have a chance to wrestle with it in the pulpit.

JESUS HEALS THE GERASENE DEMONIAC (5:1-20):
OMITTED FROM THE LECTIONARY

The narrative is a miracle story, more specifically, an exorcism. It contains many of the typical features of the form. When one considers the length of this exorcism, a full twenty verses, a few things stand out. This exorcism elaborates on certain features and draws them out: the description of the demoniac's behavior, the extended exchange in the confrontation with Jesus, and the especially long treatment of the reaction after the exorcism. A good way to read such forms is to consider what is treated formulaically and briefly and what gets emphasized through elaboration. These help to draw attention to what is special about this story.

The narrative also requires us to reflect on the setting in which it takes place. There is first confusion about the place: text critics are unsure about whether the text refers to Gerasa, Gadara, or Gergasa, the first two being cities of the Decapolis of varying distance from the shore of the sea. It may be sufficient to view the issue narratively rather than historically. Mark has just narrated Jesus crossing the sea and rebuking and silencing the storm. Now having crossed, he is exorcising on land in gentile territory. This latter reality also makes sense of some of the patterns of the story. This exorcism holds several features in common with the exorcism in Capernaum back in 1:21-28: the man is "in an unclean spirit" (1:23), his cry is "what do we have to do with you?" (1:24), and there is the recognition of Jesus as "of God" (1:24). It may be that these two early exorcisms function programmatically—in one Jesus carries out a paradigmatic exorcism in Jewish territory, in the latter among gentiles. It is also important to remember that this story takes place within spitting distance of the sea. As soon as Jesus climbs out of the boat, the Gerasene demoniac approaches. By the time the spirits leave him, they are rushing headlong back into the sea to drown in watery chaos. Jesus can best evil and is clearly one who holds sway even over the chaotic, demonic sea.

For all these connections with prior exorcisms, settings, and contexts, this particular text is so fascinating for its strikingly unique features. The description of the man at the beginning of the pericope is telling both in content and style (5:2-5). Mark repeatedly uses different words for the place where they find him and the man dwells: the tombs. The description of their inability to tie him down and keep him contained is full of negatives and double negatives, a kind of anti-divine passive, and run-on sentences, which all conspire stylistically to make the scene seem even more chaotic. Mark describes his situation in a way that is both colorful and terrifying to the reader. More than that, he describes a tragic existence for the demoniac: a divided life spent alone, among the tombs, and exposed. He is a man in an unclean gentile context, with unclean spirits, in a most unclean place of death. The judgment of the narrator in v. 5, that no one had the strength to subdue him, lays the groundwork for the confrontation to follow. The word for strength reminds the reader of opening scenes in Mark's

Gospel: John the Baptist's prediction of one "more powerful than I" in 1:7 and Jesus' statement about binding the strong man in 3:27. The statement of the lack of anyone strong enough in 5:5 lays the basis for engagement with Jesus in 5:6ff.

The confrontation with Jesus is likewise elaborated narratively. The man approaches Jesus twice (5:2, 6) for emphasis. In addition to the standard crying out and recognition of Jesus, the demoniac actually adjures Jesus "by God" not to torture him—a near reverse exorcism! In all these things this story stands out. It is only in 5:8 that it becomes clear that the demoniac's reaction has already been triggered by Jesus' prior action. In a parenthetical statement, the narrator discloses that Jesus was already busy trying to call the unclean spirit out.

From here, the exorcism proceeds in more typical terms. Jesus asks the spirit what his name is. He discloses not so much a name, but a corporate presence: legion. While some might argue that this reference is not obviously political, it clearly gains meaning in a place under Roman domination. A legion represented some thousands of troops. The region was under varying forms of occupation, depending on whether the locals were inclined toward revolt. It is interesting to note that one important, well-known legion posted to Palestine had as its symbol a boar's head.[12] The idea that the spirit would then request not to be sent away from the region but be allowed to enter two thousand pigs feeding nearby would seem to be both humorous and insightful when one reflects on the legions' reputation with local populations. The upshot is this: if not political, clearly the scene is evocative of the struggle of life under Empire. Interpreters may wish to reflect on how the demonic is not just some realm of pious superstition, but also reflects the deepest struggles and aspirations of people who live with evil and can sometimes only imagine how to be rid of it.

When Jesus does finally permit the legion of unclean spirits to enter the herd, the event proves to be the undoing of both the legion and the unclean pigs. They rush over a cliff and drown in the sea, which we recall, Jesus just vanquished with a word in the previous pericope. The scene thus helps to underline Jesus' apocalyptic significance and reframes demonic possession from an individual problem to a cosmic one.

But this apocalyptic, cosmic exorcism immediately ushers in surprising responses. Most exorcisms end in amazement. This one causes a kind of strange, local fear. The several verses that Mark devotes to the reaction are telling—his lengthy description is not typical for the form.

---

12. M. Eugene Boring, *Mark: A Commentary*, New Testament Library (Louisville: Westminster John Knox, 2006), 151. Boring does not wish to advocate for an overtly political reading, but views the text as evocative nonetheless.

The reaction begins in 5:14 with the herdsmen fleeing to announce the news in city countryside and it seems their report is sufficient to generate a crowd who comes to check it out. They are surprised to see the "demonized" one cleaned up, properly clothed, and in his right mind. But what is key is their reaction: they were afraid. Those who witnessed tried to explain it. The result is not some happy ending, but a request to Jesus to *leave*. Jesus mysteriously obliges and gets back into the boat. The "demonized" man asks to come along. But Jesus does not let him. However, Jesus does send the man back to his own people as a kind of missionary. The man then tells them what God has done and how God has shown mercy, which in turn begets the amazement proper to exorcism stories.

A story like this deepens the mystery of Jesus' incursion into gentile territory. The story is an incredible demonstration of his apocalyptic power. The territory is cleared of demons, though it is not cleared of trouble. At this point in the story, however, the issue is not just Jesus' power, but the resistance and rejection he meets. Now Jesus' parable of the soils makes more and more sense. The seed is sown, but it does not always take root, perhaps not immediately. The exorcism provokes faith; yet it also provokes fear. Preachers need to be aware that this is no comic book Jesus. His ministry ushers in cosmic change and powerful transformation with corporate consequences. It also engenders corporate resistance and fear. While we cannot give up on the seed of the word—the demonized man, the text says, *proclaims* in the Decapolis—its way forward is not a straight line, but something of a mystery even now.

The absence of this text from the lectionary is problematic, especially because its unique angle of vision on exorcism and its connection to God's reign is thereby lost. One good option would be during Year B to find some point to add this lection during a Sunday in Ordinary Time, preferably after the parable of the sower has also been added as a kind of semi-continuous reading in Mark. It would allow the preacher to explore the Markan Jesus' mysterious reign-of-God message. For a disestablished mainline church, it might also be a powerful way of exploring what God's promises mean in a context where both transformation and opposition, where both faith and fear, are evoked. It may just be an invitation to a deeper contextualization of the gospel today.

These final texts in this subsection of Mark are included in the lectionary. While these stories of Jesus' wonderworking power almost "tell themselves," preachers would be wise to remember the mysterious context in which they take place. Mark helps by pairing two miracle pericopes (the previous 5:1-20 and the upcoming 5:21-43) with a troubling story of Jesus' rejection in Nazareth and his *inability* to work wonders there. Mark is not satisfied to narrate a Gospel of the gospel that moves from success to success. All along the way, the failure of the seed of the word constantly accompanies its startling manifestation of growth. Preachers drawn to such stories would be wise to recall the mysterious, parabolic gospel that this section has so carefully planted in our minds as readers, too.

LECTION: A GIRL RESTORED TO LIFE AND A WOMAN HEALED
5:21-43; PROPER 8

With this well-loved Markan intercalation, or "sandwich" story, we see the apocalyptic mystery deepen yet again. On the way, Jesus crosses the sea, the source of chaos and haunt of demonic swine, to return to a Jewish rather than gentile environment on the other side. The two intercalated stories involving Jairus's daughter and the woman with a flow of blood help demonstrate Jesus' character not just as a healer, but as connected to "saving" in matters of death and life. "Saving" is important here because the Greek word has overtones of both salvation and healing. Life and death are mentioned because the healing is not merely from infirmity, but a restoration of two "daughters" from a deathly existence to life.

When stories are sandwiched like this, they are designed to be mutually interpretive. Often intercalation means sandwiching two narratives to ironic effect. In this case, there is an interesting contrasting movement in both. With the case of Jairus's daughter, the initial complication of her sickness unto death is compounded by the announcement later of her actual demise. As Jesus moves toward her room, he first sheds disciples, taking only three, and drives out mourners and crowds at her house. What starts off as a public call to heal becomes a private miracle of resurrection through Jesus' touch for a passive, twelve-year-old girl. The woman with the flow of blood offers a stark contrast: her *disease* was twelve years old, its ritual implication meant she privatized her pain in isolation, and she had to approach Jesus with *active* stealth in a public place so she could touch him. The contrasting stories also relate in this key way: by attending to one, Jesus runs the risk of not attending to the other. For halting to ask who touched him and enter into a public conversation, Jesus seems to forego the option of healing the dying girl at Jairus's house. But that would be to read the story apart from the eschatological vision of apocalyptic mystery. With Jesus there is healing, rather salvation, and life to go around. The "daughters" (the young girl in 5:23 *and* the woman in 5:34) in all their differences are restored.

5:21-24

In this part of the intercalated stories, Mark narrates Jesus crossing the sea back to Jewish territory. Now the terms of uncleanness at stake have not so much a gentile feel (legions and swine), but a Jewish one marked by concerns around touching, sickness, blood, death, and even gender. They involve purity concerns for which Scripture prescribes certain procedures and expectations (Num. 19:11-13, Lev. 15:19-30) among the people of God.

So when Jairus, the local leader of the synagogue approaches, the story is set in motion. Here we have a Jewish leader, but now one who welcomes Jesus' arrival. Although other Jewish leaders have opposed Jesus until now, this one falls at his feet in the hope that Jesus' touch might save his daughter, that is, heal her and return her to fullness of life. Jesus goes right away. Jairus trusts that Jesus can do this. With this, however, the crowd returns, pressing upon him as before (3:20, 31-32; 4:1)

5:25-34

In the midst of this crowd, however, the narrative shifts to the intercalated story on the way. While Jesus makes his way to Jairus's house, a woman with a long-term flow of blood is described. The Greek here has a strange shape. In a single, long, participle-loaded sentence her suffering, attempts at healing, mistreatment, and deteriorating health are described until the final main verb arrives at the end of periodic statement all the way in v. 27: she touched his garment. Why the convoluted syntax? The effect of the syntax is to underline her suffering. The grammatical focus places her as the agent. This is confirmed in v. 28. The woman reasons to herself. She is sure that if she touches his garment, it will be enough. She will be saved/healed. The context here also enriches the description both of her suffering and her agency. Because of her impurity, she cannot do what she does in an open and public way. Because she is a woman, she likely acts in a way that at least outwardly might be left unobserved in a societal order that would not permit it. It is enough to touch Jesus' garment—that is her faith talking. It is also necessary for her to exercise her agency "from behind," amidst a pressing crowd.

The result is immediate in v. 29. The narrator cues in readers that she was healed. Confirmation ensues from the woman herself. The narrator discloses she knew it in her body. The narrator also lets us know that Jesus sensed what had happened. Jesus likewise immediately poses the question of who touched his garments because he felt the power going forth. The disciples, unlike Mark's readers, do not have a clue. While we readers have been privy both to the woman's suffering, agency, and healing as well as Jesus' uncanny awareness, the disciples are incredulous. A little whiff of mystery here—those closest to Jesus do not always grasp what is key! But the narrator keeps us on the inside. When in v. 32, the narrator describes Jesus as looking around to see who touched him, the "who" word in Greek is in the feminine gender!

In the final scene of this intercalated story, the woman comes forward in fear and trembling—possibly the fear typical of an epiphany scene more than anything else. She falls down and says everything. Jesus names her "daughter," now restored in peace and health because faith has saved/healed her.

5:35-43

We now return to the outer edge of Mark's intercalation sandwich, but now the first narrative intrudes on the second. During the conversation with the now-healed woman, a man comes telling Jairus that his daughter has died (v. 35). But Jesus, perhaps with the woman's faith still echoing in his ears, urges Jairus not to succumb to fear, but to keep faith. Here Jesus begins to winnow down the crowd. He takes only three disciples with him now and begins to leave the public behind. The ensuing scene at the synagogue leader's house would seem to indicate the presence of professional mourners. Jesus' question to them, as in the last scene, provokes incredulity. Professional mourners know that death is for keeps, and so they laugh at Jesus' statement about sleep. However, the notion of sleep represents more than the denial of death; it is also eschatological language that indicates that God's ultimate purposes are still in play. Since this scene is no longer about a healing proper, but the approach to a now-dead little girl, the stakes are higher. Jesus sends everyone out, thus further privatizing this moment. Perhaps such epiphanic moments are not for all eyes. At any rate, Jesus once again risks impurity and touches the little girl by grasping her hand.

In a way reminiscent of other healers of the time, he speaks foreign words, translated from the Aramaic for the benefit of Koine Greek readers: "Little girl, arise." The Greek words for "arise" and "get up" in vv. 41-42 are more than about locomotion. They are resurrection words. Perhaps as well the proclivity to report not only her movement about, but the charge that she should eat, is a common feature of some resurrection narratives (Luke 24:41-42) and a sign of her restoration to shared life, too.

One feature at the end seems rather strange. Jesus commands those still present to silence. As with other such charges, there seems to be a concern that this news needs to be understood properly in context. Perhaps much of what Jesus does in preaching the gospel that is God's reign (1:15) and Jesus himself (1:1) also needs to be understood in terms of Jesus' own cross and resurrection. For a story that ends with a strong affirmation of an apocalyptic Jesus whose mystery is disclosed in death's very presence on the other side of the chaotic sea, it may just be that the story's end casts light even on this episode's deep, dark shadows.

This text is the prescribed lection for Proper 8 [13]. The struggle with this text will be to find a way to preach it in its intercalated unity. One way to do this is to juxtapose the two stories with Jesus himself. He is willing to risk impurity for his apocalyptic mission. He crosses the sea, walks headlong into the face of death, and offers power for healing to those as good as dead. But his presence does more. For those who are dead, he raises to life, grasping hands with those who cannot even grasp back. At the same time, it is his presence and the promise of healing that prompts others to find their agency, to reach out and touch across boundaries that keep apart. Such a sermon would be a sermon of profound solidarity and grace. It would also be a sermon of far-reaching, cosmic liberation.

LECTION: THE REJECTION OF JESUS AT NAZARETH [AND THE MISSION OF THE TWELVE] 6:1-6A [6B-13]; PROPER 9/14

With this final portion of this subsection's narrative, we see the strange mystery deepen now in Jesus' hometown. His power has emerged through a series of revealing encounters on both sides of the chaotic sea. At the same time, its disclosure has met with both fear and faith, and sometimes opposition, too. Oddly, it is those closest to him who seem to have the hardest time grasping who he is and what this all means. This first half of our lection (6:1-6a) is an apt summation of the deepening apocalyptic mystery that is Jesus.

The first verse transitions him back to his hometown, while noting that the disciples follow. A small parenthetical remark like this sets up part of what follows. Jesus appears in his hometown as a teacher—with his disciple entourage, yes, but also with astonishing teaching. In many ways, this text, which leads to a pronouncement at the end of the pericope, parallels Mark 1:21-28. In both cases, Jesus is in synagogue on the Sabbath and teaches with the result that the hearers are amazed. The difference, of course, is with the unfolding reaction. Whereas the Mark 1 text eventuates only in his fame spreading from Capernaum (1:28), here the astonishment among the hometown crowd goes south. But this is precisely the point here: the seed is sown and meets with tragic opposition.

The nature of the opposition becomes clear as v. 2b unfolds in a series of questions. People want to know the source of Jesus' teaching, the wisdom "given" to him, and the deeds of power that take place through his hands. The wording of these questions implies that people know the power is greater than his. At the same time, the question of its "source" leaves open whether it is God or an anti-divine force. The downward spiral continues in v. 3 with the kinds of questions usually used to level insults. Is not this person just a carpenter—probably a builder for hire? "Is he not Mary's son?" subtly teases at Jesus' legitimacy by placing him in a matronymic rather than patronymic line. By speaking of Jesus' brothers and sisters, they see Jesus as just another villager like them. This the narrator summarizes with an important verb: "And they took offense at him." The root Greek word of the phrase "took offense" is essentially "scandalize." The verb is an important one in early Christian literature for describing the way Jesus meets with rejection and offence, by calling to mind the language of the prophet in Isa. 8:14. The word's earlier use in Mark 4:17, in the midst of the parable of sower, gives it an important shape here as the final section of this part of Mark. The mystery of Jesus includes his surprising offense, and specifically to those closest to him: his family in 3:21, 31-35 and his hometown here.

The pronouncement in v. 4 then caps off this subsection. In this way Jesus himself is indeed like the prophets. The closing material in vv. 5-6 then exemplifies this painfully. Jesus could do no miracle there, just the odd healing. The rejection was such that it caused Jesus to marvel at their unbelief. The text thus tries to come to terms with the hard-heartedness of Jesus' hometown by relating it to the wisdom of the soils in chapter 4. It is there to come to terms with the mystery: not the mystery of faith and the disclosure of God's realm, but the mystery of unbelief and the roadblocks to its growth.

The lection for Proper 9/14 includes this and the following pericope, 6:7-13. The RCL added 6:7-13 to our text (the Common Lectionary had split them between Propers 9 and 10) despite the fact that many biblical commentators view 6:6 as a key transition point in Mark's Gospel and not a whole unit. Because this text is so important for starting the next section of Mark's narrative, we will also treat it separately there in addition to the material here below.

Turning to 6:6b-13, we know that Mark has established the mystery of Jesus' word of promise as encompassing apocalyptic disclosures and rejection by those closest to Jesus. The narrative now turns to highlight Jesus' relationship with his disciples. The ones whom he called to follow were to be the very ones who did the will of God and those who would constitute his new family (3:31-35). With the rejection of his hometown still ringing in his ears, Jesus now makes a new move and invites his disciples to a life of risky following.

The second half of our lection begins with Jesus' first response to his hometown's rejection: he makes a local circuit. Whatever his mission is, he does not let opposition sway him. However, perhaps even in reaction to his rejection in his hometown, Jesus establishes a pattern for those whom he called to be the Twelve whom he sends. Some argue that this commissioning may also reflect early Christian postresurrection practice.

Jesus first sends them two by two. This may be indicative of the importance attached to having two witnesses. As a practical matter, two travelers would have each other's back. The content of their ministry, and their connection to Jesus' own ministry in Mark 1–5, becomes clear. The Twelve are given authority over unclean spirits. As the Twelve, symbolic of the tribes of Israel, they are to go forth and do battle with Satan as representatives of God's reign.

Their mode of travel in 6:8-9 is modest. While some commentators compare their meager outfitting with that of travelling cynic philosophers, one could also say that Jesus does the cynics one better.[13] The Twelve are to go *without* a bag, one of the distinguishing marks of the cynics. If Joel Marcus is correct, all this is really to underline a theological point. The Twelve, sent two by two, were to rely on God, as a kind of participation in the "New Exodus."[14]

Their journey presupposes that they will find welcome. Yet, like the preceding narrative in 6:1-6a, it also anticipates resistance and rejection. In vv. 10-11, Jesus gives direction for both: how to receive such welcome, and the witness to bear when it is lacking. The horizon is an eschatological one. For

13. Ibid., 175.
14. Marcus, *Mark 1-8*, 389.

a place to reject their reign-of-God ministry invokes a coming judgment to which the shaking off of dust points even now. Here the two-by-two disciples bear true witness against those who reject its offer.

Mark 6:12-13 then summarizes their activity. They proclaim repentance, drive out demons, anoint, and heal. They engage, in short, with Jesus' own authority in a ministry much like Jesus' in Mark 1–5.

The juxtaposition of this text in Mark with 6:1-6a is at first blush a little odd. One closes out an earlier section about the mystery of opposition to Jesus' apocalyptic realm. The new one commissions disciples to give it a go themselves. At the center stands Mark 6:6b. Jesus, after experiencing the opposition of his hometown, doubles down. He makes a circuit teaching, returning to where he started. The notion is an odd one, but helps make sense of the two-sided reality of the disciples' ministry going forward in 3:6b-13. They are given Jesus' own authority and the shape of their ministry stays roughly the same. The disciples, too, double down on Jesus' reign-of-God ministry. They are clearly guaranteed no less opposition. In fact, they are asked to assume an incredible vulnerability for the task. Yet Jesus sends them *and empowers them*. This, too, can be a strange blessing for a disestablished church today in a place of privilege yet growing vulnerability. Ministry in Jesus' name goes on. However, success is not guaranteed. What is promised is a living word and the means to persevere. It is, in its own modest and mysterious way, good news.

4

The Rocky Way—
The Word of Promise
and The Disciples' Misunderstanding
(6:6b—8:26)

Having established the mystery of Jesus' word of promise as encompassing
apocalyptic disclosures and rejection by those closest to Jesus, the narrative
now turns to highlight Jesus' relationship with his disciples. The ones whom
he called to follow were to be the very ones who did the will of God and
those who would constitute his new family (3:31-35). With the rejection of
his hometown still ringing in his ears, Jesus now makes a new move and
invites his disciples to a journey of risky following. This rocky way will lead
to a mountaintop disclosure that will only underline the disciples' own tragic
misunderstanding, even as readers gain new insight into Jesus and are invited to
see and do what the disciples cannot. For even as the disciples misunderstand,
they are surrounded by signs of Jesus' reign-of-God ministry: signs of feasting
and bread.

The Rocky Way—The Word of Promise
and The Disciples' Misunderstanding:
Sending and Feasting (6:6B-56)

Introduction

This subsection as a whole represents the first feasting complex. It juxtaposes
Herod's ghoulish feast with Jesus' eschatological one. Yet that is not all. Jesus
and those who follow him are on the move. They are sent in 6:6b-13 and along

the way we become accustomed to much coming and going in the narrative. Amidst the signs, there is still tragic misunderstanding.

PASSAGES OMITTED FROM THE LECTIONARY

The RCL omits two key passages in this subsection: the feeding of the five thousand and Jesus' walking on the water. The problem with these omissions is twofold. First, the feeding should properly be related to Herod's feast and the death of John the Baptist. Mark's interest in narrating that story in chapter 6 is not just to set up a lurid scene, but to contrast that with Jesus' own miraculous feast thereafter. Second, the omission of the feeding story and the story of Jesus' walking on the water detracts from the powerful eschatological sense of the whole section. Preachers may want to set a context for the lections that are included by delving deeply into these two important omitted pericopes.

FEEDING THE FIVE THOUSAND (6:35-44):
OMITTED FROM THE LECTIONARY

Here the story shifts from the anti-feast of Herod in 6:14-29 to the stunning feast of Jesus. By placing these two stories back to back, the narrator asks us to contrast the two stories about food. The first is a story of a banquet with a lecherous "king," his scheming wife, and an unseemly scene where their daughter dances for the gathered men only to participate in intrigue to execute a holy man. With Jesus' feeding story, however, the crowd is in the open, clearly in need, and miraculously fed. The contrast to readers could not be greater. Yet even now, the disciples show they are slow to understand. In this way, the feast is different both with good and yet tragic dimensions for Jesus' reign-of-God ministry.

The immediate context of this feeding story is Jesus' teaching of the crowd in 6:34. The only problem with Jesus' teaching is that the instruction lasts long enough to pose a hazard for the crowd that has gathered. In v. 35 readers learn that it was getting late. The disciples seem to carry this concern because they say the obvious to Jesus in vv. 35b-36: "This is a deserted place, and the hour is now very late; send them away so that they may go into the surrounding country and villages and buy something for themselves to eat." While the disciples' analysis and prescription sound practical, it is important to remember what just happened. They had just been sent in Jesus' name (6:6b-13) and given authority for mighty deeds like casting out demons. Still, they failed to discern properly the situation they were in. So when Jesus suggests in v. 37 that *they* take care of getting something to eat, they think of the task consistent with their own prescription: if *we* buy the food we'll need two hundred denarii (a denarius was a day's wage) to do so. For people charged with Jesus' reign-of-God authority, the Twelve and Jesus are clearly assessing the situation and resources in quite different ways. So in v. 38 Jesus tasks them with finding out how many loaves they had. The disciples return with the food inventory: five (loaves) and two fish. The exchange is important enough, but is designed to show the difficulty the disciples have in understanding—they become the narrative foil for the unfolding action to follow. Commentators are fond of noting the numerical symbolism of what was found. Loaves/bread are sometimes a symbol for the Torah. The Pentateuch has five books. If you add two fish, you approach the divine perfection of seven. Be that as it may, the groundwork for the feeding miracle has been laid even as it connects deeply with the disciples' lack of understanding.

From here on out in vv. 39-44, the issue of feeding is not understood through the disciples' obtuseness, but through Jesus' own shepherd-like leadership. In v. 39, Jesus orders the disciples to get everyone to recline in *symposia* or groups. The Greek word evokes the sense of a festive banquet. This is to take place, of all things, on the green grass—which again echoes the language of Psalm 23. They recline, a posture for such festive eating, in groups or companies of hundreds and fifties, again evocative of Exodus typology where Israel is similarly ordered in the wilderness (Exod. 7:4).

When in v. 41, Jesus starts the feeding, he is the central agent. It is Jesus who takes, blesses, breaks, and gives. The situation is not simply eucharistic, but it does connect with it, both with respect to Mark's own portrayal of the Last Supper in 14:22 and, as we have noted, in connection to the powerful symbolism of Exodus manna with an eschatological twist. The key to this interpretation comes in v. 42: all had their fill. This is not just some general feeding miracle, but an eschatological sign of fullness. To the limited degree it might help us understand eucharistic practice, it does so by pointing forward to God's purposes, for Mark, the purposes of God's reign. This is borne out by the excess of fragments in v. 43 as well as the surprising number disclosed only at the end in v. 44: five thousand men were fed. The mentioning of the men is, of course, a vestige of androcentric thinking. At the same time, it breaks open the possibility of an even greater eschatological sign: with women and children those fed may have been even more!

The lectionary splits off this text from the immediately surrounding material in 6:30-34 and 6:53-56, which for Proper 11 paints a very different picture. It conveys the sense of the important need that Jesus encounters in his ministry and also the way in which Jesus meets that need with presence and healing. This is not an unimportant vision for understanding the feeding itself: Jesus as the shepherd king. This frame is important for understanding our feeding story, which is why the omission of 6:35-45 in the lectionary is such a loss. The difficulty, of course, is that the undertow of this whole section about the disciples' misunderstanding is thereby missed. It may be a powerful epiphany that Jesus offers here in the feeding miracle (and the subsequent walking on the water in 6:45-52), but these moments Mark gives meaning in relation to the disciples' struggle to grasp this powerful identity. Preachers on Proper 11 who make reference to 6:30-34 and 6:53-56 may wish to read and preach on the important, missing middle of this rich material from Mark to help make sense of the whole.

JESUS WALKS ON THE WATER (6:45-52): OMITTED FROM THE LECTIONARY

Once again, with a crossing of the sea, Jesus' disciples meet their greatest fears. Just as in 4:35-41, they encounter an element of apocalyptic mystery. While this earlier disclosure on the sea came on the heels of the parable chapter, this one comes after the feeding miracle. The fact that these stories are both Markan doublets (Mark 4:35-41 > Mark 6:45-52 as well as Mark 6:31-44 > Mark 8:1-10) would be sufficient to underline the idea that the apocalyptic mystery that is Jesus meets tragic misunderstanding from his disciples. Their lack of understanding is emphasized by the relation of repeated actions with their repeated obtuseness! What makes this connection of doublets doubly interesting is that Mark in this pericope links the disciples' misunderstanding of this epiphany of apocalyptic mystery on the sea precisely with an inability to grasp what was revealed with the loaves in Mark 6:52. The language of apocalyptic disclosure here joins the Exodus typology of loaves in the wilderness with the Exodus symbol of mysterious epiphanic presence, the language of "I am" from the burning bush and the "passing by" of Sinai.

In vv. 45-47, Mark lays the narrative groundwork for the unfolding epiphanic scene. Just as with the earlier story in Mark 4, Jesus compels his disciples to get into the boat (4:35/6:45) and dispenses with the crowd (4:36/6:45). The setting of evening is also the same (4:35/6:47). The separation is of course what drives the narrative: how will Jesus and his disciples reconnect? The story takes on added weight when the stipulated narrative separation is joined to the setting of the sea, the place of chaos. In Mark 4, the sea is the site of demonic storms, which Jesus then exorcises in a disclosure of apocalyptic mystery. In Mark 6, the chaos of the sea is an occasion for a somewhat different disclosure of apocalyptic mystery, and one that hearkens back to the immediately preceding story of the miracle of the loaves. This is anticipated already here when the identified separation is given a reason: Jesus is going up on "the mountain" to pray. The idea of "the mountain" and prayer can take many forms, since the mountain is indeed a powerful symbolic meeting place between heaven and earth. However, the immediate context here, where the Exodus typology of loaves and wilderness meets the "I am" disclosure of Jesus while walking on the water, may indicate a more specific Sinai intertext.[1]

Having set the scene of separation, the action ensues in v. 48. Jesus is able to see them "straining at the oars against an adverse wind." At first blush this language sounds problematic but not quite theological. The seeing itself should make us wonder. Jesus is apart from the disciples on the sea and it is dark! Peering behind the English translation, however, we also see the phrase "straining at the oars" means essentially "tortured" or "harassed" while rowing. This may not be just some neutral maritime hazard, but possibly an eschatological evocation.[2] The reference to early morning places the action in Greek during the fourth watch, that is, right before the dawn. Jesus may come toward them here in their need, but he intends to "pass by them." Some contemporary pastors may be familiar with the simple power of the "ministry of presence"—few pastoral leaders would buy into a "ministry of bypass!"

What the passing by language may point to is the Exodus typology. On Sinai, God discloses Godself to Moses not directly, but indirectly, that is through "passing by" (Exod. 33:17-23). What stands at the core of this story is mystery in an apocalyptic mode. The question is whether the disciples will get it.

The disciples' reaction to this epiphany in vv. 49-51 is thus all the more jarring. Seeing him walking on the water (and summoning also thereby Exodus Reed Sea typology), they thought Jesus was a ghost and cried out. The narrator underlines this problem by pointing out that all saw and all were terrified. Jesus, however, continues. In v. 50b, he encourages them and says "it is I," which would seem to be solely about recognizing him. In Greek, however, the word choice is more loaded. Jesus says *ego eimi*, or "I am," the Greek rendering of

---

1. Joel Marcus makes a detailed case for this in light of other possible readings as well in *Mark 1-8*, Anchor Yale Bible (New Haven, CT: Yale University Press, 2009), 422–23.

2. Marcus, *Mark 1-8*, 423.

divine self-disclosure in Moses' burning bush and elsewhere. The scene here is not merely miraculous, but is freighted with epiphanic meaning.

The story takes an odd turn when this Jesus gets in the boat with the disciples and the wind dies down. The disciples are exceedingly astounded. A good miracle story could end right there and be just fine.

However this story is not over. For Mark the issue needs to be spelled out in v. 52. The disciples' astonishment is because "they did not understand about the loaves." Mark is tying in the disciples' failure to understand the epiphanic nature of what the feeding of the five thousand meant with continued failure to understand here. The idea in v. 52b that it was due to the disciples' hardened hearts, casts an even greater pall over the story. This language points back to the mysterious rejection of understanding that goes back to the Parable of the Sower in Mark 4:12-13. Are Jesus' disciples now becoming like outsiders? This narrative is moving in a disturbing direction. It may be about promise and epiphanic presence. Yet it is also about tragic misunderstanding, and perhaps even now, about hardened hearts. Even here it is important to note something. This information is being *given* to us readers—and we have been repeated recipients of narrative disclosure as well. By the end of the Markan narrative in 16:8, we will need to note what we readers understand, we who have witnessed both the promise of presence *and* the disciples' failure to understand.

This text is also left out of the lectionary. It is unfortunate, of course, because Mark drives home his theological point through the use of repetition with stories in doublets. The failure of the disciples to understand becomes all that more prominent in the context of Jesus' repeated apocalyptic disclosures. The lectionary therefore runs the risk of perpetuating the telling of miracle stories without adequately grasping the tensive relationship of these miracles with the disciples' failure to understand. Homiletically, it may be necessary to resist this move. Preachers could highlight this when the Mark 4 text appears in the lectionary and draw the two stories into relationship in the sermon. Thematically, it is important to grasp. For a disestablished church struggling in its own way with both presence and failure, such a move is an invitation to deeper theological reflection. Is the struggle with disestablishment about divine absence? Is the presence of God a kind of institutional panacea? Or in some sense does "passing by" include both mysterious presence *and* struggle? Mark may be inviting us all into a deeper sense of gospel here and now.

Again, reading some of these lections below apart from the two omitted pericopes above leaves a lot to be desired. It is important to note that Herod's feast *has* an Exodus-like eschatological counterpart in the feeding of the five thousand. Similarly, the questions of Jesus' identity in light of the walking on water story give a depth to the stories of Jesus' miraculous action and following. While the lection on Mark 6:6b-13 is not affected by this loss, the other texts are. Preachers would be wise to consider this whole crucial section when they preach the Gospel lections for Propers 9–11 below.

Lection: The Mission of The Twelve
6:6b-13; Proper 9 (see 6:1-6a in previous chapter)

Although we treated Mark 6:6b-13 in greater detail in conjunction with the last chapter's final lection (see chapter 3) to keep the reading together, the substance of this second half of the text belongs right here. For here it suffices to say that Jesus' relationship with the disciples moves front and center. The fact that he sends them out two by two after his rejection, and empowered to do a ministry like his in Mark 1–5 clearly indicates a major shift. At the same time, the rejection that Jesus experienced in 6:1-6a is still problematic. Mark 6:6b-13 makes it a point to anticipate opposition the ministry of the Twelve going forward. This becomes a major key for understanding why this text belongs here at the beginning of this new major unit. The opposition is highlighted by the text that happens between the disciples' going out (6:6b-13) and the disciples' return (6:30). This intercalation is important for understanding the disturbing story that happens in between: the death of John the Baptist.

Lection: The Death of John The Baptist
6:14-29 (and 30); Proper 10

The presence of this story here seems odd. Jesus has just sent his disciples out two by two in mission in 6:6b-13. Yet all of a sudden the narrative shifts in 6:14 to Herod's household. Why is this? There are at least two things to note before we make a foray into this narrative excursus on the beheading of John the Baptist, which has generated so many stories and great works of art. First, the story ends with his disciples' return in v. 30, which makes this extended narration one more Markan intercalation. Mark wants to tell this beheading story that ends with John's disciples in relation to Jesus' commissioning of his disciples and their ultimate return in 6:30. Second, we need to read the story of the death of John the Baptist in light of this middle section in Mark that portrays the way of discipleship in terms of food and feasting. The over-the-top royal banquet in this section of Mark 6 serves also as a gruesome, lurid anti-feast to Jesus' reign-of-God ministry from here forward, especially the miraculous feeding in 6:35-44. Discipleship, whether in Galilee and gentile regions or outside the King Herod's own court, may be connected with food and feasting, but there's also a cost—a tragic, deadly cost.

The connection between the previous commissioning in 6:6b-13 and this ensuing narrative becomes clear with the transitional material in vv. 14-16. Herod is introduced. He has "heard of" what the Twelve had been doing in connection with Jesus' name. His "hearing" reprises an earlier notion of Jesus' fame spreading (1:28), though connected now with the Twelve acting on Jesus' authority in 6:6b-13. This situation prompts the question of Jesus' identity: is he John the Baptist raised, is he Elijah, or some kind of prophet? The reader of Mark's Gospel knows these are dead ends. John the Baptist is portrayed like Elijah (1:6) as eschatological forerunner, so Jesus is certainly not some John the Baptist returned! Prophet may be more apt, so long as one sees them as eschatological prophets, whose commonality seems to be connected with preaching repentance. So neither one is exactly like the prophets of old. At any rate, for all this casting about for an explanation, Herod settles on a raised John the Baptist, because Herod himself had beheaded him. At this point, where the issue had been focused on Jesus' mysterious identity, it becomes necessary for a narrated flashback. The last thing that the readers heard about John was that he had been arrested (1:14). So Mark chooses precisely at this point to do a kind of "flashback" or backstory to relate *how* John had died. The idea here in the juxtaposition of the intercalated stories is to disclose something about Jesus' identity and the reign-of-God ministry that the Twelve were just now starting—a ministry that will lead to feedings and feasts.

One of the great struggles here historically is to get at this character of King Herod in Mark's narrative. The consensus among scholars is that Herod Antipas mentioned here was not actually king but tetrarch. Unfortunately, the confusion even goes beyond Herod's identity. The text mentions that the Tetrarch's wife, Herodias, had been married to his brother Phillip. Mark seems to have gotten certain facts a little wrong in this case, perhaps including the daughter's name as well.[3] The most charitable reading is to say that Herod's subjects may have regarded him as king. That being said, it may be better to ask why Mark portrays him thusly. The story here trades not solely in history, but in a kind of biblical way of reading the events around John the Baptist's death. In this scene, Herod and Herodias act a bit like Ahab and Jezebel, famous opponents of the prophet Elijah, whom the Markan narrative already connects to John the Baptist himself (1:6). The portrayal of a lecherous king, who is willing to give up half his kingdom, calls to mind the story of Esther. The point is that Mark has his own theological agenda about the portrayal of this scene, especially since it is introduced not in Mark 1, but here in chapter 6 as a flashback. It is remembrance at the service of a narrative-theological agenda. It may not be impeccable history; it is, however, a focused part of Mark's plotting of the good news.

In vv. 17-20, Mark sets in motion the subsequent action at the banquet. The description places Herod, Herodias, and John the Baptist into a triangulated relationship. John the Baptist said it was not lawful for Herod to marry his brother's wife (Lev. 18:16). For this, Herodias would have been happy to see John the Baptist killed. However, her husband Herod merely had John arrested and put in prison. In v. 20, we get to the nub of the matter: Herod was afraid of John and was essentially protecting him. He was a conflicted "king," since he was both perplexed by and yet enjoyed hearing John. In these four verses the narrative conflict is set.

We are now prepared for the grisly banquet scene in vv. 21-29. There is something untoward at the very least about this situation. It is Herod's birthday and all the leading men are in attendance: courtiers, military officers, and local aristocrats. In the presence of all these men, the king's daughter comes in and dances. The word describing how this "pleased" Herod and his guests has sexual overtones. In an impulsive act, much like King Ahasuerus does in Esther 5:3, Herod offers to give her what she likes, up to half his kingdom. The narrator pauses for emphasis here and has Herod swear to it—and that in front of all his guests. The fact that that the girl has to go out to ask her mother reveals that this a gender-separated affair, which of course underlines the sexual oddness of

---

3. Adela Yarbro Collins sorts out the historical data with incredible care and thoroughness in her commentary *Mark* Hermeneia, (Minneapolis: Fortress Press, 2007), 305–7.

Herod's daughter dancing before a room full of male guests. But it also gives the story a chance to move forward. Now outside, the little girl asks her mother advice about what to ask for. Herodias, Herod's wife, has the perfect gift in mind (6:19): John the Baptist's head. The narrator loves to make the action move quickly ahead and obliges with extra adverbs to make her request of Herod. She does her mother one better in that she asks for the Baptizer's head *on a platter*. Suddenly the juxtaposition of royal banquet and gruesome, lurid death becomes clear. In reacting, Herod in 6:26 is still conflicted as ever (6:20), but now has to keep his oath in front of his guests, or as Joel Marcus puts it, "Herod has to decide between saving face and saving John's head."[4] The orders are set in motion, and now it is Herod who is sending (cf. Jesus' "sending" in 6:6b-13) the soldier of the guard to do the deed and return with John's head. Yet when the head returns on the platter, it is not given to the "king" who gave the orders, but to the girl and then to her mother. With all this, Herod does not look so kingly after all.

All that is left in 6:29 is to give a nod to John's disciples, who at least took the corpse and laid it into a tomb. And with this the connection back to Jesus becomes complete. He, too, has disciples. He, too, will be a corpse. But here, in the end, is one key difference: his own disciples will not be the ones to bury him. In this moment, the flashback has become something of a flashforward. For these two intercalated narratives are "sandwiched" for a reason. They are, whether indirectly or directly, about Jesus, his disciples, and the connection of his coming feasts to his coming death.

And with this, now in an orphan v. 30 (the RCL's lection ends at 6:29) Jesus' sent Twelve return to be with him after their commissioning in 6:6b-13. Now they report all that they had accomplished. The strange thing here, though, is that Jesus was the one who gave them authority do deeds of power like casting out demons (6:7). Could it be that this last verse, together with the closing line of the John the Baptist story, cast a negative light back on the Twelve? Given the tragic misunderstanding that accompanies Jesus' own reign-of-God ministry around feasting, this suspicion may not be far from the mark.

This particular text shows up on Proper 10. Its boundaries end at 6:29 instead of 6:30. While lectionary committees have their own reasons for subdividing texts, we have seen that this particular lection uses verse 30 as a means of forming the intercalated "sandwich" of the two stories: the sending of the Twelve and their return around the gruesome story of Herod's feast and the death of John the Baptizer. While the story of Herod is weighty enough itself to

---

4. Marcus, *Mark 1-8*, 403.

preach on, it is more a sad story of court intrigue and death than anything else. John the Baptist does not bear brave witness; his death is not even portrayed at all, but mentioned in a kind of narrative aside. It is the juxtaposition with 6:6b-13 and 6:29-30 that gives the Herod story its true theological weight and power. Preachers may find it more helpful to include 6:30 to ground this episode more in Jesus' spreading fame and tragic feasting with his disciples in Mark 6-8.

Lection: The Twelve Return and Healing The Sick in Genessaret
6:(30), 31-34, 53-56; Proper 11

Mark 6:30-34

The narrator actually uses v. 30 to transition from Herod's banquet in 6:14-29 to Jesus' feeding in 6:35-44. This transition requires not just a change of location, but a change of tone. The disciples' accomplishments and success *should* prepare them well for the miracle to come—*should*.

So Jesus then responds in v. 31 to the disciples' return from their mission by inviting them to retreat to a "deserted place." In narrative, the shift of scene is not merely accidental. The desert, the wilderness, is a place fraught with meaning (1:12-13). Readers need to take note. It is one thing to realize that the feeding of the five thousand is a banquet in contrast to the gruesome anti-banquet at Herod's. It is another thing still to note the eucharistic overtones of feeding miracles that take great pains to narrate the familiar take/bless/break/give pattern. It is quite another thing to place such an event in the desert wilderness. The change of scene evokes a typology of wilderness wandering and manna that is absolutely central to grasping what follows. Mark's narration of the change of scene is thus no small matter. Mark is also careful to note the harried existence of his Twelve and the people gathered around them. The disciples struggle to find leisure to eat. There is much coming and going. When Jesus shows up, crowds go crazy and try to anticipate his next move. The emerging scene evokes something quite different from Herod's banquet with military officers and aristocrats. What follows our lection will be a feeding miracle set in relationship not to human power, but need and desperation. The positive side is that Jesus' ministry is still generating thronging crowds and positive reception even while opponents gather and the disciples themselves struggle to understand. Finally, the transition is important because of what it communicates about Jesus in v. 34. His reaction to the thronging crowd's need and the deserted place is so much different from Herod's: "he had compassion for them, because they were like sheep without a shepherd." The language here likewise makes sense in the wilderness. This is kingship language that emerges out of an ideal sense of what kingship is. Moses and David were shepherds (Num. 27:17 is paradigmatic for this) and God was the ideal shepherd (Psa. 23). The ideal king is such, and, in the case of Moses, again reminds of wilderness wanderings where, yes, food was provided (Exod. 16), but leadership itself was compassionate. Jesus' response is to teach them "many things."

MARK 6:53-56

This final scene at the end of chapter 6 in vv. 53-56 helps to underline the disciples' developing misunderstanding. While the disciples fail to grasp who this Jesus is and what the events around them mean, the people on the other shore in an area called Gennesaret welcome him.[5] If faith seemed painfully absent both in the run up to the feeding of the five thousand and as the winds blew against the boat on the sea at night, it is present in full form in this text. In fact, if anything, Jesus' appeal is growing. Although this summary statement reprises narrative elements earlier in the chapter (the recognition of Jesus and people running about [Mark 6:33]), here the story goes a bit better. Now they bring the sick on mats and settle for even touching the fringe of his garment. Jesus' healing is available and their faith is palpable. This summary text stands sharpest in relief to the disciples' lack of faith on the boat in 6:45-52.

For the lectionary, this brief summary statement is the second half of the lection for Proper 11 (see material for 6:30-34 above for the first half). Again, however, the juxtaposition of these two portions of Mark 6 *apart from the material in between* (the feeding of the five thousand and Jesus' walking on the water in 6:35-52) fails to do justice to the disciples' misunderstanding. While it teaches much about Jesus' compassion and healing power, it misses a core part of Mark's unfolding narrative theology. Preachers may need to bring the tension in themselves to help bring this home homiletically.

---

5. The landing in Gennesaret, a plain and not a city, is a bit odd given the fact that they were aiming for Bethsaida. Some commentators argue that this is due to this being redacted material.

THE ROCKY WAY—THE WORD OF PROMISE
AND THE DISCIPLES' MISUNDERSTANDING:
MISUNDERSTANDING AND BOUNDARY CROSSINGS (7:1-37)

INTRODUCTION

Chapter 7 is important as a crossroads for our section in that it features a boundary crossing of its own. The shift to a debate with Jewish religious leaders about the law and purity related to eating with unwashed hands would seem like a non sequitur. However, its placement between two crucial Markan feeding miracles in chapters 6 and 8 helps to illumine its purpose. The fact that the first feeding is in Jewish territory and the second among gentiles is also crucial. Debates about law become important as Jesus and his disciples stand on the threshold of reaching out to gentiles both in the coming chapter *and*, at the time of the writing of Mark's Gospel, about a gentile mission and a very Jewish heritage about the law. In light of this, the misunderstanding of the disciples' only deepens here as they require extra help to discern Jesus' meaning in vv. 17-23. Still, the miracles that follow point the way ahead. Jesus' ministry among gentiles will meet with a jarring and surprising receptivity in vv. 24-37. Yet this receptivity only underlines the difficulty that the disciples face in understanding.

LECTIONS

These two lections come up for Propers 17 and 18 in year B of the RCL. There is an advantage to reading them successively if one keeps in mind that the feeding miracles of Mark 6 and 8 bookend these lections. The misunderstanding of Jesus' disciples and the tensions in the Jewish context juxtapose with the miraculous moments with two gentile interlocutors in 7:24-37. The feeding stories in Mark 6 and 8 remind us that Jesus' miraculous care is for both, which keeps Jesus deeply connected to his Jewish context even as the struggle to understand ensues in 7:1-23.

LECTION: THE TRADITION OF THE ELDERS
7:1-23; PROPER 17

This chapter seems to break the flow of Jesus' breathtaking kingdom ministry of healing and feeding in chapter 6 with a strange, convoluted discussion between the Pharisees and Jesus' disciples about the law and purity traditions. The odd way this discussion develops in the Greek text of Mark 7 (full of parentheses, hyphens, and broken off sentences) reflects all the problems writers have when the subject matter is just too complicated or touchy to pull off. The lectionary reading for the day would seem to try to clean things up by offering snippets of our pericope, excising vv. 9-13 and 16-20. However, it may just be better to wade through these difficult sections to get a grasp for what is going on here. It mattered a lot to Mark, even if his reputed stumpy-fingered clumsiness came through (see Introduction). Perhaps if we understood his context, it might matter more to us, too.

The language in vv. 2-4 is one of the first blocks of confusing material. The question about eating with unwashed hands is characterized as one of tradition, not Scripture. The idea that "all the Jews" did so is overdone. Practices on washing and eating may have varied in the Diaspora as opposed to Palestinian Judaism. The question of washing utensils is biblical (Lev. 11:32, 15:12), though actually for priests. In any event, the Pharisees interpreted such requirements more broadly in such a way as to make holiness not just a priestly focus but inclusive to the people as a whole. The question of the "fist" in v. 3 is a long-standing problem for translators. It may refer to various ways or measures of washing one's hands.

Two aspects of context may be important for understanding this text. First, Jesus' two-tiered discussion with the Pharisees and some scribes from Jerusalem and ultimately in private with his own head-scratching disciples happens at an important turning point in the Markan narrative. At the end of chapter 6, Mark has narrated Jesus touching and healing Jews, providing bread, and thus feeding Jews in Galilee. After this pericope, Jesus goes on touching (7:31-37) and healing (7:24-30), but this time it is in decidedly gentile regions! The same goes for his bread and feeding ministry (8:1-10). This concern about some disciples not washing their hands comes at the threshold of a change in Jesus' kingdom ministry. In Mark 7:1ff, he pauses between a Jewish ministry and a gentile mission. The concern of the Pharisees thus makes sense: whether about traditions of hand washing before eating or the examples Jesus cites about food and what *really* defiles, the concern about purity makes sense given where Jesus' ministry comes from and where it is going.

The discussion of *Korban* in vv. 9-13 is hard to follow, but offered here as an instantiation of Jesus' prophetic charge in vv. 6-8. *Korban*, meaning a gift to God, was a practice of making an oath that dedicated a certain asset for temple use. Jesus complains that Pharisees use or allow others to use the tradition of *Korban* in a way that obviates observance of the law concerning honoring mother and father, which had an economic meaning attached to it with respect to parental support. If the Pharisees countenanced such a use of a tradition about oaths like *Korban*, they were essentially using tradition to nullify the law.

Part of the confusion of this text, however, may also lie in the way it reflects a two-level conversation. Mark's story is one about Jesus in his ministry— toward the end of Mark 6, a Jewish ministry in a Jewish context, thus provoking Jewish debate on the law. Nothing new here! Jesus was a Jew and has a Jewish debate over the law and traditions. But in the second half of the text, where Jesus explains his "parable" of digestion to his disciples, *their gentile* context is more likely in view. Mark writes, of course, sometime around the destruction of the temple. In such a catastrophic historical crisis, Judaism and the small Christian sect within it are forced to redefine themselves. The disciples recall this debate about the law, purity, bread, and touching, but now in light of their post-temple crisis situation. In the late first century, the future of the Christian movement likely appears to be more gentile than Jewish (as a Gospel written in Greek and having to explain Jewish customs so awkwardly itself attests!). Thus Jesus' criticism of the Pharisee's use of the law and traditions in the first half of our lection, becomes applied parenthetically ("Thus he declared all foods clean" v. 19b) in a way that would have only made sense to gentile readers. While Jesus critiques certain interpretations of the law, and with critical prophetic help from Isaiah in vv. 6-7, the parenthetical remark in 19b practically abrogates the law with respect to food (e.g., Leviticus). In a new context in the late first century, Jesus' critique is taken to a new level. While Paul quotes a tradition about this with respect to food (Rom. 14:20) and Luke narrates a similar shift as a postresurrection act of the Spirit in the story of Peter and Cornelius (Acts 10–11), Mark uses the parenthetical remark, within the parabolic explanation to the disciples, to draw a sharper conclusion for a new, gentile day. This context, the context of the *writing* of Mark, seems to move this teaching in a direction that goes beyond intra-Jewish debate about the law for the sake of a food-law-free gentile mission as far as the disciples' eyes can see.

Because of this, today's largely gentile Christians need to speak carefully with this text. The old Christian canard that paints Pharisees as legalists and Jesus as free and easy is flat out wrong. In the first half of our text, Jesus argues *like* a Pharisee and within a Jewish frame of reference. Even his final statement about "nothing going in" as defiling is phrased in a way that is still consistent with Jewish legal debate. It is not so much about what goes in, but more about what comes out that defiles. Jesus, in this view, does not so much oppose ethics and ritual, but *prioritizes* them. However, when in the context of Jesus explaining the parable, the Markan narrator adds a parenthetical comment that applies Jesus' statement to a new largely gentile context, we need to realize that the debate is now happening in that new context: not between, say, Christians versus Jews, but law-observant Christians and non-law-observant Christians. Toward the end of the first century, Mark writes down his Gospel to help his late first-century fellow disciples figure out a way forward in a crisis-riddled, temple-ruined world. Will Christians continue with Jewish identity? Or will they move ahead more vigorously in a gentile mission that sets parts of the law aside? We modern gentile Christians are the result of their late first-century theological discernment and struggle. In the end, we cannot hand off that theological judgment by turning the forerunners of rabbinic Judaism into a foil for our own dilemmas.

Ironically, it is this way that we can make our preaching of Mark precisely more relevant theologically. This text shows up piecemeal (Mark 7:1-8, 14-15, 21-23) for Proper 17. In this moment, however, we can still join Mark in the "unfinished theological task" (see Introduction) of proclaiming the gospel. In such moments, the Pharisees no longer need to be anti-Jewish projections of what is, in reality, our own worst fears about ourselves. Instead, we can place ourselves in the theological dilemma of identity and mission and discern the promise of God anew. Who knows? We may just do so in the presence of a risen, crucified Lord who even now teaches with a surprising authority. His authority reveals our own shared human defilement in our ever multiplying evil inclinations and foolishness while nonetheless offering us an apocalyptic revelation, a word that "declares" a new opening toward the reign of God.

LECTION: THE SYROPHOENICIAN WOMAN'S FAITH
AND JESUS CURES A DEAF MAN
7:24-37; PROPER 18

The famous text about the Syrophoenician woman is even more powerful when read in connection with the first part of Mark 7. Now Jesus is venturing into gentile territory. He has just had this dispute over the law. In the course of discerning the evolving argument of 7:1-23, it becomes clear that matters of purity and gentiles are changing. At the same time, there are attempts to maintain connections with Jewish tradition—for all the modification there is a great sensitivity to the Jewish context. The fascinating narrative of Mark 7:24-30 embodies many of the same features, this time told not as a legal dispute but as an argument embedded in an exorcism story. We can and should learn from both.

Mark narrates a change of scene in 7:24 to make his point. Jesus sets out from this conversation with Jewish leaders and his disciples. "From there," Mark notes, he goes to the region of Tyre, in gentile country. But it is more than that. Tyre is a major city that commands an economic relationship of superiority with the Galilean world that Jesus knows.[6] Tyre is an important enough city that the Galilean countryside provides agricultural resources for it. This means Tyrean persons are fed, while Galileans eke out an existence with a cash crop—perhaps with a little hunger thrown in. It is a relationship of economic inferiority. Mark has Jesus go not generally into the gentile world, but into a city with a special, troubled relationship with the Jewish people, especially Galileans. Jesus may have just declared all foods clean, but food is a complicated matter in Tyre both because of Jewish/gentile relations and because of the economic context. Jesus, of course, still does not want to be known and hopes to enter the town without drawing attention. He, however, could not escape notice. This is consistent with his desire to keep the messianic secret under wraps, which is apparently all but impossible to do!

Jesus' reputation has preceded him in 7:25-26 with this foray into the heart of gentile territory. A woman with a daughter with an "unclean spirit" has heard about him and engages Jesus in a humble fashion, like many other Markan supplicants. The fact that the spirit is described here as unclean is significant, especially on the heels of the clean/unclean disputes in the first half of Mark 7. The narrator pauses to describe the woman as "Greek" (translated here as gentile) and specifically of Syrophoenician origin. Above all, it is important

---

6. Eugene Boring, *Mark: A Commentary*, New Testament Library (Louisville: Westminster John Knox, 2006), 209.

to note that this healing miracle in the form of an exorcism is actually not so much about the actual healing—it is talked about as happening "off-stage" and the narrative shows only the results. The story is really about *her* and her controversy with Jesus. As a woman speaking in public, she is crossing not only ethnic and perhaps socioeconomic boundaries, but also gender boundaries. And, by the end of the all-important dialogue that follows, she actually seems to get the best of Jesus. This fact, too, becomes important for understanding why this story follows the long struggle over the clean and the unclean in 7:1-23. Despite all these boundaries, she nonetheless pleads for Jesus to cast the demon out of her daughter.

Mark 7:27-30 is the real heart of this text—the healing itself almost becomes an afterthought. The controversy begins when Jesus asserts an idea of Jewish priority in the things of God: "Let the children be fed first, for it is not fair to take the children's food and throw it to the dogs." Commentators and preachers have tried to smooth over this rough text. Sometimes people note that the word for dogs here is in the diminutive form, but it is not about puppies. Dogs, doggies, puppies—they are all looked down on in a Jewish context where dogs are not cuddly household pets, but scavengers and signs of uncleanness. Jesus is not the first to refer to gentile dogs, so readers cannot give Jesus a pass here. Upon closer inspection, it is important to notice two details of his statement that at least place the offensive metaphor in context. First is the word "first." The idea of the children being fed first speaks to the priority that early Christians within Judaism understand as the way of the gospel in relation to God's chosen people: first to the Jews. Even for Christians (who are still a movement within Judaism in this period), the gentile mission must be explained in the context of God's election. The language of first embodies that concern. Second, is the word for "fed" in v. 27. It is the same word of eschatological, feeding in fullness that was used in the feeding of the five thousand in Mark 6:42. In his quoting of Jesus, Mark opens up an eschatological horizon by highlighting just this word for feeding and satisfying. The image offends, but it reflects also a vision of the gospel for God's people spreading out in eschatological fullness as it goes.

The Syrophoenician woman's reply in v. 28 is startling. The fact that she talks back is itself a sign of boundary-crossing persistence. Even so, her address is respectful. The word for "sir" is the Greek word that also means "Lord," and she is the first to address Jesus in the vocative in Mark's Gospel. The respect continues insofar as she adopts the metaphoric frame of Jesus' statement. The genius of her reply, and perhaps in reflection of her desperation for her daughter, is to hold the offensive metaphor back to Jesus in the hope that he acts consistent with both his exorcising power *and* his mercy. Dogs receiving crumbs, what's the harm in that? She engages Jesus in a clever, rhetorical riposte that while not undoing the offense of naming, breaks and thus bests its logic.

Then, what truly amazes is that Jesus welcomes her challenging response. He seems to recognize in it something akin to persistent faith. "For saying that," Jesus says in v. 30, "you may go—the demon has left your daughter." Jesus declares this as past fact. Please note also that the only time the daughter appears is in this final verse cameo. There is no trace of the demon.

Clearly this is not your father's miracle story. This extended dialogue has taken up the action, for that is its real focus. The healing is almost an afterthought, because what matters after the clean and unclean of 7:1-23, of the struggle between Jews and gentiles, is the idea that a reluctant Jesus, and through him a reluctant Christian movement, finds itself impelled to move out to the gentile world and an eventual mission. They say only Nixon could go to China. This text bears witness that God's promises to Jews are not null and void, even if "all foods are declared clean." It takes such difficult dialogue and discernment for this Jewish Jesus and his movement of Jewish origin to see its way clear to bearing witness to a reign-of-God feeding that spills beyond Jewish borders. But go it does: the next feeding of the four thousand is in a gentile area, too.

This first half of the lection is important because the cross-cultural barriers that so complicate this text complicate our lives still—especially at this point of growth and challenge for North American churches. How will we deal with each other in all our otherness? How will we who once had cultural hegemony, who are now being disestablished, respond and relate to others who have different narratives? The challenge of this text—and its bold inclusion in Mark's Gospel—refuses to leave us too theologically settled. There is some sense in engaging others that we bear witness to the truth of what we say in the gospel, but also that the gospel may be surprisingly enlarged as we do so. The exchange with Jesus is telling. The gentile woman works cleverly within the metaphor that Jesus uses. But in doing so, she breaks it open for newness and healing. Can those of us who are used to running the show open ourselves in relation to the one she called "Lord"? That may be our gospel challenge in a new day, too. This pericope is the first half of the lection for Proper 18. It could be one surprising Sunday for the people of God.

Yet the surprises only continue in the second half of our lection in Mark 7:31-37. With this text in chapter 7, Mark continues his narrative circuit through the gentile world. The route Mark has Jesus take, from Tyre, through Sidon, to the Decapolis makes no sense geographically. What looms larger than geography here is the continued interest in space and culture. Jesus is moving about the gentile world and in a way that keeps emphasizing Jesus' power as a preacher, teacher, healer, and prophet. But it also relates those aspects of his identity to his reign-of-God ministry. We know from the beginning the gospel of Jesus (1:1) is intimately connected to the gospel of God's reign (1:14-15). Therefore, this episode takes on special significance given the nature of the healing and its scriptural resonance. The story follows the common features of the healing story, even going into some interesting details about the physicality of the healing. Where it truly stands apart, however, is its connection with a thoroughgoing gentile context and in the Scripture quote at the end from Isa. 35:5-6. In this way, Mark shows us why this story of Jesus and the unfolding news of God's reign are so important to consider here.

In v. 31 Mark sets the narrative context. Jesus makes his roundabout trip from Tyre to Sidon, toward the Sea of Galilee and the "middle" of the Decapolis region. Trace it out on your Bible map and you will see that this narrated trip is really cartography at the service of theology.

In Mark 7:32-35, we have the central parts of the healing story. Friends bring a man who is deaf and has a speech impediment. The word in Greek indicates that the person struggles to speak. Jesus responds to their request and the narrator is sure to add fascinating, earthy details of what Jesus does: fingers, ears, spitting, and tongue touching! In v. 34, Jesus again looks up to heaven, sighs, and speaks a word in Aramaic, which is immediately translated in Greek as "be opened." There were at the time those who practiced healing by a kind of word magic using exotic foreign sounding words to do their work. The fact that the word is translated as everyday speech may be there to assure that this is no hocus pocus act, but genuine healing. With v. 35, the healing takes place. The language has eschatological overtones: the ears are "opened" and the tongue "released." NT scholar Eugene Boring argues that this release language belongs to the sphere of exorcism and demons: "Mark's conception of Jesus' ministry as a whole as a divine liberating onslaught against the demonic powers that bind human life, the victory of God over demonic power in the Christ event as a whole."[7] At the end of v. 35 the healing is effected so that the man "spoke plainly." In the culture of the time, which was oral-aural, such a healing meant a restoration and participation in shared life.

In the conclusion to this text in vv. 36-37, Jesus tries again to keep the healing quiet, but the crowd keeps speaking up. The tension here is more than an affirmation of Jesus' popularity, but underlines the importance of considering Jesus' actions here in light of his coming death and resurrection. Again, Mark wants to keep both parts of gospel good news together: the coming kingdom

7. Ibid., 217.

and Jesus' identity. Their affirmation in v. 37 highlights two scriptural connections. The language of doing all things well reminds of Gen. 1:31, where God sees that God made all things good. In this way, note several commentators, the healing miracles are connected to "new creation." The language of making the deaf to hear and the mute to speak is evocative of Isa. 35:5-6. The healing story thus helps to advance Mark's narrative-theological agenda as well.

This second half of our lection can be an important text to preach. In fact, since the lectionary holds this text together with the immediately previous one in 7:24-30, it can be a powerful occasion for preaching. With the combination of texts in the lection for Proper 18 (see above) preachers have the opportunity to preach Jesus' boundary-crossing ministry, which certainly has resonance for us today. It also continues the emphasis begun with the concern for the clean and the unclean in 7:1-23.

Another option, equally good, would be to focus on Mark 7:30-37 separately in order to deal with the question of healing and disability. Here one could focus on the cultural differences between then and now by noting that the conditions that isolate the man in this text have changed significantly in our day, when communities of persons exist whose communication and cultural life exist in rich relationship. What does "healing" look like when the predominance of oral-aural communication does not have to be assumed? What *different* boundaries might Jesus be crossing today in the lives of people who find new lines of solidarity across differences? This new context could offer the preacher a new opportunity to name the gospel for today. It might even be a different way to take up the emerging theme of "new creation" that the text points to in 7:37.

The Rocky Way—The Word of Promise and The Disciples' Misunderstanding: Feasting, Again, and More Misunderstanding (8:1-26)

INTRODUCTION

With this final subsection of the "rocky way," we see both misunderstanding and promise reinforced in crucial ways. Jesus feeds now four thousand persons in gentile territory (8:1-10). What has become clear to the reader about Jesus' reign-of-God ministry does not quickly seem to dawn on the disciples. At the same, the divisions with Jewish leaders only deepen when the Pharisees, immediately after the feeding, ask for a sign and only intensify Jesus' frustration

(8:11-13). This causes him to warn the disciples about the Pharisees and Herod, but this, too, only leads to misunderstanding and head scratching about the feeding that had just taken place—perhaps even leading the reader to a similar frustration after all the obvious questions that Jesus poses (8:14-21)! With the pericope about healing of a blind man at Bethsaida, the story sums up the difficulty. As with the blind man, any healing of the disciples' misunderstanding may require more than one healing attempt on Jesus' part (8:22-26)! But does this mean that the disciples will never understand, or that Jesus has not given up on them yet? As such, it offers a fitting conclusion to this central section of Mark's Gospel underlining both promise *and* misunderstanding.

PASSAGES OMITTED FROM THE LECTIONARY

All of the material here at the beginning of Mark 8 is omitted from the lectionary. This is particularly sad in light of the healing story with which it concludes: the healing of the blind man at Bethsaida (8:22-26). This text, above all, sums up the troubling misunderstanding of this section and personifies it for the reader. The fact that Jesus just prior to it asks such difficult rhetorical questions only underlines the healing's narrative function in this regard. Preachers may not see a need to repeat all of Mark's doublets, of which the feeding of the four thousand (8:1-10) is an example, as well as the material about the "yeast of Herod," which can be difficult to communicate. For those preachers who want Mark's theology to come through, however, the healing story at the conclusion of this section would make an excellent choice for an added lection for reading and preaching, perhaps during Ordinary Time. It would also help to highlight themes that are important throughout the readings for the Propers in the second half of the Season after Pentecost Year B.

FEEDING THE FOUR THOUSAND (8:1-10):
OMITTED FROM THE LECTIONARY

This is the second time Mark narrates a feeding miracle from Jesus. The second story is not identical to the first. Still, the similarities are such that it is clear that it functions as a doublet. Mark uses this second feeding story to move the disciples closer to being on the outside, and the readers more on the inside. In this rocky way of discipleship, here moving through gentile territory, the misunderstanding of the disciples becomes exceedingly pronounced. This becomes clear as chapter 8 unfolds and moves toward a key moment at Caesarea Philippi.

The situation is described in Mark 8:1. "In those days" not only connects this story to the preceding narrative in gentile country, it also invokes a sense of the eschatological. The scene that follows presupposes that end-time frame. The word again reminds the reader, perhaps, that we have been here before. By now the reader may be even growing weary of the disciples' obtuseness! The crowds are still "great," but this one had nothing to eat. We notice this situation is described a little differently from the first feeding miracle in Mark 6:35-44. Back then, the disciples took the initiative. Here, the narrator sets the stage, and the action is set in motion by Jesus' compassion for the crowd in the next verse. The disciples play thus *less* of a role in setting the scene.

Jesus' compassion is disclosed in the first person in vv. 2-3. The idea of this being a gentile crowd may make this significant in two ways. First, it places it in continuity with the first healing miracle: one in a Jewish context, the second miracle in a predominantly gentile context.[8] Second, it distinguishes this gentile scene from the other by reason of its motivation. Jesus' concern in chapter 6 was expressed through Exodus typology and the desire to see the sheep of Israel have a shepherd. Here, the reason for Jesus' action is as a compassionate response. They have been there three days (here the eschatological frame meets up with a resurrection allusion), they are in the desert far enough that they could grow faint, and some have come from a great distance (as gentiles are stereotypically wont to do, since they are "far away" from God). Jesus' motivation for doing this for gentiles is thus not identical with the first feeding. It has its own logic, perhaps one consistent with the gradually accepted turn to the gentile mission—which has been an important subtheme since the beginning of Mark 7.

The disciples' response in 8:4-5 only points to their befuddlement. Despite the feeding miracle that they witnessed only a few verses ago, they do not know how they are supposed to feed this crowd. The way they phrase their question is particularly telling: the English translation says "how?" but the Greek asks "from where?" Jesus responds by following almost the same procedure as in Mark 6:35-44. He asks how many loaves they have. The disciples respond with a biblical "seven."

Jesus directs the action in vv. 6-7 once again by having the crowd to sit down. When he takes the bread, he does so in quasi-eucharistic fashion: taking, giving thanks, breaking, and giving. When he does give the bread, the

8. Cf. Yarbro Collins, *Mark*, 378.

disciples are the ones who distribute to the crowd. The presence of some fish accompanies the miracle as well, likewise blessed and distributed. Jesus is in charge, and yet the disciples play a role—perhaps significant for the role they play in the post-Easter church.

But this is not just any meal in 8:8-9. Now in these verses the eschatological miracle itself comes into view. They ate "and were filled," signaling the fullness of the end time. As if to emphasize the point, the narrator highlights that seven baskets of leftovers were taken up. The note of the four thousand persons present underlines the miraculous feat; as with the first feeding story in Mark 6, this is disclosed at the end of the story. Now Jesus can send them away.

In the final verse Jesus and the now resume their frantic pace. Immediately they embark on the boat and go to Dalmanutha. Scholars are unsure what this refers to, as no place by that name is attested in ancient sources.[9]

That this text does not appear in the lectionary is, together with the story in Mark 6:35-44, a great loss. The two together become important for understanding the eschatological nature of Jesus' reign-of-God ministry in light of our own struggles to understand, too. The repetition of the stories is crucial for the developing misunderstanding of the disciples as well as the inclusion of the readers in the story going forward. Preachers wishing to include these stories may wish to do them in tandem as a way of highlighting their importance. For those communities that celebrate Holy Communion, they can become a rich resource for preaching on God's eschatological purposes and the ways in which even our celebrations point forward to the eschatological banquet. Here Mark's apocalyptic theology fills out and deepens our own sense of what Eucharist means and why God's future matters in communities that struggle with understanding their vocation in the present.

The Demand for a Sign (8:11-13):
Omitted from The Lectionary

In this brief interlude, Jesus stops long enough in Jewish territory to get in a further dispute with the Jewish leaders, the Pharisees. The context of this has played out during the first half of Mark. There were the first whiffs of opposition in questions about Jesus' legitimacy with some of his early ministry in Mark 2. Beginning in Mark 3:6 the Pharisees had begun conspiring with the Herodians to put Jesus to death. The last opportunity when they were

---

9. Marcus, *Mark 1-8*, 498.

together, they were disputing with Jesus' disciples over a matter of practice around purity in 7:1-23. This latest scene thus seems to highlight a growing split between Jesus and the Pharisees. They do not contest what is happening; they do, however, wish to clarify what it means.

When the Pharisee's challenge Jesus in 8:11 Mark as narrator surmises that they are testing Jesus. The word *testing* is a loaded one. The language of such testing goes back to Jesus' temptation in the wilderness by Satan in 1:13. This way of narrating the dispute with the Pharisees aligns them with those opposed to God's purposes and frames what they ask for: "a sign." By seeking a sign from heaven it may be that the Pharisees ask for some incontrovertible proof that the things Jesus does are indeed from God, and not from Satan. They do not dispute the healings and the exorcisms; rather they want proof that they are divine in origin.

Jesus responds by sighing in vv. 12-13. The narrator uses the same word in Greek to describe Jesus before he heals the man who was deaf and had a speech impediment in 7:34. In doing so, the narrator's description may be to help us relate the inability of that man's lack of hearing with the incapacity of the Pharisees to understand. With his invocation of this "generation" Jesus also links the Exodus typology of the previous stories around feeding (Moses, manna, wilderness) with the desire for a sign. Joel Marcus argues that Mark is recapitulating part of the Exodus narrative that in Exod. 16 describes feeding with manna and in Exod. 17 describes the request for a sign and by a faithless "generation," as also in Deut. 1:35, 32:5, 20 which have shaped the NT use of the term.[10] Given the proximity of our text to the second feeding miracle in Mark 8:1-10, that request seems all the more ironic. Jesus goes on to respond in the form of prophetic speech with his "Truly I tell you" language. He is making an important statement here that may imply an oath with an implicit curse.[11] The intensification of the language may point to an important break in the developing way of Mark's narrative. Jesus' ministry has encompassed in the last few chapters both Jewish and gentile contexts, the latter of which is seen as something that Jesus does not engage as a first choice (7:27), but as an act of compassion (8:2). With this, however, Jesus' ties to Jewish religious leaders have become strained. Jesus sees their recalcitrance as a desire for something more than has been given in his many signs and wonders. His departure in 8:13 for the other shore may be more than just another narrative shift. It may imply, after such a short visit with his disputants, a looming break.

---

10. Ibid., 501, 503–4.

11. Yarbro Collins, *Mark*, 385.

Again, this text has been left out of the lectionary. Its presence provokes both problems and opportunities. The problem touches on matters of relationships. The struggle in this text is one that plays out with first-century Jewish religious leaders. Our take on that first-century struggle usually is overlaid by a long, troubling history of Jewish/Christian relations. Preachers willing to go with Mark into these troubled waters will need to do so with care, not simply replicating medieval or modern struggles, but understanding the unique nature of the conflict in the first century. The opportunity, however, is a theological one. Mark seems in this text to be making a point about the nature of "signs" and the quality of human expectation vis-à-vis God. The Markan narrative offers all sorts of demonstrations of power that relate to faith. Much of the first eight chapters of Mark has borne witness to this. The request for signs, however, especially a sign *from* heaven, Mark seems to be saying, demonstrates a desire to move behind faith to something else—perhaps a wish to manage the divine in human terms.[12] Here we preachers may have the opportunity to wrestle with Mark about the quality of faith and its relation to what God is doing.

THE YEAST OF THE PHARISEES AND OF HEROD (8:14-21): OMITTED FROM THE LECTIONARY

With an almost accidental beginning, this little scene sharpens the conflict of the previous chapters around bread and the disciples' misunderstanding. On the heels of Jesus' sharp disagreement with the Pharisees, it seals by immediate narrative juxtaposition (8:11-13/8:14-21) the increasingly troubled relationship between Jesus and his disciples in light of the growing opposition of the Pharisees. From the readers' standpoint, it concretizes the increasing frustration with the disciples with an almost comical feel—comical, were the misunderstanding not so tragic. In doing so, it cements the relationship between Jesus and the readers, who are now becoming more insiders to his identity and his reign-of-God ministry, the two sides of the gospel proclamation that is Jesus himself (1:1) and the kingdom he preaches (1:14-15), a gospel he has been announcing from his first, promising beginnings.

The comedy of errors begins with a deadpan, subtle disclosure from the narrator in v. 14: the disciples had forgotten to bring bread—all they had was a single loaf in the boat. This plaintive statement becomes the ground for the irony of the situation as well as the misdirection of the conversation that ensues.

---

12. Eugene Boring explores this with great care in *Mark*, 223.

Jesus then gives a strict warning in 8:15-16 by piling on imperatives of seeing: keep alert and watch out. Jesus warns specifically of the leaven of the Pharisees. Leaven may be a symbol of corruption. Just a little alters the lump of dough. In a broad sense, this is true, but that may not do the term full justice. Adela Yarbro Collins points out that leaven is sometimes a metaphor more broadly of influence, thus explaining why Jesus needs to qualify it here: the leaven *of the Pharisees* and the leaven *of Herod*.[13] Is there something about their influence, the Pharisees and Herod's, that poses a special problem for being receptive to Jesus and his claims? If so, the alignment of Jesus' boatload of disciples in 8:14-21 and Jesus' opponents in 8:11-13 and elsewhere does not bode well along the way. Joel Marcus takes it a step further and identifies leaven with Passover practice interpreted eschatologically.[14] Is there something of the "old age" in the Pharisees and Herod's influence?

With almost comic relief the disciples say to one another, "It is because we have no bread." Clearly, they are not grasping the moment or the meaning of what Jesus says. By this time, even the reader might become exasperated. The disciples and Jesus seem to be talking past each other.

Jesus picks up on their conversation in vv. 17-21 and poses a series of questions, many of which voice the perspective also of the exasperated reader who has lived through two feeding miracles and another in-the-boat misunderstanding of Jesus' epiphanic identity in relation to the loaves (Mark 6:52). Just as in that difficult boat journey, Jesus raises the question not just of a failure to understand, but the possibility of hardened hearts. This language harkens back not just to the apocalyptic mystery of the parables of Mark 4, but to the strange language of the prophet Isaiah that its wording evoked. Another question pulls in other narrative connections: do the disciples have eyes and fail to see (cf. Mark 8:22); do they have ears and fail to hear (cf. Mark 7:31-37)? Then Jesus goes into detail with the lessons that could have been learned with the two feeding miracles. Here the distance between the readers and the disciples becomes deeper. Jesus not only recalls elements of the stories in Mark 6 and Mark 8, he uses the same numbers for the loaves and for the people fed, the same words for the two kinds of baskets in each of the stories. We readers *get it*; the disciples do not. The disciples remember, but only under duress. Though they may have passed the math test for counting loaves, it appears they failed the fullness of the eschatological exam. Jesus asks in sum, "Do you not yet understand?"

---

13. Yarbro Collins, *Mark*, 386.

14. Marcus, *Mark 1-8*, 507.

The final question is rhetorical and hangs in the air, answered really by the next episode in the sequence, the story of the blind man in Bethsaida. Jesus has revealed an apocalyptic mystery of the gospel in Mark's narrative. However, for some reason the disciples are now just about as oblivious to it as Jesus' sign-seeking opponents. The rocky way with the disciples is nearing an end. It was strewn with promise, yes, full of demonstrations of the kingdom's power and Jesus' identity. At the same time, it is also strewn with the debris of tragic misunderstanding. In this sense, the gospel comes even to us as a mystery. The gospel is sown in promise and yields more than enough for a banquet or two even as it meets with incomprehension. However, there is no guarantee that every seed sprouts to life. Here, at the end of this rocky way of discipleship, this tragic dimension of faith becomes palpable. The religious leaders resist. The disciples misunderstand. Both may be suffering from cardiosclerosis. And yet, the promise does its work, perhaps most of all . . . in the reader.

This text is likewise omitted from the lectionary. Still its inclusion allows preachers to explore the mystery of faith in a distracted age. How does Jesus' word of promise meet us? How does his invitation to break bread impact us? Hopefully, the promise can still even now take root in us even as we go with Jesus and his disciples on the way. But take heart: we readers know that Jesus' word has the power to open eyes and ears, even our own. It is important to remember that Jesus' question in v. 21 is "do you not *yet* understand?" It still is possible—even for recalcitrant disciples—that they yet will understand. In fact, the next story even underlines this mysterious possibility of eventual insight.

Jesus Cures a Blind Man at Bethsaida (8:22-26): Omitted from The Lectionary

With this new healing story, Mark helps to show just the kind of dawning vision that the disciples need. It is an important healing story for the unique way it proceeds relative to its placement in Mark's narration of the rocky way that the disciples are walking.

Bethsaida, mentioned in v. 22, is a village on the northeastern side of the Sea of Galilee. The action moves immediately to a situation involving people bringing a man who was blind before Jesus to be touched. Certain things here are already familiar to the reader. The form of this healing is not unlike that of 7:31-37. The view of Jesus' healing power in his touch was already described in Mark 3:10 and 6:56. Yet there is one thing in particular unique to this story. Coming on the heels of Jesus' urgent questions in 8:14-21 to his disciples on the boat about *their* inability to see and understand, the scene with the man who was blind is doubly poignant for readers.

What makes this healing unique is its two-step process in 8:23-24. The healing at first is only partial. The value for connecting with the disciples' struggle to see and understand becomes clear. At the same time, it also emerges as a struggle for Jesus and his healing power.

The scene proceeds with Jesus leading the man who was blind out of the village and putting saliva on his eyes. Yarbro Collins argues that the location of the healing is for the sake of privacy, while the saliva itself was thought to have healing properties at that time.[15] Marcus and Boring add the thought that the "leading by the hand" and the actual healing of a blind man play on prophetic intertexts in Jer. 31:32 and Isa. 42:6-7, thus giving this healing a peculiarly eschatological feel.[16] The unique element of this healing, relative to the typical form, is the two-step progression of the healing process. When asked if he can see, the man replies in v. 24 that the people he sees look like "trees walking." His vision is thus not fully resolved after Jesus' application of saliva and laying on of hands.

With a second laying on of his hands directly to the man's eyes in vv. 25-26, the man is able to see, his sight referenced in three clauses to make the point. His instruction to go home, but not to the village, may be consistent with the way the recipients of such miracles are charged to keep it secret. This becomes all the more important in the subsequent verses when Jesus' identity and its correct understanding become central for the unfolding Markan narrative.

For the contemporary interpreter, the preaching of a text that equates blindness with ignorance becomes problematic. For hearers with blindness, such equivalence is an extra burden for living a full life. While Mark is clearly trying to relate the blindness of the disciples with their inability to understand on a metaphorical level, contemporary preachers as interpreters need to find ways to bring these texts into close proximity with persons who are not ignorant and actually possess deep understanding.[17]

---

15. Yarbro Collins, *Mark,* 393.

16. Marcus, *Mark 8-16,* 598 and Boring, *Mark,* 233.

17. Preachers who wish to explore these aspects of interpreting texts may wish to consult Kathy Black's *A Healing Homiletic: Preaching and Disability* (Nashville: Abingdon, 1996).

As with most of Mark 8, this pericope is not part of the RCL cycle of readings. Again, its absence means that we hear some of the language of Jesus' ministry and identity without the benefit of reflecting on the disciples' misunderstanding and the struggle to help them discern correctly. While the text poses problems for interpreters today as noted above, it is helpful theologically for the church to wrestle with the mystery of who Jesus is in relation to our very real struggle to follow faithfully today. The fact that Jesus follows through to heal the man on the second try also shows his dedication to the mystery of his promise. Like the ending of the previous unit in 8:21, this implied promise points forward even while the two-stage healing underlines the hard-won insights that will be necessary for the eschatological truth ultimately to dawn through suffering and resurrection.

5

Gospel Interlude—
Revelation on the Way
(8:27—9:13)

INTRODUCTION

Much like the prologue, this brief section serves as a revelatory reflection in relation to the unfolding narrative. If throughout most of the narrative the relation of Jesus' identity and gospel proclamation of the divine reign prompts rhetorical questions and amazement, here the language broaches mystery not with such indirection, but with openness, address, and even apocalyptic symbolic depiction on a mountain. As mentioned in the introduction, Jesus' baptism, transfiguration, and crucifixion are all portrayed as key revelatory moments at the beginning, middle, and end of this narrative. The material around the transfiguration story—with its use of gospel language, direct address, and references to Elijah and other prophetic figures as well as its setting at Caesarea Philippi and the mountain—sets this section apart as an interlude that discloses Jesus' identity "openly" in relation to all these things. Yet such revelation, which to us seems so strangely apocalyptic and symbolic, is given right here at the farthest point in Jesus' ministry. It is given not at the beginning or the destination but "on the way." It is, nestled within this narrative, an oddly apocalyptic glimpse given proleptically to the disciples to help correct their vision (Mark 8:21-26), even if it takes during this interlude a series of questions, rebukes, special teaching, and mountaintop revelations to help them see as they follow on the way.

The material progresses in a very challenging way. It begins with Peter's confession in 8:27-30. In a surprise to readers, given the misunderstanding of the previous section, Peter seems to have insight into Jesus' identity, and in way that conforms to that which has been revealed to the reader along the way since Mark 1:1. Yet Jesus' charge to keep silent about this in 8:30 pushes right back into mystery. Then in 8:31-38, the conflict reemerges in the narrative. Jesus gives his first passion prediction about the Son of the human, and Peter rebukes him. Jesus shares the sentiment and rebukes Peter right back, thus heightening the paradox of misunderstanding. It even forces Jesus to do a little extra teaching about discipleship in 8:34ff. In the final part of this brief revelatory interlude, we ascend the mountain with Jesus, Peter, James, and John to join with them in a revelation of Jesus' identity that bears striking similarities to his baptism in 1:9-11 though this time described with quasi-resurrection language. Again, this key revelatory interlude at the midpoint of Mark's Gospel narrative necessitates further teaching about the significance of suffering in connection to eschatological hope in 9:10-13.

LECTIONS

The RCL includes crucial pericopes from this interlude section. However, there are some verses, namely 9:1 and 9:10-13 that do not appear in the lectionary at all. Because of the extra context they provide, I will be treating them in connection together with the prescribed lections for their respective days in the calendar. Venturesome preachers may choose to include them on a Sunday as well—if nothing else to provide a richer context for Jesus' first passion prediction and the transfiguration.

LECTION: PETER'S DECLARATION ABOUT JESUS AND JESUS FORETELLS HIS DEATH AND RESURRECTION
8:27-38 (9:1); PROPER 19
8:31-38 (9:1); LENT 2

This extended section with Peter and Jesus sets up the revelation in the transfiguration scene. Already here Jesus connects questions and claims about his identity with the kind of discipleship that actually "follows" from it. The section features not only direct address in dialogue, but three "rebukes," which underline what is at stake in connecting Jesus' identity, the gospel, and discipleship.

We begin by noting the setting in 8:27-30. Before we even get to Jesus' first question, "Who do people say that I am?" in this crucial hinge moment for the Gospel of Mark we need to contend with two things. First, we note that the location of the action is Caesarea Philippi. The name indicates that the city was named after Caesar. However, since another Caesarea nearby shared that name, it is distinguished with the second name Philippi, referring to Phillip, one of Herod's nearby ruling sons. Digging deeper, one notices that this region has a symbolic significance for our revelatory interlude at the mountain of transfiguration. The region, as Adela Yarbro Collins points out, was connected not only with Mount Hermon, but it was also an important location for worship associated first with ruler cults stretching back to the Ptolemies and as recent as a new Herodian temple "in honor of Augustus."[1] In short, this revelatory discussion is happening in a region of imperial religious significance. It is no mere bit of local color or backdrop, but is central to understanding the give and take that results in Peter's confession. Second, the narrator goes out of his way to describe Jesus' initiatory question in the dialogue as happening "on the way" in v. 28. "On the way" is discipleship language. We are thus engaging the back and forth of question and response, rebuke and rebuke, in the material that follows not as an intellectual exercise, nor even as one about christological speculation, but as one connected deeply to discipleship and the nature of the gospel itself.

In light of this, Jesus proceeds with his question: "Who do people say that I am?" The disciples reply with answers, many of which have already emerged in the previous narrative. They respond with the names of prophetic figures, most of whom have clear eschatological significance: John the Baptist, Elijah, or one of the prophets. Jesus, however, wants to press the question deeper and asks his disciples: "But who do *you* say that I am?" Jesus asks the question in the second-person plural "y'all." We are no longer in the realm of hearsay or rumor. Peter answers with a confession: "You are the Messiah." The language in Greek, of course, is the word for Christ. It is here clearly spoken and connects profoundly to the titular reference in Mark 1:1: "The beginning of the gospel of Jesus Christ . . ." In this sense, Peter's confession is not merely his, but offers now a second anchor to the narrator's work of connecting the gospel to the identity of Jesus and explicating that identity as Christ or messiah. Finally, the reader, who has known this since 1:1, hears a major character—the first named disciple, Peter—corroborate that early disclosure. It is a clear turning point, a crux, for the narrator's vision.

---

1. Eugene Boring, *Mark: A Commentary*, New Testament Library (Louisville: Westminster John Knox, 2007), 237.

It would be easy to see the language of "Christ" here and begin assuming overly flat pre-conceptions of christological titles. The received messianic designation "Christ" is a loaded one—and part of what is loaded on to it is our belief about what that means in the contemporary Jewish context. For some time, it was asserted that there was some generic messianic expectation afoot in the Judaism of the time. Sometimes we as Christians tend to speak monolithically of such expectations, effectively rendering Jews as a foil in the process, as in the question, "why couldn't the Jews see that Jesus was the expected messiah?" The problem is that Judaism in this time is far more diverse in this regard than today's Christians properly give it credit. While there was some messianic expectation in the period, it was not universal. And where it existed, the expectation was diverse. The Dead Sea Scrolls, for example, even talk about *two* messiahs: one royal and one priestly. It is probably enough to know that messianic anointing pertained to kings, priests, and prophets, too. The rest of the term's meaning, in fairness, is usually filled in by the person doing the defining. Mark's Jesus obliges us by defining what "Christ" means with yet another title in Jesus' teaching in v. 31 to follow. So please do not assume just yet that we know what "Christ" or messiah means either. Stay tuned for Jesus' teaching below.

This subsection ends in 8:30 with Jesus' mysterious charge to say nothing. Again, we see the so-called messianic secret motif. The Greek word translated as "charged" is an odd choice. It means "rebuke" in other settings and appears in Mark also in exorcism scenes. Could it be that a Markan gospel knows that even divine revelation can be misunderstood and misapplied? The fact that the demons sometimes get it right in Mark should be a sobering thought for interpreters today. By charging them to keep silence, Jesus seems to imply that silence is the order of the day for now. Perhaps, from our theological view, following the logic of the messianic secret, the meaning of such confessions can only make sense later—not just after the teaching that follows, but perhaps after crucifixion and resurrection, too.

For reason of clarifying these matters, Jesus seems to dig deeper in 8:31-33. In v. 31, the narrator makes the point with the phrase "began to teach them." This was, as we shall see, the first of several occasions where Jesus fills in what his messianic role means. This text marks the first of three Markan passion predictions: suffering, death, and resurrection (cf. 9:31 and 10:33-34). This news would be shocking enough except for two things. First, this suffering/

death/resurrection is described as "necessary." The word *necessary* (*dei*) in Greek is an impersonal construction that has something like the force of a divine passive. The necessity refers to God and God's purposes and brings with it in this case an eschatological overtone. Second, and this is where the messianic specification takes place, it is the "Son of the human" who suffers. Yarbro Collins argues that here the term "son of man" is understood as equivalent with Christ or messiah and perhaps connects to the secrecy motif above by virtue of the tradition of the "hidden" son of man in an apocalyptic writing called the Similitudes of Enoch (*1 En.* 37–71).[2] If so, the hiddenness of the charge and the messianic vision is tied to a later eschatological judgment that is to be the public vindication. It is in this sense that Jesus' identity here as Christ and Son of the human is understood as secret: one that is hidden for now, but will be revealed in eschatological fullness. As Yarbro Collins puts it, "one factor in the secrecy of Jesus' messiahship may be the idea that the Son of Man is revealed to the elect in a secret and anticipatory way."[3]

The title "Son of the human" is a tricky one. Again, we will find ourselves frustrated if we assume there is some monolithic understanding of the term or title in the Bible. Sometimes the phrase is simply a reference to humanity, a synonym for human being. Sometimes in Mark the term is used with reference to Jesus' authority in, say, legal interpretation. Sometimes the language of Son of the human, whether in the NT or in other apocalyptic writings, refers to a kind of divine, heavenly figure associated with judgment.[4] It is probably most helpful to keep the clay wet as Mark narratively helps us to sculpt a theological vision. In this way we understand the use of the term in each context while realizing that Mark's gospel is there to help us unite some of these understandings in service of defining Jesus' messiahship as "Christ."

Joel Marcus argues that the "necessity" here goes beyond the divine purpose to include some connection with Scripture.[5] The fact that Jesus

2. Adela Yarbro Collins, *Mark: A Commentary*, Hermeneia (Minneapolis: Fortress Press, 2007), 402

3. Ibid.

4. This trajectory of the Son of Man begins with Daniel 7, even though Daniel seems to envision the Son of Man in human terms. Over time in the apocalyptic tradition, the Son of Man becomes this quasi-divine figure in the Enochic literature and in the NT itself. Mark's contribution may well consist in holding some of these different traditional strands together in connection with Jesus' earthly ministry, passion, resurrection, and role in ultimate judgment.

announces this "openly" in v. 32 does two things. It is for the disciples revealed and not hidden like in parables and in other places. Second, it also connects deeply with Jesus' own bold, candid purpose. There is a lot riding on this revelatory teaching moment.

Yet if all this is the case, it only heightens the shock of the next scene in v. 32b-33. If the idea of connecting suffering/death/resurrection to a messianic vision of a suffering Son of the human were not offensive enough, the idea that Peter would now rebuke Jesus *contrary to God's purpose, the Scriptures, and Jesus' bold revelation* heightens the conflict of this particular scene. The reversal here in the action is telling. Peter pulls Jesus aside, and begins (or keeps on) "rebuking" him with the same Greek verb described above. Given the fact that this unit started off as a teaching moment, the usual relationship of teacher/student has been overturned with Peter's action. As a result the action reverses again, this time with Jesus taking the lead. First he "looked at the disciples." This is not just Peter's problem; it is something all of them need to consider. Second, he rebukes Peter and compounds its exorcistic sense by referring to Peter as Satan. Lest we think that Peter has now been consigned to the apocalyptic ash heap, it is important to note in v. 33 that Jesus' command to Peter is to "go behind me." This phrase does not just mean "get out of my face," but also tries to restore Peter to his proper place: behind Jesus, as a follower (yes, even to the cross), as a *disciple* and not a teacher to Jesus. The meaning of the whole becomes clear with the explanatory statement. Peter's view is human centered, not oriented to God.

In the subsequent section, Mark 8:34—9:1, all the talk about Jesus' identity and teaching is linked to discipleship. Now the crowd is brought in and Jesus makes clear to both them and the disciples what discipleship entails. Along the way, it is also connected to the gospel itself—once again, a chief concern of the prologue in 1:1-15, too.

First of all, following Jesus entails self-denial and the taking up of a cross. The language is in the third person singular. Discipleship makes that kind of personal claim. More important than that, however, is the *reason* for such discipleship. Trying to save life on one's own terms leads only to losing life. Paradoxically, Jesus teaches also that losing one's life actually means gaining it—so long as one does it for the sake of Jesus and his gospel. Notice, here, the close connection between Jesus' identity and the gospel he proclaims. This thematic of the gospel, so important in the prologue in 1:1, 14, and 15, now gets hands and feet in this teaching on discipleship. Losing and saving are not

---

5. Joel Marcus, *Mark 8-16*, Anchor Yale Bible (New Haven, CT: Yale University Press, 2009), 613.

generic principles, but are connected to Jesus' identity and the gospel of God's reign that he proclaims. The opposite choice, that is, saving one's own life, is pilloried by means of a series of rhetorical questions. In the end, such a tragic choice even misses out on a more foundational, if eschatological, truth. Being ashamed of Jesus and his words (the gospel) now in this evil generation will only beget similar treatment from the eschatological Son of the human, who will come with angels and glory. To this threat, Jesus ends this teaching by adding a final promise for those hearing: "Truly I tell you, there are some standing here who will not taste death until they see that the kingdom of God has come with power." For all this talk of Jesus' identity and gospel word, it hinges in the end on a promise to his hearers.

This particular verse in Mark 9:1 has vexed interpreters for some time. For many scholars in the pursuit of the historical Jesus it was an important text. Jesus' apocalyptic expectations and saying here have been disconfirmed by history. No doubt all his hearers have died and yet the kingdom has not come with power. There is little solace here for the historically minded. The material fits with the preceding text. It uses a participial verb in the perfect to convey a completed action. The notion of not tasting death is metaphorical, but certainly cannot be stretched too far. The upshot is this: this text makes a prediction about the kingdom that did not come to pass. What it does offer, however, is a vision that the future present is not for someday, but for now, in this place, where discipleship is "on the way." And yet it precedes a vision on the mountain. Some have ventured that the epiphany scene of the transfiguration is itself the fulfillment of this promise. It is so, perhaps, in part, but still leaves questions open. If this promise does connect with the transfiguration, it does in a partial and proximate way. It begins already to make present the forward-looking promise that God's reign is indeed on its way.

This particular long section corresponds only piecemeal to the lectionary. Mark 8:27-38 (without the embarrassing prophecy of 9:1) is the lection for Proper 19. Mark 8:31-38 (without Peter's confession at Caesarea Philippi) is an alternative lection for Lent 2. The reduced choice in the latter makes some sense for the Lenten season, but does so at a cost. We have tried to show that christological meaning and discipleship are intimately related in Mark 8:27—9:1. The lectionary risks severing that connection and turning Jesus' teaching into a generalized ethic. Both texts miss out on the interesting theological reflection that would be provoked by including the problematic prophecy of Mark 9:1. Perhaps in this way the lectionary could be pushed to go deeper: not to reinscribe us into a lectionary world of fulfilled typologies and hopes that move naturally from promise to fulfillment. Indeed, by including 9:1 we engage more profoundly in the unfinished task that is Christian theology. The verse invites us to try making sense in the face of mysterious realities that plague us still: hopes that have not come to pass, or that do so in part, or even visions that while compelling are only a resting place on the way. Perhaps a life of discipleship lived in deep connection to Jesus' mysterious identity may also help us, on the far side of history's many tears and disappointments, to name the gospel anew with our words and lives in the very shadow of such disappointment and in the dawning light of its still inviting promise.

Lection: The Transfiguration [and The Coming of Elijah] 9:2-9 (10-13); Transfiguration and Lent 2 (Alt.)

In this section, Mark sets out visionary material that parallels nicely the prologue in 1:1-15. We have argued both here and at the beginning of Mark's Gospel, that Mark offers something to help frame his narrative about the gospel: namely, Jesus Christ and the reign of God that Jesus himself proclaims in word and deed. In this case, Mark has begun this frame by asking questions of Jesus' identity that connect deeply with his sense of the gospel and the nature of discipleship. Jesus may have been the great miracle worker, exorcist, teacher, and preacher of the gospel of God's reign. His revelatory actions on the waters of chaos may have provoked profound reflections on his powerful identity. Yet this same Jesus has just now announced his seemingly contrary destiny in suffering, rejection, death, and resurrection. Although acclaimed Christ by Peter, Jesus is quick to add that this understanding is linked to a vision of the Son of the human ("Son of Man") that includes precisely this destined reality both for him and his disciples—suffering and death. The mutual rebukes, the questions, the responses have not made for an easy transition. With this text, however, teaching is supplemented by vision. Years ago, biblical scholars might have argued that its unusual character represents a resurrection story now transposed into this earlier section of Mark. The theory does not presently have many advocates among NT scholars. Yet it is fair to say that this visionary material invites the three disciples who witness it (along with us readers) to keep before our eyes that Jesus' suffering and death, along with the disciples', needs to be understood in light of his resurrection life. Yarbro Collins argues that the text that follows is an epiphany.[6] While different from a resurrection narrative proper, it does make deep connections both to apocalyptic traditions and Greco-Roman ones. We are still, after all, in the region of Caesarea Philippi. It commends itself as well for other reasons. Its chief biblical connection is to the story of the theophany to Moses in Exod. 24. These important connections help to clarify our mysterious text while relating it more deeply to Mark's unfolding narrative purposes going forward.

Here in the transfiguration story proper, the stage is set with the first verse. The narrator discloses in 9:2 that six days pass before the event happens. Scholars and commentators over the centuries have puzzled over this number of days and their meaning. It may just be that the narrator is harkening back to the Moses theophany of Exod. 24:16, in which Moses climbs the mountain and waits six days for the divine voice to speak from the cloud. With the second part of the setting, however, something foundational is disclosed. The location of this event on the mountain has not only an intertextual connection with Exod. 24, but a general appeal to mountains as places of divine disclosure. A mountain is a meeting place between heaven and earth. It is also important to note who is present for this meeting. Jesus calls Peter, James, and John. Throughout this scene they play a representative function for the disciples inasmuch as the ensuing dialogue takes place in the first person plural "we". The point here is that the story is not for private spiritual consumption, but connects deeply to the very issues we have been raising in our interlude: the relationship between the mystery of Jesus' identity and the disciples who are called to follow. This verse closes by lifting up the most peculiar character of the epiphany itself. Jesus himself is "transformed," as the Greek verb describes. The use of the passive form here indicates divine agency.

The description in 9:3 of Jesus' clothing or appearance is common in such epiphany stories. The reference to such clothing and its connection with heavenly, divine realities also extends to the clothing of witnesses and martyrs in heaven, say, in the book of Revelation. The comparative language to what a human being can do as a whitening agent again confirms it as a divine act.

With v. 4 the Markan narrator describes the epiphany scene in ways consistent with the theological emphases thus far. The two exemplary biblical figures "appear" with the passive form of the Greek verb to see—again implying divine agency on the mountain. Curiously, the two figures are named as "Elijah with Moses." Some have speculated that they represent the Law and the Prophets—and indeed the later tradition assimilates them to just those roles. However, Moses is not just the law giver; he is first among the prophets. In

6. Yarbro Collins, *Mark*, 416–19.

Mark, moreover, we have already seen how Elijah plays a key role precisely because of his place in eschatological scenarios—an issue that is taken up yet again in the subsequent post-epiphanic debriefing with the three disciples in 9:9-13 below. As if this were not enough, they are described as conversing with Jesus, and not he with them! This is not your run-of-the-mill epiphany.

This becomes clear in Peter's representative response to the event in 9:5-6. As is typical with many such epiphanies and theophanies, Peter and his cohort are afraid, even terrified. He all but trips over himself in order to offer to build "dwellings" for the three figures on the mountain. The dwellings may be reminiscent of the Festival of Booths. Peter also shows his hand by addressing Jesus as "Rabbi," which in the time could mean teacher, but could also function as a more generic, honorific title. The narrator concedes that Peter did not know how to respond; he and those with him were apparently flummoxed by the scene.

In this climactic part of the scene in v. 7, the theophanic cloud appears and overshadows them. The cloud is an important sign of divine presence all the way through the Exodus narrative. Now a voice comes from the cloud and makes an important pronouncement concerning Jesus' identity: "This is my Son, the Beloved; listen to him!" Unlike the voice at Jesus' baptism, this disclosure is in the third person. Given the fact that this is precisely done in the presence of and for the disciples whom Jesus called to go with him, it is appropriate. It probably also explains the command at the end. Presumably disciples confused by a miracle-working figure who also now announces the necessity to suffer and die need to hold this mysterious, odd paradox of Jesus together. For all his mystery, disciples should listen to him. As if to underline this, everyone else disappears on the mountain. All they can see is this same paradoxical Jesus alone with them.

The text that follows, Mark 9:9-13, is a bit of an orphan in the history of the tradition. Some treat it as part of the transfiguration itself, others do not. Some attach the first verse to the previous pericope; others explain any discontinuities with subsequent verses by asserting Markan redactional work. The problem carries over to the issue of form. It probably should simply be treated as the text functions. Here Jesus works through some teaching issues that have eventuated through what the disciples saw on the mountain and heard from Jesus in chapter 8. It will function for us to round out this brief revelatory interlude.

This first verse at Mark 9:9 is important in the history of interpretation for the role it plays in Wilhelm Wrede's theory of the messianic secret. In the final part of the verse, Jesus charges the disciples to remain silent about what they had witnessed "until after the Son of Man had risen from the dead." This certainly underlines the contention that the transfiguration story, while not a resurrection narrative, was functioning as a resurrection preview here in chapter 9. While clearly the idea of resurrection is emphasized here—a key element of Wrede's thesis—two other things loom here both with connections to what precedes and follows. First, the one who is to rise is the Son of the human. This was precisely Jesus' recent teaching and disclosure in Mark 8:31. Whatever this text is about, it deals at least with helping the disciples wrap their heads around the necessity of Jesus as Son of the human to rise again. Second, the phrase here about the resurrection refers to Jesus rising "from the dead." Some commentators note that the Christian conception of Jesus' resurrection *apart* from the general resurrection at the last day was a problematic notion. It was not part of a general conception of resurrection alive at the time.

For this reason, the disciples' actions in vv. 10-11, and the question they formulate, begin to make sense. They have witnessed this epiphany, a kind of resurrection preview featuring the temporary transformation of the one who was confessed Christ by Peter and who himself linked this to the divine necessity of the Son of the human's suffering, rejection, death, and resurrection. There is enough here to scratch your head about. Why should a messianic conception be linked to a suffering Son of the human? But the specific issue here is also the notion of resurrection itself: just what is "this rising from the dead"? Most would link a resurrection to a *general* resurrection. And then everyone knows that a general resurrection is a Day of the Lord event. And no Day of the Lord event is going to happen without Elijah coming first (Mal. 4:5-6). Hence, the disciples' question: what gives?

In this case, the truly tricky part is in Jesus' response to their question in vv. 12-13. It may necessitate some redefining of terms along the way.

The logic of the argument is a bit of a crossing between terms. In v. 12, Jesus agrees that Elijah must come to restore all things (Mal. 4:6). Jesus adds to the stipulated premise about Elijah another premise of his own that he expects the disciples will agree to: that the Scriptures say that the Son of the human will suffer and be treated with contempt.[7] However, if you hold to both premises, they cannot make obvious sense in tandem. If the forerunner "restores all

---

7. Even this premise of scriptural warrants for a suffering Son of Man is a tough one to take at face value. Yarbro Collins points out that many scholars have struggled to find clear scriptural references that confirm this confidence (*Mark*, 430–31). She goes on to point out that his is even more the case with respect to the final line of 9:13, which presupposes that there are scriptural warrants for a suffering, eschatological Elijah. The best case for it is to assert a general suffering of prophets—it seems to be their lot in Scripture.

things," then why is the Son of the human going to suffer and be treated contemptuously? As a result, in v. 13 Jesus seems to redefine the terms as they fit Elijah. He reminds the disciples that John the Baptist was the Elijah forerunner (of course, the narrator also cued the reader in on this several chapters ago) *and* that people did with him whatever they wanted. Faced with this reality, the nature of Elijah's forerunner status to the eschatological restoring of all things has to be reframed—at the very least consistent with a suffering Son of the human figure.

Admittedly, the solution is less than satisfactory. Yet, from the standpoint of a compliant reader of Mark, the solution is not implausible. As it is, a suffering Son of the human will probably necessitate a reworking of multiple eschatological scenarios. It just was not in the cards at the time. Yet the solution is also more than that. Joel Marcus points out what this means *to the disciples.*[8] John came and spoke the word and he suffered. Jesus came and preached the gospel and he suffered. One way to see your way through the confusion and chaos of the final three decades of the first century is to be familiar with the characters and the storyline, too. True disciples should know what to expect. This strange identity of Jesus is revealed for his disciples on the way.

The first portion of this particular text, Mark 9:2-9, shows up in the lectionary on Epiphany and Lent 2 as an alternate. It tends to leave out 9:10-13, which has the difficult reflections on resurrection, Elijah's role, and the suffering Son of the human. In one sense, this edited version may be sufficient. The scriptural move in vv. 10-13 is not easy to follow. At the same time, the underlying theological issue is worth the struggle. The idea of a suffering, rising Son of the human did indeed pose problems then. And an understanding of divine revelation through suffering, not as a general principle (as if any kind of suffering would bring us closer to God), but as a specific issue for the gospel and our engagement with it as disciples on the way, is indeed worth struggling with. Perhaps in this way the story of transfiguration is told is such that its revelation is not ethereal but having hands and feet in the strange gospel that is Jesus Christ *and* the reign of God.

---

8. Marcus, *Mark 8-16*, 650–51.

6

Teaching and More Misunderstanding on The Way (9:14—10:52)

This next section then highlights the juxtaposition of what has just been revealed with the struggle to understand on the disciples' way through Galilee and Judea. Mark invites us to live this paradox with Jesus, whose identity and reign-of-God ministry are fraught with the same conflicts. This section explores those conflicts as moments of *teaching* and the disciples' continued misunderstanding even while moving forward "on the way." As we begin this part of the narrative, Jesus' title as teacher becomes more prominent. For the first time since 4:38, Jesus is addressed as "teacher" (*didaskale*) in 9:17 and subsequently in 9:38, 10:17, 10:20, and 10:35. In the final scene, a healing, Bartimaeus addresses him as "master," using the word for rabbi (*rabbouni*). In short, Jesus' role as teacher here is played out in a uniquely strong way. The address as "teacher" is not peculiar to this section alone. In Jerusalem others will speak to Jesus in the same way. At the same time, the references here are important. They do not merely report about Jesus' teaching authority, as was done earlier in Mark. Now they represent some of the content of his teaching. At the same time, they demonstrate the continued need for helping the disciples understand—whether by speaking or asking pointed questions in moments of private disclosure (9:28, 9:33, 10:10). There is teaching going on here—complete with occasional private tutorials—and yet the disciples' misunderstanding persists. This is only highlighted by the two final passion predictions in this unit: 9:31-32 and 10:33-34, which likewise only seem to flummox the disciples. The revelation on the mountain and its heavenly voice's command to "listen to him" seem to be slipping from the disciples' memory.

It is also important to remember in this section that we are not just "on the way," but eventually on the way to *Jerusalem*. This section of Mark is thus important to readers because of the deepening misunderstanding between Jesus and his disciples and thus the greater insight that is granted the implied reader in the moment. These realities for us readers will be important for comprehending the action that will unfold in Jerusalem from Mark 11–16. Yet in the midst of it all, the gospel promise continues. When Peter, representing the disciples, frets about what they have given up to follow Jesus, Jesus points to the gospel itself and promises for its sake a hundredfold for all that had been left (10:28-31). Even now, in the midst of teaching and misunderstanding, and impending signs of failure, Jesus points to the gospel promise and makes his way with them through Galilee (9:30) on to Judea (10:1) and ultimately to Jerusalem (11:1).

TEACHING AND MORE MISUNDERSTANDING ON THE WAY: TEACHING DISCIPLES ABOUT FOLLOWING THROUGH GALILEE (9:14-50)

INTRODUCTION

In this subsection, Jesus teaches his disciples in situations that emerge on the way. There is teaching and private disclosure that happens in the story of the epileptic boy in 9:14-29. There is the teaching and the disciples' misunderstanding around Jesus' second passion prediction in 9:31-32. In private, Jesus uses the disciples' own discussion about greatness to teach them something new about servanthood in 9:33-37. A question about another person casting out demons prompts questions about who *really* follows Jesus and is "for us" in 9:38-41. Finally, the subsection concludes with warnings of hell in 9:42-50. There are ample opportunities for Jesus' disciples to learn. The open question is still whether they actually will.

PASSAGES OMITTED FROM THE LECTIONARY

Only one part of this subsection is not one of the RCL readings. The healing of a boy with a spirit in 9:14-29 lays important groundwork for what follows in Mark concerning the disciples' difficulty. The disciples are struggling to resume the reign-of-God ministry with which they have been charged. They cannot seem to understand what has gone awry with this exorcism. In light of this situation, Jesus needs to speak to them privately. As such, the story sets the stage for the teaching and misunderstanding to follow.

The Healing of a Boy with a Spirit (9:14-29):
Omitted from The Lectionary

In this episode, Jesus' ministry resumes. Statements of identity and confessions are still ringing in the air since Caesarea Phillipi. For the disciples who accompanied him up the mountain, the visions are still on their mind. However, the confessions and visions about Jesus' identity are not speculative, spiritual matters. They are, rather, about discipleship. So here in this text they are "on the way" yet again.

It is fitting that the first story after this revelatory interlude of the transfiguration is the final exorcism of Mark's Gospel. Mark's apocalyptic mode includes a view of the world as oppressed by the demonic. Whatever Jesus is about, it is not about making good people a little better. His world is tragically beset by evil and struggling with forces beyond human control. Somehow the confession and vision (the promise, as it were) are given in the midst of chaos and failure. Nowhere does this become more apparent than in the chaotic, extended exorcism narrative of 9:14-29.

To call the narrative extended may be a misnomer. Some scholars argue that this text is really two stories stitched into one. There are indeed some mysterious turns here, some non-sequiturs, which may well be more evidence of a clumsy editorial hand. It is possible, however, to read the story as a compositional whole precisely in light of what has been happening. This reading assumes that this exorcism stands as it does for a reason—right here.

In Mark 9:14, Jesus approaches his remaining disciples for the first time since going up the mountain. He comes back to a scene that includes them, a crowd, and some scribes in dispute. The scene it sets, right after the heights of epiphanic vision on the mountain, is sobering. The earlier narrative references to the scribes in v. 14 may lead the reader to assume that this is more than just friendly conversation. The crowd's response of being "overcome with awe" in v. 15 seems a bit much. Just why are they so amazed and emphatic with their greeting? Some scholars have speculated that the narrative is playing intertextually with elements of Moses' return from the mountain. Perhaps Jesus still had traces of some epiphanic glow. The text itself and its possible intertext of the Moses' story in Exodus do not square all that well. Moses' crowd may have had a strong reaction to his return, but first it took the form of being afraid to come near him (Exod. 34:30), not running up to greet him! It is probably best to assume that this reaction is a continuation of Jesus' reputation for healing and teaching since the beginning of Mark's Gospel. At any rate, Jesus' response is key. In v. 16, Jesus asks what the reason is for the dispute. Now that he has approached all his disciples, the crowd, and the scribes once again, the question permits the action to move forward.

With vv. 17-19, we enter the miracle story, more specifically in the form of an exorcism. A man answers Jesus' question by providing a little context. He had brought his son to Jesus for healing. The malady that he describes in the surrounding verses sounds a lot like the disease of epilepsy. Within the ancient world, the sickness of epilepsy was often explained in spiritual terms. The man attributes his son's sickness to the presence of a "speechless" spirit. It may well be that the epileptic seizures rendered him unable to hear or speak, at least during the seizures themselves. The key issue here, however, is not so much the diagnosis as the problem of a prognosis. The man had spoken with the disciples about casting it out, but they were unable.

This lapse on the part of the disciples may sound unremarkable, except for one key fact. In Mark 6 the disciples *were able* to cast out demons in Jesus' name. At the center of this controversy is therefore a theological problem: why? Why are the disciples unable to do now what they were able to do just a few short chapters ago? Once again, we struggle in the space between identity and discipleship, perhaps even between promise and failure.

So instead, Jesus offers his diagnosis not of the malady, but of the whole gathered scene. His comment in v. 19 is full of pathos and carries even more meaning in the context of chapter 9 as a whole: "You faithless generation, how much longer must I be among you? How much longer must I put up with you? Bring him to me." Jesus sees the problem as one of faithlessness. Whose faithlessness is not yet clear, although the word "generation" would seem to leave little room for anyone to hide. The language about how much longer would seem to highlight the very identity issues that surfaced in the revelatory interlude of Peter's confession and the transfiguration. There is something about Jesus that is not quite of this world. If so, it represents *his struggle* on the way. And yet his statement continues right through the pathos and paradox of his condition. "Bring him to me," Jesus says. For all the frustration, the reign-of-God ministry carries on.

Now that the unusually poignant theological question has been broached, the typical track of the healing story's exorcism can resume with 9:20-24. Once again the text says that they brought the boy to him (the difference being that the first time the intention resulted in bringing the son to those charged to cast out in his name and authority). The reaction of the boy to Jesus' presence is similar to that in previous episodes in the narrative. This prompts a question on Jesus' part about how long the boy had been ill. The question gives the father the opportunity to express himself on not only the appalling duration of the disease, but the dangers it has been posing to the boy, even in "fire" and "waters." The severity also affects the father who tells these details in response to Jesus' question. So the father in his concern for his son and himself puts it to Jesus: "if you are able to do anything, have pity on us and help us."

Here we need to pause to consider the father's words. What makes this miracle story stand out is precisely the odd interruptions in flow. Now in v. 22 it is the father's turn to offer a plaintive cry. The first part becomes key for the balance of the narrative: "if you are able." When the father speaks, it is not out of unalloyed faith in the promise. It is both grammatically and therefore theologically conditional. Nonetheless, he goes on to underline his deep concern. In v. 22, he asks for mercy using a Greek verb for deep embodied feeling of solidarity (*splanchnistheis*). If Joel Marcus is correct, the term may also have liturgical overtones.[1] In the midst of his doubt, he nonetheless holds to some implicit faith that God—and only God—can have such mercy. The solidarity extends as well to his pronouns: not just help him, but help *us*. If forms are important for understanding the communicative force of biblical texts, it is equally true that the deviations from the form are usually crucial. Part of the effect of this now final exorcism in Mark is to place the paradox of identity and discipleship in the midst of deep human pain and the intransigence of evil and the demonic. For all the unusual features of this particular story, I suspect that it is powerful precisely in this post-confession, post-visionary context (see above) of the latter half of chapter 9.

Jesus' response in v. 23 then sharpens the issue further, thus helping to bring the strange story into thematic focus. For Jesus, it is about faith. We should take note of the way his statement is worded: "If you are able!—All things can be done for the one who believes." By quoting the man's words back to him and linking it to the man's faith, he not only clarifies the presenting issue, but names exactly that which has been troubling him since coming to this scene (Mark 9:14-16). The words for "faithless" in v. 16 and "believes" in v. 23 share the same root in Greek. On the surface, this may not sound like good news. This not-enough-faith gambit is sometimes used among dubious faith healers as a way of explaining their failure to heal. As a result, it can cause persons seeking help to question not only their situation, but now their own faith. But please note that Jesus' words preserve an important difference. The Markan narrative as a whole talks about all things being possible for God (10:27 in response to the disciples' question about the rich man and 14:36 with respect to Jesus' own

---

1. Joel Marcus, *Mark 8-16*, Anchor Yale Bible (New Haven, CT: Yale University Press, 2009), 661.

anguished prayer in the Garden of Gethsemane). While faith is key, it is faith *in God*. The translators of this verse in the NRSV help to capture this in a nuanced way with a kind of English divine passive: "All things *can be done* for the one who believes" (emphasis mine).

Even then, Mark succeeds in going even deeper. The man, in all his ambivalence, confesses faith, yet a profoundly struggling one in v. 24. It issues in a quote that has rung true for many through centuries of living with both the promise and the failure: "I believe; help my unbelief." Again, here after the open confession and the mountaintop vision it is good to know that identity and discipleship connect precisely in the depths of life.

With all those unique preliminaries out of the way, the narrative can now continue with the exorcism proper. In Mark 9:25, Jesus notes the crowd forming and then addresses the unclean spirit with an exorcistic rebuke. The subsequent convulsions render the boy "like a corpse," which has at least the proximate effect of making the actual miracle even more decisive and allowing the crowd to bear witness to its severity (v. 26b). Jesus takes him by the hand and this "corpse" now "rises"—with all the resurrection implications in tow. Indeed, all things are possible, for this freeing from the demonic is more than self-improvement. It is through Jesus' apocalyptic engagement and struggle a movement from life to death, a harbinger of resurrection. And these things, of course, are possible only to God.

This immediate context of the exorcism itself may also help to unify what is otherwise an odd tagline to the whole controversy in vv. 28-29. The narrator is allowed, post exorcism, to pick up the thread of the disciples' earlier inability to cast out the demon in 9:14-16. Jesus' response that this one requires "prayer" would seem to prompt more questions than it solves. If that is true, then why does Jesus succeed in *his* exorcism prayer-free? It is perhaps telling that the disciples' question betrays them: "Why could *we* not cast it out?" (emphasis mine) Their focus is still on themselves. In light of this, Eugene Boring makes an important point. It may well be that the reference to prayer is designed to help even authorized disciples to see that such authority to act in Jesus' name is not a possession, but an even deeper reliance on God.[2]

It is sad that this text is omitted from the RCL. It is in many ways quintessentially Markan and has the added benefit of taking on the "healed by faith" notion that is a theological problem elsewhere for many of today's homiletical interpreters of Mark. The text probes matters of faith and unfaith

---

2. Eugene Boring, *Mark: A Commentary*, New Testament Library (Louisville: Westminster John Knox, 2006), 276.

and yet sets its hopes even in the face of struggle all the more deeply on God. Perhaps preachers would be wise to include it for some Sunday in Ordinary Time as a substitute Gospel lection. It offers an opportunity for homiletical-theological reflection that other texts pass by.

LECTIONS

The lections that follow continue the themes of teaching and misunderstanding with the disciples. Since they appear in succession for Propers 20 and 21, they give the preacher the opportunity to explore these themes more deeply in Ordinary Time. The idea of teacher is also important, however for large sections of Mark 11–12, which are not well covered by the RCL. Perhaps here preachers can also point forward to Jesus' teaching in Jerusalem and the important conflicts with religious leaders that his teaching occasions. For these teaching moments also contribute to understanding the conflicts that emerge in Propers 26–28 that lead ultimately to the prediction of the temple's destruction in Mark 13. Preachers who do so will lay important groundwork for future Markan lections to come *and* embody the intention of the narrative, which even now locates Jesus' teaching with his disciples in connection to passion predictions and the future events in Jerusalem.

LECTION: JESUS AGAIN FORETELLS HIS DEATH AND RESURRECTION AND WHO IS THE GREATEST?
9:30-37; PROPER 20

The setting changes, but the key themes about the implications of Jesus' disclosed identity, the life of discipleship, and misunderstanding are still in evidence. Mark does this by juxtaposing the second of Jesus' explicit passion predictions that includes a suffering Son of the human with a disciple-initiated argument over "greatness" along the way. One would think that, for the disciples, the shock of Jesus' revelation had not yet worn off. The two brief sections to follow in 9:30-32 and 9:33-37 show that the revelation and its implications have not only failed to sink in, but in a sense are being resisted. This reality points to a difficult struggle that continues all the way through the end of Mark's Gospel.

Mark 9:30-32 is the first part of our lection and the second of the three Markan passion predictions. What makes it particularly interesting is the setting and motivation. Jesus and the disciples have departed and are thus in action "on the way." The reference to "passing by" Galilee indicates, perhaps, a more distant destination. The most telling part of this initial description, however, is that Jesus did not want anyone to know. Here is someone who was acclaimed in Galilee in his early ministry. But now that the news is out—that his disciples know that his messianic future is not one of national victory, but suffering, rejection, death, and resurrection—Jesus wants to keep it under wraps. This action is consistent with the messianic secret motif we have mentioned thus far.

As if to corroborate this, the narrator cues us in further on Jesus' motivation in v. 31. The imperfect form of the verb "to teach" indicates that this was a continuous activity, not a one-off teaching. This time the passion prediction is a little different. Instead of the more particular warning about the elders, Jesus simply says that the Son of the human will be betrayed into the hands of *people*. The shift to people from his concern with Jewish elders in chapter 8 signals a Markan vision about the problem of human evil and its reach. The term translated "betray" here misses an interesting nuance with the Greek text. The Greek verb here is *paradidōmi*, a verb that means something more like "handed over." This verb has resonance with a tradition in other texts, especially suffering servant texts (Isa. 53:6, 12 LXX), where that figure is "handed over" by God. This will become an important theme in the Markan passion narrative. The mention of his rejection has disappeared, but both his death and resurrection are present.

What makes this particular prediction so interesting from the standpoint of discipleship is his own disciples' reaction to his ongoing teaching. The text says they did not understand his saying and were too afraid even to ask. If Mark desires in his portrayal here to link Jesus' now disclosed messianic identity as suffering, dying, and resurrecting Son of the human to *discipleship*, the going will apparently be difficult. The disciples do not comprehend and seem to resist even knowing.

Mark 9:33-37 is the second half of our lection. In this brief section, Jesus seems to teach the implications of his identity for the disciples. What follows are no longer predictions about himself, but an exploration of a different way for disciples to live out the surprising identity he has revealed to them. Their struggle to comprehend this and his other recent teachings in particular plays again on the theme of the disciples' misunderstanding. Here, the focus is on children.

It is important to note that the view of children in the ancient world is not like that of our own. Childhood in the West receives a kind of romantic treatment, especially after the rise of the American suburb where childhood is portrayed as a time of innocence and play. In the ancient world, children were not so romanticized, nor was there any prospect of children living carefree lives of innocence and play. While neither age has a corner on the problem of the mistreatment and abuse of children, the ancient world at least did not have ideas about childhood as some kind of ideal. This context helps to make Jesus' teaching that follows all the more unusual.

The text of vv. 33-34 (including the remaining teachings of chapter 9) locates Jesus and his disciples in Capernaum where much of his early ministry took place and from which several of his disciples hailed. Mark also immediately places the setting of this conversation in private, namely, in a house. The issue is prompted by Jesus' notice that the disciples had been arguing "on the way" (!) and Jesus' question about its subject. The disciples' silence in response might indicate that they knew Jesus would not be pleased to learn that they had been arguing over who was greater. Clearly this would not be an endearing topic for a messianic Son of the human who had just twice predicted the necessity of his suffering and death as well as teaching about the importance of self-denial in chapter 8! The scene for Jesus' teaching on discipleship is now set.

The teaching begins in Mark 9:35-37 by describing Jesus as being seated, the traditional posture of teaching. He makes it a point to call the Twelve to him, perhaps as a special leading subset of the disciples as a whole.

The teaching is comprised first of a statement designed to overturn the disciples' expectations of greatness and rank. To be first in Jesus' reign-of-God perspective is to be servant of all and least of all. Given Jesus' own strange identity, those who follow him operate out of a different perspective. To make his point he takes a child, places the child in the midst of the disciples, and embraces the child. The resulting teaching takes the point now a step further. To welcome such a one, who has so little value, in Jesus' name is to welcome Jesus himself. Furthermore, to welcome Jesus is to welcome the One who sent him. At this point, the teaching widens out to offer an even deeper theological claim. Jesus takes the issue of his humble and yet messianic identity to a new level in relation precisely to the weakest and the least: a child. In this way, the notion of Jesus' own suffering, rejection and death becomes instructive for the disciples' own lives of following on the way.

This is the prescribed lection for Proper 20. Although it breaks up the line of teaching that extends to the end of Mark 9, its pairing with the second prediction of the passion makes for a weighty and productive juxtaposition for preaching. The temptation is to preach Jesus' teaching about children as simple moral exhortation. The connection to the second passion prediction aligns Jesus' claims for the disciples with important issues of Jesus' own identity as the messianic Son of the human who suffers, dies, and rises. The hiddenness of his messianic identity in this difficult path grounds nicely the vision of embracing and welcoming those considered of little or no value in the time. It places Jesus' concern for children within the horizon of a theology of the cross that transvalues all our values as disciples.

Lection: Another Exorcist and Temptations to Sin
9:38–50; Proper 21

The links here between the several sayings about exorcism and temptations to sin that comprise this lection are upon first reading quite difficult to discern. It is no wonder that many redaction critics are drawn to read 9:38-50 as barely assembled batches of pre-Markan material.

On the other hand, there are two features that help to unite these into a section with a bit more singular orientation. First, it uses a series of catchwords that hold it together at least through verbal links: casting out, stumbling, salt—all of these words recur with frequency through these sayings. Second, all of them seem to be concerned with the nature of the Markan community in relation to its sense of discipleship. As such, it carries forward the idea that disciples who follow this Jesus have both a different vocation *and* a different kind of life together. Using vivid and unusual apocalyptic language, Mark's Jesus continues to try to help us readers see the implications of following him—especially since in chapter 11 he will be arriving in Jerusalem. This teaching moment in Capernaum may be important because it is the last opportunity to gather things together before the passion events are set into motion.

The initial section of teaching in vv. 38-41 occurs in response to John's statement about the exorcistic activity of someone who is not a disciple. Its concern about community boundaries and acting in Jesus' name may be indicative of a post-Easter origin. Two things deserve special notice in the way this statement sets up Jesus' teaching in response after v. 38. First, the person performing the exorcism does so in Jesus' name, that is, with an invocation of his authority in the act of casting out demons. This name language also serves as a verbal link with the preceding teaching episode in 9:37. Second, the disciples, who earlier failed with their own attempt to perform an exorcism earlier in the same chapter, try to prevent an exorcist acting in Jesus' name because that person does not follow "us," that is, the disciples. Thus early in the setting of this teaching, it is clear that the disciples are still struggling to understand what it means to follow—not themselves, but rather Jesus, as the heavenly voice from the cloud made clear earlier in chapter 9 with the command to "listen to him"!

In response, Jesus corrects their misunderstanding by offering a more generous and inclusive vision of engagement for the reign of God. Working deeds of power in Jesus' name is something that is open to others, especially since they are unlikely in the same breath to speak ill of Jesus! Jesus continues by drawing out a general principle that whoever is not against us is for us—again, a more generous vision of cooperation with others. In verse 40, finally, Jesus even expands this notion to a broader theological claim, this time to include those who give a cup of water to those in Christ's "name." Such persons can count on not losing a reward for that act of mercy, here expressed eschatologically.

Why does Mark go so far as to include such a generous, inclusive vision of God's reign? Are not apocalyptic theologians like Mark more likely to sound sectarian? Joel Marcus points out that there are two sides to the reign of God.[3] On the one hand, Jesus does point out that the kingdom is in radical opposition to the ways of the world. On the other hand, it is also true that the apocalyptic kingdom is also secretly growing in the world. Here Mark plays to a generous hiddenness of the apocalyptic gospel.

The section in Mark 9:42-48 is complex not just because of the loose thematic links, but also due to its textual history. There is much disputed material here, which is why there is no v. 44 or 46 in the NRSV! We will work with the available English translation, but curious readers are encouraged to investigate this further in commentaries featuring more detailed scholarly background about the text's manuscript tradition. Suffice it to say that the text uses much repetition, both of terms and of structures, to give us a feel for its direction and thus some openings to understand why this chain of sayings belongs together. Again, the quality of the disciple community becomes a guide for grasping its unusual and vivid apocalyptic language.

The initial saying about "stumbling" in v. 42 stands alone. It is not structurally parallel with the others that follow immediately afterward. Still, the concern is "causing to stumble" and the "little ones," presumably persons in the community who like the child of the previous unit are worthy of care, concern, and welcome. While the watery outcome of the saying for those causing such stumbling in v. 42 is startling and even terrifying, the unifying idea behind it in this section is the safeguarding of persons in the community. Implied

3. Marcus, *Mark 8-16*, 687.

in this wording is that even the worst human punishment is not as bad as the potential eschatological punishment. Community solidarity with the "little ones" is therefore a high value and any human punishment for such disruption pales in comparison with God's commitment to preserve them at all costs.

By contrast, Mark 9:43-48 has a basic structure of thought holding it together. It builds on the theme of "causing to stumble," so apparently the welfare of the community's "little ones" is still in view. It places the consequences for such failures within a startling eschatological frame of punishment, Gehenna, a common figure of judgment in apocalyptic writings prior to and contemporaneous with Mark's Gospel.

Some have interpreted these warnings in sexual terms, pointing among other things to traditions where the hand, foot, and eye are connected to sexual sins.[4] The fact that Matt. 5:27-32 interprets Mark in this direction would seem to give credence to this point of view. Some of this begins to fall apart on closer inspection. Joel Marcus points out the logical inconsistencies of such a view in several respects, including the idea that that the call for the cutting off of the offending foot (understood as penis) in 9:45 would result in a man choosing to enter the Kingdom either as "lame" or Gehenna with *two* feet![5] It is probably best to assume that the concern for the little ones at the beginning of this section and the concern for a community that is "at peace with one another" (9:50) governs the use of this material. Mark's Jesus is concerned that disciples as leaders take others into account and in such a way that honors the fabric of the disciple community.

The structure of this section is remarkably consistent. If some part of the body causes someone to stumble, it is best to cut it off and enter the reign of God than either to enter or be thrown into Gehenna, here rendered as "hell."

In describing the figure of Gehenna as a place of judgment, Mark is drawing on an apocalyptic tradition with roots in the Hebrew Bible. Isa. 66:24 provides the important themes of worm and fire, here associated with a this-worldly judgment of God's enemies. The particular valley represented by the Greek term Gehenna refers to a place outside of Jerusalem that had been linked to child sacrifice and idolatry within the

---

4. Will Deming, "Mark 9.42-10.12; Matthew 5:27-32, and b. Nid. 13b: A First Century Discussion of Male Sexuality," *New Testament Studies* 36 (1990): 130–41. Although revising Deming's thesis, Adela Yarbro Collins pursues a similar line of interpretation in *Mark: A Commentary*, Hermeneia (Minneapolis: Fortress Press, 2007), 449–54.

5. Marcus, *Mark 8-16*, 696–97.

wider biblical tradition and had later become a kind of city dump. The apocalyptic tradition later develops a similar pit or abyss of judgment as a place of fire in some of the books of Enoch and *4 Ezra*.

The point here is therefore not a literalistic one. The language is designed to get leaders to think about how they exercise power in a community of "little ones," not to advocate an ethic or policy of self-mutilation. The use of the apocalyptic imagery of judgment is to provide a frame for the difficult task of discerning how leadership should be carried out. Such an abuse of power, such sin as "causing to stumble," is an ultimate problem for this community. The apocalyptic language is designed to help make that point clearly.

Again, in vv. 49-50, the logic of the verses about salt moves more by linguistic connection. The language of fire continues, but this time with reference to the figure of salt. Mark 9:49 begins with a categorical statement of eschatological force: all *will be* salted with fire. Yet here fire is viewed as a double-sided reality. Now more than judgment is in view, since fire is also a kind of purgation. Salt shares at least in part in this idea. Salt is painful in a wound, but has conserving and cleansing properties. Perhaps salting by fire indicates how fire is also a necessary testing. Its connection here through the figure of salt may just be that this unique, salty identity helps to hold the community together, to live "at peace."

This amalgam of teachings and sayings, from exorcisms, to stumbling, to fire, and to salt all are read together for Proper 21 in the lectionary. This text poses problems for the preacher, in part because its unity is contested, if not downright elusive. Preachers would be wise to hold to the Markan frame about community concern. While the hyperbolic language of cutting off members and the dire apocalyptic consequences of failing to do so make this text difficult to preach in the early twenty-first century, they do succeed in placing the fabric of community life at the center of our concern and God's ultimate purposes. In an age when congregations are struggling to see their way forward and therefore make choices that marginalize others or occlude the "little ones," perhaps a text like this can help us see others not as threats but as important partners for naming the gospel of the messianic, "hidden" Son of the human and the reign of God that he announces even now.

Teaching and More Misunderstanding on The Way: Teaching Disciples about Family and Possessions in Judea (10:1-52)

Introduction

The cultivation of Jesus' role a teacher here in relation to the disciples' misunderstanding continues. This subsection features Jesus' teaching on divorce (10:1-12), his blessing of little children (10:13-16), the conversation with a rich man about eternal life and the commandments and its relation to possessions (10:17-22) along with Jesus' continued explanation of this to his disciples afterward (10:23-31). The third passion prediction (10:32-34) places all of this teaching in light of Jesus' identity and what will be happening in Jerusalem: the Son of the human's suffering, death, and resurrection. Almost as if they had not even heard that third prediction of suffering and rejection, James and John make a request of Jesus to sit with him in glory—to which Jesus responds with even more teaching (10:35-45). The section concludes, of all things, with a healing of the blind beggar Bartimaeus (10:46-42). While this does not appear to be a teaching episode at all, Bartimaeus addresses his concern to Jesus by calling him rabbi or teacher (v. 51) and expressing his desire to see. Even at the end of this tour of misunderstanding through Galilee and Judea on the way to Jerusalem, Jesus the teacher offers the prospect of seeing—a perfect bookend paired with the disciple's "rocky way" in our chapter 4, where a blind man was healed at Bethsaida through a two-step process of emerging sight.

Passages Omitted from The Lectionary

The only text omitted in this subsection is the third passion prediction, Mark 10:32-34. The repetition of the prediction is, of course, important for underlining the disciples' misunderstanding and Jesus' identity and steadfastness. The impact for the reader is this deepening divide with the disciples, since the readers know and perceive the strange misunderstanding on their part. At the same time, its omission is not absolutely crucial so long as preachers keep Jesus' identity in mind through the texts of this section, for it is an identity whose messianic sense is shaped by rejection, suffering, death, and resurrection in Jerusalem. Preachers should attend therefore to what is unique about this third prediction to understand its special significance for the other lections going forward.

A Third Time Jesus Foretells His Death and Resurrection (10:32-34):
Omitted from The Lectionary

This is the third and final passion prediction. To the reader it may seem repetitious. To those following Jesus in the narrative, however, it continues to be a matter of struggle. It is important to note that this third prediction is the most explicit of the three. Many commentators note that it has an almost programmatic relationship to the events narrated in 14:1—16:8. If Jesus' first two passion predictions were hard for the disciples to digest, Jesus with this third prediction is exceedingly detailed and explicit.

The introductory verse in 10:32 is confusing with respect to the actual referents of "they" and "those who follow." Yet the verse is absolutely crucial. It sets an important note first by pointing out that they were going up to Jerusalem. The journey that wound its way from Caesarea Philippi and the mountain to Capernaum and to Judah and the Transjordan is now moving to its concluding point. This fact alone calls up the earlier predictions. Although Jerusalem was not explicitly mentioned in either one, the first did speak of rejection by the elders, the chief priests, and the scribes. The narrative is clearly moving to its central moment and the now explicit mention of Jerusalem highlights it.

The introductory verse also goes out of its way to say that Jesus was "walking ahead of them." The sense of the Greek is that Jesus was "going before" them. This theme is an important one, especially for Jesus' promise in 14:28 and the resurrection scene in 16:7, which use the same Greek verb with reference to the return to Galilee. Jesus is freely accepting the events about to happen and in this sense of "walking ahead" or "going before" actually embodies this in the scene.

What happens behind Jesus, however, is the confusing part. This is true both grammatically and descriptively. The verse is full of "they" pronouns that make it hard to sort out. Perhaps the best way to think of it is to assume that not all the "they" references are coterminous. The larger group accompanying Jesus was amazed, but those who followed, in particular, were afraid. This becomes the exigence for Jesus to take the Twelve aside along on the way. These Twelve, Jesus decides, need to hear yet again what was about to happen to him.

In Mark 10:33-34, Jesus then says with great explicitness and clarity what will happen. He repeats the narrator's reference to Jerusalem, inviting his hearers to "see" it. He speaks of the Son of the human and his being "handed over"—a use of the divine passive that reminds hearers and us readers of God and God's purposes in doing so—and invoking again the language of the suffering servant of Isaiah from the LXX. Those to whom he will be handed over include the chief priests and the scribes who will condemn him and hand him over to the gentiles, a reference that situates the Roman crucifixion afterwards. The idea of handing him over to the gentiles reflects a particularly strong sense of rejection and abandonment—this was a practice done only to the worst of offenders, given the hatred felt toward the Romans. What the Romans do is described in careful detail, and in way that corresponds to the passion narrative to follow. At the same time, the prediction eventually breaks off the continued pattern of condemning, mocking, spitting, flogging, and killing to yield to a final verb where Jesus is the subject: and he "will rise again." This third prediction is clear, detailed, and difficult. And yet it is still a promise in the midst of it all. It helps, also, to make sense of the actions of Jesus' disciples in the following pericope—as all of these passion predictions follow with powerful stories of the disciples' profound misunderstanding.

LECTIONS

The lections here correspond to Propers 22–25 in Year B of the RCL. This gives the preacher the opportunity to cover them in a roughly continuous series. Again, given the prominence of the passion predictions for grasping the misunderstanding that shapes the disciples' response to Jesus' teaching, preachers would be wise to invoke that prediction and the movement of the narrative toward Jerusalem. These themes are especially important for laying future homiletical groundwork in dealing with the teaching and prediction materials in connection with the temple in Mark 12:28-34, Mark 12:38-44, and Mark 13:1-8 for Propers 26–28 at the conclusion of Year B. Since the lectionary skips over much of Mark 11–12, these teaching texts here may be the best opportunity to prepare hearers for Jesus' teaching conflict with religious leaders in Mark 11–12, which eventuates in Jesus' prediction of the destruction of the temple in Mark 13. It is, in some ways, an extension of the notion of Jesus' teaching in connection with misunderstanding, now leading to rejection and opposition.

LECTION: TEACHING ABOUT DIVORCE
AND JESUS BLESSES LITTLE CHILDREN
10:1-16; PROPER 22

The material here now turns decisively toward family matters as they relate to discipleship. In this chapter, subjects like marriage, children, and even inheritance are in view. With this shift in subject matter comes also a shift in place. Now Jesus has left Capernaum and has arrived at the boundary of Judah. Jesus is nearing Jerusalem and takes this crucial opportunity to continue to teach his disciples along the way.

Mark 10:1 provides the shift of setting, although not without some problems. The language of "beyond the Jordan" does not really make sense. However, two familiar motifs about the context of Jesus' ministry reemerge. First, people are flocking to him. Just as with his earlier ministry, Jesus can still draw a crowd. Second, he is teaching them. Mark's Gospel does not always give us much about the content of that teaching, but does want to make sure that Jesus appears here as an authoritative teacher.

The content of this text on divorce takes the shape of a dialogue in vv. 2-10. Now the Pharisees reappear and ask him a question. Two things about their approach in v. 2 merit comment because they seem strange. First, the Pharisees are described as testing him. This language is reminiscent of earlier difficult encounters and evokes a note of malevolence, especially since it was Satan who first tests Jesus back in 1:13 when he is in the wilderness. Second, the issue around which they are testing him is not really the presenting legal issue about marriage at that time. The question is not *whether* divorce is permitted, but under what circumstances. The unreality of the question may point to the idea that the Pharisees are aware of Jesus saying something unusual about divorce elsewhere and hoping that he will say it publicly here.

Jesus responds to their question in 10:3 about permission with the language of commandment. He tries to reframe the Pharisees' question, therefore, by adding the name of Moses as the one who does the commanding. The unfolding dialogue shows why this important.

In 10:4 then the response to Jesus' question reverts back to the language of permission. Moses did indeed "permit" a letter of divorce to be written for a wife to be dismissed (Deut. 24:1).

The practices around divorce are markedly different from what we know. In traditional Jewish practice, divorce was the prerogative of a male as evidenced by Deut. 24:1-4. There was dispute over how wide or narrow the grounds for divorce were, but the law around providing a letter of dismissal was not really contested—which is why Jesus' teaching so stands out in relief. The letter was important because it also allowed the wife to remarry. This, of course, was a small respite in a patriarchal system, but it could help life to go on. It may be that the question of *mutual* divorce and the possibility of adultery against either marriage partner, as Jesus portrays it later in this pericope in vv. 11-12, reflect a wider Roman context where most commentators agree that it was indeed possible for women to divorce their husbands. Depending on where Mark wrote his Gospel, it may be that the framing of the issue reflects more than just its narrated Jewish context here.

Jesus responds by trying to place Moses' command in a narrower context. What Jesus proceeds to do in v. 5ff is to juxtapose the later commandment with God's purposes in the creation stories of Genesis. A common practice in scriptural interpretation is to bring two texts into such juxtaposition. The idea is not to bring two texts into open conflict, but to argue that one has a more far-reaching meaning while limiting the scope of the other. Jesus' perspective here is that God's purposes for creation (Gen. 1:27 and 2:24) represent the overarching purpose and context for understanding the later command in Deuteronomy. In this sense the commandment concerning divorce is a narrower concession to "hardness of heart." In this way, Jesus' reading is actually consistent with the Pharisees use of the term "permission"! The law is an accommodation to human weakness, but finds its fullest expression in God's purposes in creation. Joel Marcus also points out that the reframing also plays into the eschatological interests of Mark's apocalyptic thinking. A teaching about marriage and divorce that recognizes God's purposes at the beginning also points forward to God's ultimate purposes in going back to an Eden-like state.[6] Thus matters of marriage and divorce for disciples are concerns for the reign of God and God's new age.

In Mark 10:11-12, the disciples show that they continue to be confused by Jesus' teaching by asking him in private about it. Jesus elaborates by drawing on the implications of his interpretation of Genesis as reflective of the divine purpose. Because God has made two people one, divorce afterwards is tantamount to adultery. Here the question moves decisively to the issue of what

---

6. Ibid., 710–11.

is allowed *after* a divorce—that is to say, whether divorced persons are allowed to remarry. This statement has two important implications. First, Jesus expresses it so that both the male and female marriage partner are potentially committing adultery *against* one another. The cultural practices of the time would have problematized female adultery much more than its male counterpart. Second, by calling it adultery Jesus relates this teaching to one of the Ten Commandments.

Jesus' teaching on divorce here is quite distinctive. It also proves problematic in the tradition. Already in Paul (1 Cor. 7:10-15) and Matthew (5:32), certain exceptions are brought in that also account for other theological values. While this can be somewhat unsettling, it is also an opportunity for today's homiletical interpreter to take up the unfinished theological task. On the one hand, how do we value marriage and acknowledge the cost of divorce in today's society? Surely there is some space for unique Christian witness here, even if we struggle to name it so. On the other hand, it is equally difficult for us to hand on uncritically a view of heterosexual desire and union as exclusively indicative of God's creative purposes. Even if we did, it would be necessary as well to name ways in which even heterosexual desire and practice does not merely point to divine purposes, but goes awry in various kinds of heterosexual contexts of abuse and misconstrual as power "over." The Scriptures here help us to take up the essence of Jesus' distinctive teaching yet again but in light of communities that are aware of ways in which human heterosexual life and practice invite us again to further theological reflection.

The second part of our lection is Mark 10:13-16. The theme of the disciples' misunderstanding continues in vv. 13-16, this time shifting from marriage and divorce to children. Whereas earlier in chapter 9, Jesus places a child in the disciples' midst, this time "they" bring children to Jesus. The interruption proves to be yet another occasion for naming their importance and value in light of the reign of God.

The introductory material in v. 13 sets the scene and by doing so places it in the context of the ongoing conflict between Jesus and his disciples. Although in chapter 9 Jesus asks his disciples to receive children as they would receive Jesus and the God who sent Jesus, clearly the disciples fail in their response to the situation. While we do not know who the "they" are who bring children to Jesus, the disciples have in short order already failed to respond to what Jesus said in Capernaum a few verses prior. In fact, the disciples again are described as "rebuking" them, a word Jesus reserved for demons and chaotic storms (and, yes, Peter in Caesarea Philippi!). Judging by the verb, the scene is not pretty. Those who brought the children only wanted Jesus to touch them, perhaps hearing of the power associated with his touch. Jesus' disciples, however, are operating form a different point of view.

Thereafter, Mark 10:14-16 describes Jesus' response of indignation, signaling to the reader a negative evaluation of the disciples' behavior. Jesus then goes on to make his point. Jesus wants children, who have no value in the culture and time (see 9:33-37 above), to come to him because the reign of God belongs *to them*. Here, unlike the earlier text, the issue is less how to receive children, but how children *receive* God's reign. They have no claim, no status, and thus stand in stark contrast to the disciples who struggle to grasp that God's reign is not about their status or striving. Such children should not be prevented, but allowed to come. Some commentators note peculiarities of the language here (the verb for stop/prevent does show up in some baptismal texts as does the laying on of hands) and wonder about associations with infant baptism, but such a view is far from explicit or even necessary in this text. Jesus then makes a stark statement: entering the reign means welcoming it "as a child." Jesus completes the action by then fulfilling the initial request implied by the intention of v. 13. Jesus embraces, blesses, and places hands on those with "no value." It becomes a graphic depiction of the proper relationship of Jesus' identity and the proper shape of discipleship.

Although we have treated the last two pericopes (10:1-12 and 10:13-16) serially, the RCL excises v. 1 and links the teaching on divorce and Jesus' response to the children. There are some helpful ways in which to treat them together. Certainly, it is helpful to view Jesus' teaching on divorce, which is perhaps just as startling now as it was in the first century, in light of his reception and concern for children. Jesus' stance about divorce is radical in its extension of concern for women in divorce (10:11-12) and the concern for children in the next pericope would at least seem to indicate a wider ethical frame for what otherwise would read as an impossible ethic. But perhaps a more important way to hold the two pericopes together is not to see them as blueprints for a contemporary family policy, but within Mark's own apocalyptic horizon. What unites the two texts is an eschatological perspective rooted in the reign of God. The proclamation of God's reign refigures both family life and the way in which children are valued and respected. This, it seems to me, would offer a much more promising way forward for contemporary homiletical-theological reflection within the frame of the lectionary. Preachers might consider what the texture of our life together looks like as we lean into God's promised future, following the messianic, suffering Son of the human, and living lives as disciples that see past status and self-seeking even in our most intimate relationships.

Lection: The Rich Man
10:17-31; Proper 23

The story that follows is about a failed call to discipleship and a teaching moment that issues from it. The story is complex in part because of its overly familiar history of reception. Please note—bracketing the common pericope title above—that Mark 10:17 initially refers to the person who hustles up to Jesus not as a rich man, or a rich young ruler. He is just "a certain man"—the disclosure of his wealth in property comes only at the end of the episode in v. 22. Preachers need to be aware about the curious way Mark is telling this story and not jump too quickly to its conclusion. Spoiler alert: his wealth will be revelatory for the failed call to discipleship that Jesus issues to him. The fact that discipleship is at issue is even surfaced here at the beginning, where Jesus is described as "on his way." The failure of *this* call, however, also in the end confirms Jesus' teaching from the parable of the Sower. Wealth can thwart the sown word of the gospel. But for now, let us follow the story on its own terms.

The man hustles up to Jesus in two ways. He begins by calling Jesus "good teacher," to which Jesus retorts with a theological claim: only God is good. He also kneels before Jesus, which seems to give a certain urgency and earnestness to the scene. Readers need to be careful about the question in v. 17: "What must I do to inherit eternal life?" We cannot read eternal life here in the Johannine sense. The key word is "inherit," a good Jewish world that recalls the promise of land to Israel. The shift to "eternal life" keys off the idea that resurrection transfers that promise to the coming age—as represented by the seamless transition into "entering kingdom of God" language in vv. 23ff. There is still something of an apocalyptic sensibility here. In response, Jesus recites commandments that correspond to the second table of the Decalogue, specifically the ones that refer to human relationships. An odd exception is the penultimate one: "you shall not defraud." It might refer to the commandment not to covet, but it could be that this particular one is worded with *this* man in view. The man's statement that he has been doing commandments since his youth might indicate otherwise, but the three final parts of the story would seem to underline Jesus' choice of interpreting coveting as defrauding. First, Jesus looks at him and loves him. Jesus, in other words, seems to see into the man's heart here. Second, Jesus discerns what the man needs to do and in a way consistent with his defrauding angle: sell, give, have treasure in heaven, and follow me. Finally, the man's response seems to justify Jesus' substitution of defrauding for coveting. The man goes away grieving for he had *many possessions.*

On the surface, it looks pretty straightforward. The demand is a condition. Yet nestled in the midst of three imperatives of v. 21 is one future-tense indicative promise: "you will have treasure in heaven." The call to discipleship is two-sided, both demand *and gift.* As biblical scholar Eduard Schweitzer sees it, the two are not so much sequential as inseparable.

"[T]he giving up of one's possessions is not a prerequisite for discipleship. It is the consequence of discipleship as it was in 1:18, 20 and 2:14; it is the concrete manner in which discipleship is carried out."[7] And yet, this is what precisely causes the problem to follow in vv. 23-28.

You see, the upshot of this failed call is unique. Jesus has failed in calling this disciple. This requires explanation for disciples and for us readers. The problem of vv. 23ff is more theological than anthropological. Because the call to discipleship in 1:16-20 to four disciples resulted in the dropping of nets and the leaving of boats and the dads in those boats, the problem here is not really "who can fulfill the demand" but how can a rich man, or anyone for that matter, *be saved?* Just as with the parable of the Sower, how can God's word be thwarted, God's call go unfulfilled—especially if God's Word, God's call through Jesus is, well, *God's?*

So Jesus turns in v. 23 to his disciples to make sense of the failure. His opening statement there is pretty strong. The disciples respond with perplexity, but why? There are traditions in the Hebrew Bible that view wealth as a sign of divine blessing, so perhaps Jesus' words are jarring. Now Jesus addresses them as children, who we know have a special place in the kingdom from the immediately preceding pericope in 10:14-16. As children, they only enter because they have *received it* as a gift. Suddenly the calculated question of the rich man (what must I *do to inherit*) seems, well, calculating. If disciples are called children, they will inherit. Entering kingdom *is hard* as Jesus' discipleship call indicates but inheriting kingdom is *receiving like a child.* Such are the jaw-dropping paradoxes of discipleship, which are about as impossible as threading a camel through a needle . . . except that God can do it. Thanks be to God, those paradoxes of radical relinquishment in discipleship and incalculable gift of

7. Eduard Schweizer, *The Good News According to Mark,* trans. D. Madvig (Atlanta: John Knox, 1970), 212.

inheritance are beyond our mortal minds, but not impossible for God, who we will already recall from v. 18 is alone good.

Peter then as exemplary disciple seems to take this all to heart in v. 28 and starts cataloging his own inventory of relinquishment, pointing out that he and his fellow disciples have "left everything" to follow. Jesus follows up in vv. 29-31 by going deeper. He inventories all they have given up for the sake of the gospel good news, but links it to an eschatological promise of a hundredfold change of fortunes not just in the kingdom age of eternal life, but right now in ordinary ecclesial life. Yet, right now includes in that inventory *persecutions*. This last saying locates discipleship in that eschatological moment of tension. Discipleship thus takes place at the same troubled intersection: a place of relinquishment, persecution, but also gospel and new community—though minus the fathers who ran the old patriarchal inheritance system (v. 30) in favor of new houses, new fields, and yes, new *family*.

Although this pericope appears in Proper 23 in the lectionary, the text here has something of a Lenten feel to it. Its vision is startling, not just to the disciples, but also to us. Homiletical theologians need to be careful not to pass over its teaching too quickly. One way this has happened, especially in the wealthier confines of mainline Protestantism, is in our tendency to soften the text's demand. So many preachers love to tone down the extravagant hyperbole of the camel and the needle's eye. Perhaps the camel is really a *cable* (the two words in Greek are about as similar as the two words in English!). Then there's the story of the gate to the city of Jerusalem, supposedly called the "needle's eye," which a camel could enter only on its knees. But all these hermeneutical gymnastics for the sake of piety, probability, and humility cannot reduce the tension of the hyperbolic figure. The text is, in the end, demanding.

At the same time, however, the story of failed discipleship and Jesus' teaching is still about the gospel. In the final section of Jesus' teaching this becomes clear. These things we do for the sake of the gospel. This call—a call that indeed demands and causes relinquishment and that goes far beyond observing the principles of non-maleficence of the second table of the Ten Commandments—results in the failure of the rich man to follow. Yet the gospel was also and is still a promise in the midst of failure and failing discipleship. It brings with it its own gifts and persecutions, both in this present age, and the age to come. Preachers who learn to live in this paradox will be faithful to the text to the benefit of hearers caught somewhere between relinquishment and promise who yet still long to follow.

LECTION: THE REQUEST OF JAMES AND JOHN
10:35–45; PROPER 24

This scene of James and John asking Jesus to do for them whatever they ask follows immediately after the third passion prediction in 10:32–34. Mark 10:35–45 does not disappoint the expectation that even with the *third* passion prediction ringing in the air, the disciples will still struggle to comprehend its meaning. In doing so, however, it brings home to the reader the inability of the disciples to grasp what it is going on. It allows Mark to narrate a scene that not only gives Jesus' response to their misunderstanding here, but in light of the spate of such scenes (8:34–38, 9:33–37) that have followed all of the other passion predictions (8:31, 9:30–31).

It begins in vv. 35–37 when James and John approach Jesus with a question. They have served a representative function before at the point of their call as disciples, at a healing, and as part of the transfiguration scene. Now, having witnessed all this, and having heard all three of Jesus' passion predictions, they ask Jesus for a favor. In a way that seems strikingly out of touch with the surrounding narrative they ask Jesus to grant that they sit at Jesus' right and left hands "in your glory." For all of Jesus' talk of the necessity of his suffering and death, they want to make sure that they are in good position in light of what they see as Jesus' glorious destiny around the corner. The idea about being "seated" at the right and the left would seem to envision this eschatological glory as connected with some sort of judgment scene. The request proleptically contrasts with those who are noted to be at Jesus' right and left when he is crucified in Mark 15:27!

What ensues in 10:38–40 is a dialogue between Jesus, James, and John. The dialogue on one level seems to highlight the misunderstanding that is present in this scene. Jesus begins in v. 38 by noting that the two disciples do not know what they are asking. This is driven home in the form of rhetorical questions that would seem to underline a key difference between Jesus and those who would follow him. "Drinking the cup" is, here, probably not a sacramental reference but points to the Hebrew Bible notion of drinking the cup of suffering or wrath (Jer. 25:15–29; Ps. 75:8; Isa. 51:17, 22). In the Christian community this may well have sacramental echoes, especially to the degree that sacramental thinking includes a participatory dimension, but the language here can be explained best in light of Jesus' own coming death. The language of baptism functions similarly here, that is, more with respect to the quality of being immersed in water rather than in an obvious sacramental sense. Again, there is a deeper meaning in the sacramental tradition around *participating* in Jesus' death (Rom 6:3–4) that is helpful indeed, but such a view is at best only implied and is not the central issue. Both images here are evocative of Jesus' coming death and thus contrast nicely with the "in your glory" expectations of James and John.

In light of this, the two disciples' response in v. 39 seems strange indeed. The two disciples think they are indeed "able." Again, the statement also seems odd in light of their *coming* behavior at the point of Jesus' own death.

In vv. 39b-40, Jesus responds and in a twofold way. First, he affirms in an almost prophetic sense that they will indeed do what they say. The disciples may not know what they are asking, or even what they are saying, but in a sense they say more than they know. Is this comment a recognition that, post-Easter, the disciples will undergo their own suffering, too? If so, this would seem to acknowledge a kind of participation in Jesus' suffering, even if the rest of the text clearly distinguishes what Jesus undergoes from the rest of the disciples (see 10:45). Nonetheless, even if Jesus does concede the possibility of their suffering in v. 39b, Jesus is quick not to presume upon a divine prerogative concerning eschatological seating charts. Such things are for *God* to give (as the divine passive "prepared" indicates).

These events then in vv. 41-45 set things in motion in the ranks of the disciples. The other disciples learn of James and John's attempt at proleptic eschatological intrigue and they are indignant because of it. So in v. 42a Jesus calls them together for yet another teaching session.

The teaching is by now a familiar topic. It is *familiar* because the disciples have been slow to learn the lessons of the three passion predictions in Mark. The teaching in part reprises themes first developed in 8:34-38 (taking up the cross and losing one's life to save it) and 9:33-37 (who is the greatest and being the servant of all). In this case however, Jesus in v. 42b turns to life among the gentiles as an example. Jesus tries hard to distinguish between the way power is wielded by people in the broader culture: they "lord it over" and act as "tyrants." In speaking with the disciples, Jesus wants to be sure that among them things should be different. The operative vision for leadership is akin to service, even slavery, not dominance. Here, Jesus links the group's identity as disciples once again to his own as Son of the human who came not to be served but to serve. Then finally Jesus connects this reality of the Son of the human to a unique part of that figure's mission: to give his life as a ransom for many.

Readers should be careful not to over-read this language of ransom. Christian interpretation has easily shifted from this to full-blown theories of the atonement that include much more than ransom as a payment for freedom. One thinks of the language of propitiation, expiation, or satisfaction—language that the tradition has developed over time to speak of the meaning of Jesus' death on the cross. While some scholars link subtle shifts in meaning of the word ransom in this way, it is probably best to let Mark be Mark and speak at face value. In the passion predictions, Mark's Jesus has not even spoken of the cross in the terms of atonement theory—that comes much later in the tradition. Mark in the passion predictions has merely highlighted Jesus' death. As such, Mark has simply let it stand here—in the briefest of terms—that Jesus' death is about the divine will and about paying a ransom. Preachers should be careful not to load onto Mark's language too much of the freight of our atonement theories.

This text comes up for Proper 24 in the RCL. While it would be better to read it in tandem with the third passion prediction in Mark 10:32-34, it should not take much for preachers to remind hearers of this context as they prepare to unpack Jesus' teaching. Its issues are still current and the need for disciples to connect their own identity with Jesus' understanding of the sufferings of the messianic Son of the human are no less important today. The place of power in ecclesial leadership is still important for us to think about.

At the same time, Mark's reticence about the meaning of Jesus' suffering does invite us as homiletical theologians to reengage on language of the meaning of Jesus' death. The complicated histories of our atonement theories and the way in which they relate to abuses of power call for great discernment. Perhaps a reengagement with the very simple language of Mark 10:45 can occasion a free and open conversation about how Jesus' unique vision might meet those today who wrestle with the place of power, suffering, and service precisely in light of the abuses that have so troubled us across gender lines, racial lines, and between adults and children in cases of sexual abuse. While this would not be an easy tack, it could open up conversation in the church's life so that persons, at the foot of the cross, meet to see each other once again as we really are in the presence of God—not only in suffering and death, but in resurrection, too.

Because even this conversation happens "on the way," it is important for us disciples to remember the intransigence that is our own inability to "see" what is going on with giving faith an overlay of power. It is not just the Markan disciples who struggle with truly seeing others who are occluded or victimized by our power schemes. We, who would follow "on the way," today need to see all this as well.

LECTION: THE HEALING OF BLIND BARTIMAEUS
10:46-52; PROPER 25

With this final text in this chapter, Mark as narrator reprises the story of healing from blindness in 8:22-26. These two texts help to bookend both the revelatory interlude of this commentary's chapter 5 and the problem of teaching and misunderstanding on the way in chapter 6. Whereas the story in 8:22-26 was a two-part healing that involved partial sight before moving onto full sight, this story represents a miracle where sight is given all at once. Throughout this chapter, the necessity of Jesus' teaching about his passion and its implications for following a messianic, suffering Son of the human has proven difficult. And yet the disciples are not without revelation or insight. The question is whether their partial sight will be sufficient to keep following Jesus on the way. This final pericope in this chapter sets up a contrast between this story's main character, Bartimaeus, who once healed follows Jesus on the way to Jerusalem, and the disciples whose continued lack of understanding renders their following at this crucial moment in the narrative problematic.

This ample treatment in v. 46 provides details of the setting. The beginning is confusing enough and has prompted some speculation about this text's final form. The first sentence indicates that the entourage comes to Jericho, thus approaching Jerusalem. In the next sentence, however, the narrator indicates that he (Jesus) encounters Bartimaeus on his way *from Jericho*. The awkwardness of the text is hard to explain but perhaps indicates in a clumsy way that Jesus is indeed on the move!

The description of Bartimaeus is a little odd as well. He is first described in Greek as the son of Timaeus (a good Greek name) and only then rendered in an Aramaic equivalent: the "bar" in Bartimaeus meaning "son." He is immediately described as a blind beggar who, like many such persons in the time, would have been seated "along the way" for the purpose of receiving alms. The wording of this in the context of our chapter, however, where "on the way" is itself evocative of the discipleship which stands at its center, helps with other parts of this introductory verse to frame the story. Despite the disciples' lack of understanding, and in light of Bartimaeus' coming insight, this too will be a story about being "on the way" as they follow Jesus to this destiny in Jerusalem.

The subsequent two verses in Mark 10:47-48 launch the miracle story proper. Bartimaeus is narrated as hearing that Jesus the Nazarene is on the way. This unusual appellation for Jesus in Mark (which does not mention Nazareth) just as quickly is joined to yet another new epithet through the mouth of Bartimaeus himself. As in other healing narratives, he cries out; yet here Bartimaeus says, "Jesus, *Son of David, have mercy on me!*" NT scholar Francis

Moloney draws special attention to this new way of describing the Jesus that we meet here at the end of chapter 10. Moloney argues that Bartimaeus perceives Jesus' humanity while addressing him as "Son of David."[8] Moloney himself would be quick to note along with other commentators that the Markan Jesus is quick to disavow "Son of David" language (Mark 12:35-37). Here the title Son of David may well indicate that Bartimaeus has Jesus' role as potential healer in view.[9] It is, however, at the very least a confession of faith that this man Jesus can help him.

The contrasting reaction of the disciples and the crowd makes for a telling relief, now together portrayed as "many" in v. 48. The NRSV tells of them "sternly ordering" him to be quiet. The Greek verb is once again the word for rebuke, which showed up with the disciples' mistaken response to the children just a few verses ago. This Bartimaeus, however, will not be silenced. The second time around in v. 48b he makes his confession even more loudly: "Son of David, have mercy on me!" Like the Syrophoenician woman, his is a faith that talks back!

With that in vv. 49-50 Jesus' coming and going in Jericho comes to a halt. The text notes that Jesus now stands and speaks: "Call him here." With a word he begins to wrestle the narrative away from a mere healing to a call story. Those responding then begin to engage as helpers, likewise calling the blind man by encouraging him to arise (the verb has resurrection overtones) and repeating for the third time in this paltry verse the Greek verb to "call" but this time with the crucial pronoun "you."

The man's response in v. 50 is striking. He casts off his cloak. In this way, his miracle story response also sounds like a call narrative. Just as the disciples left things behind to follow, so does Bartimaeus leave his cloak and get up immediately—again the urgency reminding of those initial call narratives in Mark 1 and 2.

Now that all the principle characters have been gathered for the healing event, there is really none of the typical exotic features of this healing in Mark 10:51-52—in contrast with the spittle and the touching of 8:22-26. Here in v. 51 Jesus merely poses a question: "What do you want me to do for you?" The question sounds innocent enough and makes Jesus seem downright solicitous. However, the wording is similar to the question the disciples James and John asked in the previous pericope, where they wanted Jesus to grant them proleptic positions of glorious power in the coming reign of God. Bartimaeus,

8. Francis Moloney, *The Gospel of Mark: A Commentary* (Peabody, MA: Hendrickson, 2002), 209.

9. J. P. Meier, *A Marginal Jew: Rethinking the Historical Jesus*, vol. 2 (New York: Doubleday, 1994), 689–90.

in contrast, asks out of simple need and faith: he wants to see again. In doing so, Bartimaeus refers to Jesus honorifically as "my teacher." Perhaps even here *discipleship* is really in view. For teaching here is not always about content; it is also about illumination on the way. So in the final verse Jesus merely announces what has happened: "Go; your faith has made you well." The word for making "well" here has salvific overtones. However, the real point is even more than healing. The man's response is to "follow him on the way," again, the language of discipleship—illumined for him, for the disciples, and now for us, too.

This wonderful text is read as the lection for Proper 25. It provides an excellent opportunity for preaching, so long as its troubled context in a section of Mark that deals with the disciples' struggle to understand is kept in view. This is no easy, breezy miracle. In fact, it refuses to stay a miracle and invites us to reflect on the relationship of healing to discipleship—or, to infer from Moloney's insight, of vocation to resurrection.[10] Preachers would be wise to key off of the language of calling that emerges part way through the story. In doing so, and in speaking honestly about the difficulty of following a suffering Son of the human, it will add depth for us to a text that cries out so that we understand it in the difficult literary context in which it already is situated.

10. Moloney, *Mark*, 210.

7

The Gospel in Jerusalem
(11:1—12:44)

With Jesus' arrival in Jerusalem, Mark's Gospel arrives at its climax, too. We know this is the case narratively because Mark very carefully slows down the action from here until the end in chapter 16. Jesus has been moving with rapidity and immediacy through the landscape of Galilee with the occasional foray into gentile territory. In the previous chapter, he has moved deliberately toward Jerusalem ever since Caesarea Philippi and the revelatory interlude on the mountain of transfiguration. In this final part of Mark's Gospel, the last few chapters are really devoted to seven days of action, each one carefully portrayed and delineated with references to the day. If the first two-thirds of Mark's Gospel takes us on a breathless reign-of-God tour designed to proclaim the mystery of both the coming kingdom and the strange suffering revelation of Jesus Christ, Son of God, this final portion in Jerusalem allows us to dwell in that mystery in all of its ambivalence and irony. This extends even to the Gospel's final scene, a resurrection story gone awry that ends with silence even among its few faithful female witnesses. These witnesses as a result say nothing to anyone "for they were afraid" (16:8b). Yet from promising beginnings to bitter end, Mark is faithful to his vision in this first Gospel written. It is in the midst of the disciples' failure and Jesus' rejection, a word of promise.

JERUSALEM: JESUS ARRIVES AT THE TEMPLE
(11:1-25)

INTRODUCTION

In this subsection, Mark narrates Jesus in a series of episodes having to do with Jesus' arrival in Jerusalem and the temple. These narratives are important because they highlight his arrival after the long journey from Caesarea Philippi marked by passion predictions that signaled coming conflict with religious leaders. He is now at the city and in a succession of days, enters and reenters the temple in fateful ways. The narratives here are also important in that they set up a series of verbal conflicts with many of the same religious leaders in 11:27—12:44.

Passages Omitted from The Lectionary

This complex in Mark 11:12-25 is made up of three parts, all of which contribute to a Markan intercalation (see Introduction), in other words, a literary sandwich. In the first part, vv. 12-14, is the cursing of the fig tree. In vv. 20-25, we return to the cursed fig tree and some teachings on catchwords like faith, prayer, and forgiveness.[1] In the middle of the intercalation stands what we have traditionally called the cleansing of the temple.

With intercalations, it is usually understood that the outside parts and the inside part interpret each other. In this case, what happens to the fig tree is instructive for thinking about Jesus' action in the temple. While scholars dispute the strength of that relationship here, it is helpful to remember that Mark is likely written at the time when the temple is either being destroyed or has been destroyed. This historical catastrophe is the context for writing down and interpreting these crucial traditions about Jesus. For this reason, the strange figure of the cursed fig tree also connects up with the temple in the way it helps readers reflect on what has happened. What is left open, of course, is our contemporary homiletical-theological response to the Markan narrative's use of the figure.

Cursing The Fig Tree (11:12-14): Omitted from The Lectionary

In Mark 11:12-14, the first section of the intercalated story, the narrator marks the second day of Jesus' time in the environs of Jerusalem. The mention of Jesus' hunger in v. 12 becomes the proximate cause of the unfolding incident. Jesus sees a fig tree from afar. For the purposes of the figural relationship with

---

1. Most versions omit v. 26 for text-critical reasons. Because of this, the next section will commence with 11:27.

the temple, this becomes important. Jesus notices the leaves and from that indication hopes to find something to eat on the fig tree. Yet when he gets close, all he sees are leaves—no "fruit." The narrator notes that the season is not apt for finding figs anyway—the word for season being the word *kairos*, which also has eschatological overtones here. Jesus' response to the fig tree seems harsh: "May no one ever eat from you again." As a way of setting up the second half of the story in its intercalation (11:20-25), the narrator notes that the disciples *heard* what Jesus said.

If the fig tree is a figure what does it stand for? William Telford identifies five Hebrew Bible passages that use the figure for eschatological judgment on Israel, all of which later become a source for early Christian reflection: Isa. 28:3-4; Jer. 8:13; Hosea 9:10, 16; Joel 1:7, 12; and Mic. 7:1.[2] Yet it would be wise for interpreters at this point not to overly generalize this figuration. At this point in the narrative, the critique of the figure may be not of the whole nation, but of its temple leadership, which will fail to welcome Jesus in the next pericope and be the known target of his parabolic work in chapter 12.[3] Thus, the upcoming parable of the vineyard will be important to keep in mind in this connection. Still, Mark is being written in the context of life around 70 c.e. The question is how Mark makes meaning with Jesus' actions in these sections. These will be key for us in understanding the range of the figure in the course of Mark's intercalated story.

Cleansing The Temple (11:15-19):
Omitted from The Lectionary

In Mark 11:15-19, the middle part of our intercalated sandwich, Jesus engages in a startling action in the temple. The note here is struck by the choice of verbs in v. 15. Jesus "casts out" the buyers and sellers—the same verb as in Jesus' exorcisms. This is not to say that their activity was illegitimate, but it does underline Jesus' activity in a way consistent with the action of the narrative's apocalyptic mode as a whole. Buyers and sellers as well as the provision of money changing and doves for sacrifice were all important for the functioning of the temple. When poorer persons came to participate in temple sacrifice, such access was necessary to ensure that there were acceptable animals for sacrifice

2. William Telford, *The Barren Temple and the Withered Fig Tree: A Redaction-Critical Analysis of the Cursing of the Fig Tree Pericope in Mark's Gospel and Its Relation to the Cleansing of the Temple Tradition*, Journal for the Study of the New Testament Supplement Series (Sheffield: JSOT), 142-54.

3. Adela Yarbro Collins, *Mark: A Commentary*, Hermeneia (Minneapolis: Fortress Press, 2007), 526.

and to see to it that coinage could be used that made it possible for people to avoid bringing idolatrous images into the temple proper. What we have in this text, therefore, is a prophetic action that brings temple activity to a halt. This is underscored by Jesus' other action, which is to see to it that no vessel was being carried through the temple. Scholars are not in agreement as to whether these "vessels" were ritual objects of worship or weapons, but the effect of it is to shut the temple down. This in itself seems to be the point of Jesus' action: a prophetic sign pointing to the temple's destruction. Again, we readers need to see this action in light of the events that accompanied Mark's writing: the Jewish War and the destruction of the temple in 67–70 c.e.

The teaching then in v. 17 helps to explain what has transpired. Two parts help to clarify the action. In the first part, Jesus cites Isa. 56:7, which specifically mentions "the nations," or gentiles. The "shall be" language of the quote highlights its eschatological significance. Whatever Jesus is doing in this part of the temple, it connects deeply to this eschatological sense of the temple's ultimate purpose. This might also help to explain an aspect of the prior action with the buyers and sellers. Joel Marcus points out that in Zech. 14:21, there will be no buyers and sellers in the temple in that day.[4] The vision here is at once a moment of crisis (shutting the temple down) and expansive (reminding of its ultimate purpose). In the second half of v. 17, therefore, Jesus renders his true judgment: "But you have made it a den of robbers." The term "robbers" does not quite carry the meaning of the Greek term, which was also used for bandits. At any rate, both the concern for the temple's inviolability and the "den of bandits" image can be traced back to Jer. 7:4-11 Again, Marcus goes on to make the case that this whole situation needs to be understood in light of the catastrophe of the temple's destruction and the Jewish Wars. In the temple, bandits or brigands are declaring the temple's inviolability in light of Roman threats while also insisting that gentiles be cleared out. Jesus' action here is thus over-determined with respect to his openness to gentiles and his sense of the temple's ultimate purpose. Mark is telling the gospel that is both Jesus (1:1) and the reign of God (1:14-15), but he does so as a contextual theologian in his own late first-century situation. Moreover, his way of doing so is consistent with his overall apocalyptic view of Jesus and a unique set of eschatological hopes and dreams about God's purposes.

The closing verses of this middle part of the intercalated sandwich then help to move Mark's plot forward. The religious leaders get wind of what Jesus

---

4. Marcus, *Mark 8-16*, Yale Anchor Bible (New Haven, CT: Yale University Press, 2009), 791f.

is doing and seek to kill him. The narrator identifies the leaders' fear and Jesus' favor with the crowds. With the end of the day, Jesus again departs Jerusalem.

THE LESSON FROM THE WITHERED FIG TREE (11:20-25): OMITTED FROM THE LECTIONARY

Now with the final section of our intercalated text, Mark 11:20-25, Jesus is passing by early (the next day, presumably). He and his entourage see the fig tree now withered. The careful remark in v. 19 about the disciples hearing what Jesus said now pays dividends in Peter's remembrance and observation. Peter calls Jesus "Rabbi," notes that that same fig tree had been cursed, and describes its resulting state. Interestingly, Peter uses the same verb as the narrator did in v. 20, thus emphasizing it for us readers. Jesus is also shown to be reliable in what he says. He is both prescient and true as a prophet!

The sureness of this occurrence between Jesus' word and the results gets taken up in v. 21-25 with Jesus' teaching. He therefore answers Peter's observation by talking about faith. First, he commends them to "have faith." This exhortation is joined to a solemn statement where Jesus continues to speak in a prophetic voice. The idea of moving a mountain with faith may strike us as odd, especially since the comment proceeds on the basis of an effective fig tree curse. Yet if the fig tree is indeed about the temple, or at least the temple's leadership, the language makes more sense. The temple is, of course, on a mountain. The language about being thrown into the sea is therefore barely veiled as a kind of prophecy. Faith can move mountains, seemingly insurmountable mountains of powers and institutions—even one as strong as the temple and its leadership! It is also able to trust in God even when temples fall—God can even work newness even in the midst of such catastrophe and grief. Between the curse and the ceasing of temple activities in the middle part of the intercalated sandwich, Mark is encouraging readers to trust that God can indeed do the impossible (note the divine passive in v. 23). The language in v. 24 intensifies the notion, even putting the verb for "receive" in a past tense form. To pray for it is to have "received" it; eschatologically, it is as good as done. This verse also puts the verbs in the second-person plural. This is not simply a triumph of personal faith, but something said to "y'all," to the community.

Mark 11:25 with its reference to forgiveness seems to stand alone here and even uses language reminiscent of Matthew. It has apparently attached itself here because of the topic of prayer. Perhaps the text also serves a warning to any community with such profound trust in God—it still needs forgiveness, too.

This important section of Mark 11 does not appear in the lectionary. Because of the emerging questions around the temple's leadership (Mark 12) and the future of the temple (Mark 13), this intercalated action becomes crucial for the unfolding Markan narrative. Too often, Christians have been tempted to interpret such events and meanings through supersessionism: namely, that the rejection of the temple is tantamount to the rejection of Israel and its displacement through the church. These are theological issues that Mark, however, could not have even conceived in 70 c.e. Even apart from this issue, however, the text remains significant as an occasion for thinking theologically about historical catastrophe, crisis, and profound grief. For homiletical theologians interested in taking up the unfinished theological work of the tradition, it offers a unique opportunity. As those who also live in the shadow of catastrophe and crisis, it gives us a moment to think theologically through such traumatic moments to re-envision God's presence and promise in new and renewing ways. Preachers wishing to do such difficult work may find this difficult passage to be a helpful theological conversation partner.

LECTIONS

Our one lection in this subsection is an alternate for Palm/Passion Sunday. It is regrettable that this text is read apart from its context in chapter 11, the rest of which does not appear in the lectionary at all. A perennial problem with Palm Sunday as practiced in North America is that its royal claims are heard without the strange irony that this text in particular offers. The shift to Palm/Passion Sunday has alleviated some of this problem, by relating this act more closely to the rest of Holy Week. At the very least, however, its puzzling ending in v. 11 (see below) will help the preacher stay rooted in the challenging Markan vision that has Jesus both acclaimed on the street but also retreating from the city. In doing so, the pericope invites us to pause at the words of acclamation and remember Jesus' own predictions about his passion and resurrection. NT scholar Clifton Black calls this episode a lampoon of a triumphal entry.[5] Preachers committed to preaching the mystery of the apocalyptic gospel of God's reign and Jesus' identity will want to reflect deeply about how to use such a text today.

---

5. C. Clifton Black, *Mark*, Abingdon New Testament Commentaries (Nashville: Abingdon, 2011), 238.

Lection: A Not-So-Triumphal Entry
11:1-11; Liturgy of The Palms

This "lampoon" of the triumphal entry becomes painfully clear in Jesus' arrival in Jerusalem. The story here has resonance on two levels. First, there are the uniquely Jewish traditions concerning the entrance of a royal personage or messiah in Jerusalem. Over the many years of Holy Week and its deep connection of typologies, we have become familiar with texts that are absolutely crucial for understanding our text, especially Zech. 9, 14, and Ps. 118. They provide a rich intertext from the Hebrew Bible that makes this moment in Mark's text so powerful. At the same time, Adela Yarbro Collins also points out that there are Greco-Roman traditions around celebratory entrance processions that must be acknowledged here.[6] Whether following a biblical messianic typology or the arrival *(parousia)* of a Greco-Roman hero or dignitary, a reader discovers problems here in Mark 11:1-11. In both cases, the story of Jesus' arrival prompts both powerful expectations and *disappointment* around its final execution, especially with its strange ending in v. 11. In other words, in this arrival scene so rich in meaning in the ancient world, *Jesus' welcome goes awry*. This sets a tone that both lays the groundwork for Jesus' three passion predictions and moves the narrative along in all of its revelatory power and irony. Through these conflicts, Jesus' mysterious apocalyptic gospel will be revealed. It is revealed not only in Jesus' reign-of-God ministry, but in his suffering, messianic person as crucified Son of God.

The key here in 11:1 is the geographical reference. The journey from the revelatory interlude on the mountain is now complete. Jesus has traveled with his disciples from Caesarea Philippi to Capernaum to the edge of Judah now all the way to Jerusalem. The text mentions two villages near Jerusalem where Jesus stops: Bethany and Bethphage. While we know something about the former, the exact location of the latter is unclear. From a narrative perspective, Bethphage at least offers an important place name for the unfolding plot. Its name means "house of the unripe figs." Since this story will lead quite quickly on the next day to the cursing of the fig tree, the name at least embodies the conflict about to unfold. Both villages, associated here with the Mount of Olives, bring in an element of foreboding judgment. With Zech. 14, the Mount of Olives is a place of theophany and is quite self-consciously portrayed as "opposite" the temple mount. This key geographic feature of the narrative

6. Yarbro Collins, *Mark*, 514–16.

becomes a clue for the developing action. In light of this, Jesus sends two of his disciples ahead to make the proper preparations for his arrival.

This next sequence in vv. 2-6 is devoted to showing Jesus' prescience as a prophet. He gives his two disciples explicit, detailed directions about finding a colt (in this case, given the upcoming connection to Zech. 9:9 and the context of the time, this colt was likely an unridden donkey). Jesus gives them directions not just for where to go and what to do, but how to speak if someone questions them as they untie the colt. The narrator then goes on to describe what happened and, word for word, the story transpires as planned. The narrator helps the reader to see Jesus as a prescient and reliable prophet.

Underneath this action, however, are a couple of important claims. First, it is important to the unfolding action that the colt be "unridden." This notion probably goes back to the idea of something being consecrated. It is not just for profane use; this colt is devoted here to sacred use. Second, the verbal response they are told to give to anyone who questions them is that "the Lord needs it." While readers disposed to follow the action favorably may find it helpful that these words suffice, it still leaves us in a bit of a quandary. Some speculate that the word for Lord or master here (kyrios) refers to the colt's owner. This, however, is unlikely since the disciples are told to add that the colt will be "sent back" again later. Some would argue that there is a very exalted claim of Jesus' lordship here. While it may be premature to jump to such a high Christology in Mark, clearly Jesus does instruct them to use a kind of messianic prerogative in securing the animal. It may suffice to notice that Jesus also links the language of Lord with his own Son of the human title in Mark 2:28.

With the preparations now complete, the disciples in vv. 7-10 bring the colt to Jesus. In the background, the messianic text from Zech. 9:19 helps to explain the unfolding action: "Rejoice greatly, O daughter Zion! Shout aloud, O daughter Jerusalem! Lo, your king comes to you; triumphant and victorious is he, humble and riding on a donkey, on a colt, the foal of a donkey." The action of placing cloaks upon the colt where Jesus "sat," placing cloaks on the roadway to prepare his way, and using leafy branches in celebration along the way are all means of welcoming a dignitary. As Collins points out, the spreading of garments, for example, has relevance both in Israel's history (e.g., 2 Kgs. 9:13) as well as in Roman culture as exemplified by a scene from *Plutarch's Lives* (8:260-61).[7] The underlying messianic text and the historical customs around welcome underline the importance of Jesus' entry into the city.

---

7. Ibid., 519.

Mark 11:9 then describes a procession that accompanies Jesus—a procession made up of those who were going ahead and those who were following. Given the importance of "following" for the previous section of Mark, the notion here has a deeper significance. It would appear that even if persons from the city are participating in this procession, Jesus' disciples as "followers" are part of it, too. This is important to note because elements of this entry are hard to reconcile with Jesus' own purposes in coming to Jerusalem. Some of these problems with expectations around Jesus' arrival are also borne out by what follows. The crowd shouts the words of the familiar Ps. 118. What is interesting here is not so much the quoted material, but its variations. Psalm 118 does not contain the phrase "Blessed is the coming kingdom of our ancestor David!" Here the expectations of messianic Son of David, named in passing by Bartimaeus in the previous pericope, seem to have overtaken the event. With the voicing of the expectation that Jesus as Davidic Messiah will engage in acts of power that help to dispose of the Romans, we have come a long way from Jesus' own messianic, suffering Son of the human.[8]

All of this makes v. 11 all the more strange. One might think that the highpoint of such an entrance in light of the crowd's shouts in v. 10 might involve acts of welcome by local dignitaries or perhaps even a royal installation. In this case, Jesus simply "looks around" the temple and *leaves the city*. Over the coming days, Jesus will not keep his base of operations in Jerusalem, but will alternate back and forth from Bethany. Such an ending to the periciope makes it hard to call this story a triumphal entry at all!

JERUSALEM: JESUS IN CONFLICT WITH RELIGIOUS LEADERS AT THE TEMPLE (11:27—12:44)

INTRODUCTION

In the following subsection, we shift from narrated stories to conflict dialogues with various religious leaders. A key motif throughout is the way Jesus ends up silencing his opponents. In fact, at one point, they dare ask him no more questions (12:34b)! Jesus continues to teach, however, in preparation for the

8. Joel Marcus argues that the fusing of these traditions of Ps. 118 with the Davidic language of 2 Sam. 7 in Mark 11:10 may have been understood apocalyptically in certain revolutionary circles at the time of Mark's writing. If so, this makes the final verse of this pericope all the more unusual. See Marcus, *Mark 8-16*, 780.

coming narrative conflict. Throughout these encounters, Jesus continues to demonstrate his authority even in the shadow of his looming suffering and death. Through these means, the Markan narrator continues to reveal the gospel of who Jesus is and the reign of God that he preaches.

PASSAGES OMITTED FROM THE LECTIONARY

There are seven pericopes in this section emphasizing conflict, yet five of these seven are absent from the lectionary. The lectionary picks up Jesus' teaching on the greatest commandment and the widow's offering, but leaves out both difficult indictments of religious leaders as well as some crucial theological arguments with them.

THE AUTHORITY OF JESUS QUESTIONED (11:27-33): OMITTED FROM THE LECTIONARY

On the heels of the discovery of the cursed fig tree, Jesus and those with him arrive in Jerusalem again, now the third day of their activity in Jerusalem. Jesus is described as merely walking around, in contrast to his very purposeful behavior on his first entry in the temple and the second day's prophetic action of temporarily shutting it down. Here, however, Jesus' opponents begin to take the initiative. It is important to notice that the group here that approaches him in v. 27 represents the same people he spoke about in his first passion prediction (Mark 8:31): the chief priests, the scribes, and the elders. They ask him questions designed to put him on the defensive, or perhaps even to entrap him and kill him, as 11:18 indicates narratively about the scribes and chief priests' intentions toward Jesus.

The sticky question they ask in v. 28 concerns Jesus' authority. They want to know the source of Jesus' authority to do "these things." In the most immediate sense, "these things" probably refer to Jesus' entry to Jerusalem and the subsequent day's action in the temple. In a broader sense, it could also include Jesus' teaching and healing, both of which have also prompted questions about Jesus' authority throughout the Markan narrative. At any rate, the questions are designed to make Jesus answer in such a way that either isolates him or pushes him to say something about his own identity that would constitute blasphemy. The questions could put Jesus in a sticky situation.

Jesus, however, responds with a common rabbinical tack by asking a counter question. When he does so, it not only reveals his authority, but draws into question the authority of his official interlocutors. It is in its own way a revealing moment.

In vv. 29-30 Jesus asks a question about John the Baptist that frames the subsequent conversation. John the Baptist, of course, has been an important and controversial character throughout the Markan narrative. Early on he is portrayed as sympathetic to Jesus and his purposes. The narrator provides us with a positive evaluation of him and his ministry. At the same time, John the Baptist does fall afoul of Herod and others. Jesus plays on this conflict about John and his portrayal as a kind of prophet. Now with his question Jesus wants to put the religious leaders on the spot. Was John's authority from heaven (that is, divine) or from human beings? While the content of the question is itself important, there is also a linguistic urgency around it. Jesus says he will answer his questioners, provided they answer him. Then, once he poses the John the Baptist conundrum, he says again: "Answer me." With his emphatic repetition *and his difficult question*, Jesus is putting his interlocutors on the defensive. He is, in a sense, exercising his authority by not merely submitting to the terms of their question.

With vv. 31-33a, we are party to the religious leaders' reflections on Jesus' question. In the process, the religious leaders are portrayed not just as conflicted about John, but essentially without authority of their own. The scene begins with a group discussion where they argue among themselves. The narrator breaks off a bit from the third-person description to set up competing options in the voice of the speakers: "If we say, then . . ." By showing the leaders as equivocating in their response, the Markan narrator portrays them as vacillating. By the end of v. 32b, the narrator slips back into the third person (they) in order to disclose the religious leaders' fear of offending the crowd, who held John in esteem as a prophet. By doing so, the narrator discloses that the religious leaders have no divine authority either. Their answer, "we do not know," not only means that Jesus does not need to answer their initial question to him, but also "reveals" who they really are. The reader has the pleasure of sharing in their comeuppance and in Jesus' ability, without the authority of religious precedent, to best them in their dialogue. With the final section of v. 33, Jesus says he will not answer their question. The beautiful irony, however, is that he has. His authority is *not* like theirs; and, in fact, theirs is shown to be something less. The scribes, chief priests, and elders took the initiative, but in this first round they have failed to corner Jesus on the terms of their question.

THE PARABLE OF THE VINEYARD AND THE TENANTS (12:1–12): OMITTED FROM THE LECTIONARY

In the well-known parable of the vineyard tenants, Jesus then continues the turnabout of Mark 11:27–33. Now that the religious leaders are on their heels, Jesus presses them further. In v. 1, Jesus begins speaking to them parabolically. Although his earlier practice of this in Mark 4 proved mysterious, this parable now moves more openly. By the time it ends, Jesus' opponents will have discerned that the parable was indeed addressed to them (v. 12).

The parable itself probably presupposes the Song of the Vineyard in Isa. 5. The echoes of the Scripture text set up a certain set of expectations: God has carefully tended the vineyard. But since the vineyard has failed to bear fruit (recall the fig tree in 11:11–13), the vineyard comes under judgment. Mark, however, has Jesus tell the parable with a different goal. His parable sets up the vineyard in just the same way, but sets it in the context of first-century life. The owner is departing and leases the vineyard to tenant farmers. This would have been a familiar arrangement in Jesus' time. By arranging the parable this way, the accent falls not on Israel, but on the tenants, who quickly become a figure for the religious leaders with whom Jesus is in conversation.

This allegorizing of the parable here would seem to undermine the way we have thought about parables since the landmark work of Adolf Jülicher. He argued that parables were by definition different from allegories in that parables had a single, arresting point.[9] Yet the problem here goes deeper. The idea of the parable seems to change within the horizon of the Markan Gospel itself. In chapter 4, the telling of parables requires Jesus to explain it to his disciples immediately afterward. This particular parable elicits not confusion, but resolution among Jesus' opponents. Mark is clearly having Jesus narrate parables in this Gospel to serve specific aims of his writing as a whole.

Because of this double connection, the language seems particularly evocative. The hearers would have understood the tensions involved with the owner's appropriation of the harvest fruits. At this point the story seems quite plausible, perhaps even reflecting with the sending of servants and their ill treatment some of the social tensions of the time. One way the text may gain further allegorical force is through the word chosen for servant or slave. Many

---

9. Adolf Jülicher, *Die Gleichnisreden Jesu*, 2nd ed. (Tübingen: J. C. B. Mohr [Paul Siebeck], 1899).

commentators note that such language was a common way to refer to prophets. The one who reportedly was wounded on the head might even remind readers and hearers of John the Baptist. The summary report evokes a whole history of the reception and rejection experienced by so many of the prophets.

The narrative takes a very odd turn, however, in v. 6. The vineyard owner decides after all this carnage and humiliation to send the beloved son. The text highlights this narratively by describing the vineyard owner's context and action with an odd syntactical break which sounds something like this, "Still one thing he has: beloved Son. He sends him lastly to them." The word "lastly" here is the adverbial form of the word we use for eschatology. The mention of the beloved son also brings to mind two other revelatory scenes where the designation is made for Jesus: his baptism in Mark 1 and his transfiguration in Mark 9. Again, the allegorical force of the parable leaps to the foreground. Mark's Jesus does have the vineyard owner muse about the reasoning: surely they will respect the son. But it is not so.

This next part of the parable in vv. 7-8 has caused some considerable historical consternation. Not just the motivation of the vineyard owner above, but even that of the tenants here seems a bit dicey when viewed historically. Many commentators speculate about whether a group of tenant farmers could so revolt and kill a son in the hope of wresting ownership from an absentee landlord's line. Joachim Jeremias suggests that when they saw the son, they might have assumed the father/owner had died and that they would thus eliminate the final claimant to the land in that line.[10] Given the allegorical tendency here, however, it is probably better to note the affinities here to the situation and addressees that the narrator has in mind. To whatever degree the parable fits some elements of land tenancy in the period, its aim in 12:12 is the perceptions of Jesus' interlocutors in the temple. In light of the narrator's disclosures of the intentions of these addressees in 11:18, furthermore, the telling of the parable offers a narratively consistent vision. One more historical factor also needs to be acknowledged as we consider this parable. The historical context of its writing is the final third of the first century. The historical crisis of the temple's destruction and the role of religious leaders in a temple versus a post-temple environment become important factors in the parable's retelling here in a section about Jesus in Jerusalem, in the temple, and in conflict with religious authorities. It is this historical overlay that may be the most determinative for understanding the parable aright. That being said, this particular section of the text, as it describes the killing of the son, has its own

10. Joachim Jeremias, *The Parables of Jesus*, 2nd ed. (New York: Scribner's, 1972), 74–76.

intertextual connections. There are elements of the Joseph story in Gen. 37:20 that are evoked here as well.

In vv. 9-10, attention then shifts to the vineyard owner's reaction. It is important to note here the use of the Greek word "Lord" to describe the vineyard "owner" (NRSV) in v. 9. While it is perfectly fine to describe the vineyard owner with that word, the overtones here in the Greek are also theological. While the idea of destroying the tenants may not be historically plausible, it does make sense in light of the context of the parable as narrated in the last third of the first century. The issue with the parable is not the judgment of Israel, nor even the temple per se, but the religious leadership. The leadership role in the vineyard will be given to others.

In the light of this parabolic judgment of leadership, the biblical material from Ps. 118:22-23 in v. 10 is especially telling. For one thing, the same Psalm is quoted at Jesus' entry to Jerusalem. Here it also becomes a means for reflecting on the killing and rejection of the son in light of God's purposes. It is thus no wonder that this particular text becomes so important for early Christian apologetics.

With vv. 11-12, then, the parable reaches its destination. Like much of the preceding narratives, it ends up having a dual function, even with its intended recipients. On the one hand, the telling of the parable seems to reinforce in the religious leadership a desire to see Jesus arrested. On the other hand, the same religious leaders are aware of Jesus' continuing (at least, for the moment) favor with the crowds. For now all they can really do is walk away.

This particular text is not part of the lectionary, but as part of the canon it requires both homiletical comment and ongoing theological reflection. While the text evidences a desire to displace the Jewish religious leadership of the day, its ongoing effect has become greater. Twenty centuries later, it is easier to read as a displacement of Jews in their entirety (in the form of Christian supersessionism) and the "handing over to others" as a vindication of a now ascendant Christian church. Historically, it is better to make more modest claims about these "others." We ought not be too quick to jump to our contemporary gentile church as the "others" named here. Whatever the configuration Mark's Jesus had in mind, Judaism as a whole was struggling for identity in the events around the temple's destruction. We contemporary readers ought to respect the text's open-endedness in this regard. The upshot for preachers is whether we can reengage on these issues. Can we take up the unfinished theology of the Markan text? In an age marked by violence and fear of the other, it may just be a good place to begin again.

Paying Taxes to Caesar (12:13-17):
Omitted from The Lectionary

In this second controversy story of the series, Jesus meets with representatives of the Pharisees and the Herodians. They are described as "sent," presumably by those religious leaders who heard Jesus' parable in 12:1-12. Mark signals to us in v. 13 that the Pharisees and Herodians are seeking to entrap him.

Now Pharisees and Herodians may seem like odd partners in such a venture. We know something about the Pharisees because their group eventually becomes key for the Judaism that emerges after the temple's destruction. As we have seen earlier in Mark's Gospel (chs. 2, 3, 7, and 10), they are often engaging Jesus on matters of legal interpretation. They would be concerned that Jesus' answer be in conformity with law and piety. Herodians, by contrast, are not as well known. Many scholars assume that they were Jewish leaders in sympathy with Herod and therefore accommodating to Rome. For them, an answer that bordered on sedition might prove especially problematic. With a question in the offing about the payment of taxes to the largely detested Romans, Jesus answering in their presence would place him between and rock and a hard place.

Their strategy in the encounter comes through clearly in v. 14. They butter Jesus up. The Herodians and Pharisees seem to believe that by offering some flattery, they will get Jesus to make a mistake. Then comes the question: shall we pay the tax or not? The tax they refer to is one designated by a Greek rendering of the Latin word we know today as "census." It was therefore a kind of poll tax. To pay the tax is to support the hated Romans. Not to pay the tax, or to advocate the same, was to court disaster. The way the question is phrased is unique to discussions of torah: "Is it lawful to pay taxes to the emperor or not?" Hence, it is not just politics; there is a religious question in view here.

Jesus, however, sees through their ruse. In the second half of v. 15, the narrator tells us that Jesus senses their hypocrisy and asks to see a denarius. A denarius would have likely had Caesar's image and inscription on it. It would have been the kind of coin you would need to exchange in the temple. But here the question of the coin's image, the *eikōn*, drives the rest of the story. Jesus' question about what was on the coin calls for a reply from his interrogators. Their reply that the emperor's image and inscription are on the coin allows Jesus to escape the snare. He then says, "Give to the emperor the things that are the emperor's, and to God the things that are God's." The reader is given the satisfaction of seeing Jesus avoid the trap they set. Yet, in the process, the reader is also invited to ponder the question anew: just what is God's? Is it what bears God's image? Perhaps so, but that does not say it all either. In its puzzling reply, the text invites a marveling, as the final verse indicates. His interlocutors were not merely confounded. They were also "amazed" and utterly so.

Sometimes this text is treated as if it sat all alone—as if it were just another clever saying from Jesus. The realization that it happens in the midst of conflict, both in our text *and* in the history of Judaism as it struggles with the temple's destruction and its implication for religious leadership, means that we need to see it in the light of such conflict. Jesus is not merely musing about matters of church and state, like some armchair constitutional scholar. Instead, he speaks as one invested in naming God in the midst of conflict and crisis. Preachers today who do their work in places where so much is now becoming unsettled may find just such a view an invitation to deeper theological work in their own conflicts and crises.

THE QUESTION ABOUT THE RESURRECTION (12:18-27): OMITTED FROM THE LECTIONARY

Once again, this confrontational dialogue only makes sense in light of conflict. In this case, the conflict goes to the heart of the matter: the resurrection itself. The Sadducees approach Jesus with a question designed to embarrass. Jesus, however, deals with the premise of their question in response. In the end this conflict dialogue is really about, well, the end.

The Sadducees are yet another group among the religious leaders. They are known for views about the Scriptures that are fairly limited. Unlike the Pharisees, they hold to no *oral* traditions or laws. Their religion was about the Torah, namely, the five books of Moses. The idea in v. 18 about them not believing in the resurrection reflects this notion. For the Sadducees, resurrection was a new-fangled teaching, because it was not in the Torah.

In vv. 19-23, the Sadducees then tell their story about seven brothers. The question presupposes the practice of levirate marriage, which stipulates that a brother marry and beget a child with a brother's widow if they had been childless (Deut. 25:5-6). The law exists to make sure that a line does not die out without its stake in God's promises. It may also have provided for security for widows, although the price for that seems to have been a very androcentric view of marriage and inheritance. The story itself is pretty odd. All seven brothers eventually die. Finally, the woman, now seven-times married, also dies. Yet the Sadducees are merely helping to lay the premise of the question: whose wife will the woman be in the resurrection? The question is hardly neutral. In fact, it seems to be a kind of *reductio ad absurdum*. If you, as a

Sadducee, already do not believe in resurrection, surely such a scenario can only be seen as an attempt to make the premise of resurrection untenable.

Jesus' response to them in vv. 24-27 may sound to us rather harsh. In v. 24, he says the Sadducees are *wrong*. The question here is, again, not of the armchair variety. This is not merely speculation about life after death. For Jesus, the issue of resurrection that is raised by the Sadducees' question goes to the heart of his ministry. Jesus has predicted three times that the Son of the human will rise (Mark 8:31; 9:31; and 10:34). For Jesus, therefore, the issue must be addressed. Clearly the Sadducees know neither Scripture nor God's power.

He begins by showing that the Sadducees have committed an error in kind. The new age of resurrection is not a mere continuance of the old age. Relations in one are not simply transferable to relations in the other. But then Jesus goes to the heart of the matter in v. 26. Jesus' mention of the burning bush story where God is known as the God of Abraham, Isaac, and Jacob is not just a clever use of Scripture that appeals to a present tense verb (the main verb is absent in Greek here anyway!). Instead, it makes its claim in an *earlier* text in the Torah (Exod. 3:6). If the Sadducees hold to the primacy of the Pentateuch, then even they must acknowledge such an argument. Jesus therefore concludes in v. 27 with the very comment with which he first responded. The Sadducees are just wrong.

A lot is at stake here. Jesus' ministry hinges on the resurrection, as the passion predictions bear out. But underneath this is another important theological point: *God* is God. To think otherwise is to think in merely human terms, as Jesus has already confronted earlier in Peter (Mark 8:33). Where resurrection meets the possibility of God, we have Mark's apocalyptic Gospel. It is not about cozy visions of timeless eternality. Mark's Gospel has a sense of urgency. After all, God raises what is *dead*. And in a time of catastrophe with the temple and the reality of war, it is only such a strange, suffering-tinged promise that will do.

For us, the strange notion of apocalyptic possibility is no less edgy. We either turn such language into movie special effects or eschew it as useless myth. With Mark's Gospel, we might see its value again in profound experiences of shared dislocation. All this is to say that our conflicts and struggles in difficult days also invite us to place such realities in relation to God's ultimate purposes. Again, in a moment of crisis we begin to discern in new ways the God who is the God of the living.

THE QUESTION ABOUT DAVID'S SON (12:35-37):
OMITTED FROM THE LECTIONARY

The absence of this text from the lectionary may be the result of its theological distance. It contends with scriptural problems that are not at the top of our list, but were perhaps important apologetic issues in early Christianity. Preachers who wish to use the text should be sure to remember the conflicted context of this section before dabbling in ancient exegesis and theological reflection. This one requires a little homework, but it would reward the effort, too.

This brief text follows on the end of all questions from Jesus' many interlocutors in 11:27—12:34. Although the immediately prior text, 12:28-34, features a friendly conversation between Jesus and a scribe concerning the greatest commandment, the fact that the text also indicates the end of the questions (12:34) now means that with our text Jesus will be taking the initiative. He does so with a question about Scriptures and messianic interpretation.

With the introductory verse, the narrator reminds us that Jesus is still in the temple, but now he is *teaching*. He does so as several of his recent opponents did: by asking a question. Now, however, Jesus tries to show that some common conceptions may be mistaken. He starts by questioning a possibly popular messianic notion.

His question goes to the heart of scribal interpretation. How is it that Christ is the Son of David? We know after several chapters of Mark that Jesus himself has been referred to in just such terms. Bartimaeus cries out to Jesus as "Son of David" in 10:47. The crowds cried out at Jesus' arrival in Jerusalem in 11:10a: "Blessed is the coming kingdom of our ancestor David." Yet Jesus does not seem to cultivate this appellation. In fact, he finds himself often correcting other messianic understandings with his own messianic notion of the suffering/ rising Son of the human. In fact, it is just this struggle that makes the long journey from Caesarea Phillipi to Jerusalem so important. For the sake of the gospel, the disciples need to understand what Jesus' identity is and how that relates to the coming reign of God. The Davidic messianic notion, though perhaps not rejected outright, is at the very least reconfigured. Jesus wants to understand it in his own mysterious sense.

Jesus begins in v. 36 by noting that David said something a little different in Ps. 110:1. The idea was that David was the composer of the Psalms. In order to underline the significance of what David was reported to have said, Jesus mentions a common notion of the time: that David said so under the inspiration of the Holy Spirit. By heading to the Scriptures to find a point of contradiction, Jesus does two things. First, he undermines any simplistic way of thinking about

Davidic messiahs. If "the Lord spoke to my Lord" and gave him kingship, how can *David*, the exalted ancestor, be referring to this messiah not as son, but Lord? Second, by doing this Jesus forces his interlocutors (and readers!) to ponder mystery. If this is so, perhaps this messiah thing is more mysterious than we think. Jesus, consistent with his own preaching and practice, invites people to be open to something different and unexpected—something at least more than your royal, Davidic messiah.

The response of the crowd "with delight" seems a little incongruous. Perhaps it shows yet again, in contrast to the vast majority of religious leaders, that the crowds still take to Jesus. The effect would be to isolate the majority of leaders and not to indict the whole people, some of whom may still be open to hearing good news.

LECTIONS

The two final lections in this section are Jesus' teaching on the greatest commandment and the widow's offering. Apart from the surrounding context, which concentrates on conflict, it is easy to turn the teaching into a general moral rule and the widow's offering into a sentimental example story. In context, these lections can be appreciated at greater depth. They are part of Mark's ongoing dispute with the religious leaders and what that dispute means for the temple.

LECTION: THE GREAT COMMANDMENT
12:28-34; PROPER 26

This lection, situated in the midst of conflict in Mark's important Jerusalem narrative, is too often treated apart from that context. It becomes a kind of general teaching that summarizes Jesus' view. Upon close reading, however, this particular conversation is exceedingly important precisely because of its relationship to the immediate context of Mark *and* what it says about the historical context in which it was written: the destruction of the temple. This only enriches the lectionary preacher's work in being a homiletical theologian in her own time and place.

The problem of context is not only a result of this text's seeming timelessness rather than timeliness. It is also true that it appears as the reading for Proper 26. This means that this particular text for a lectionary preacher will follow upon the reading for the healing of Bartimaeus (10:46-52) for Proper 25. Preachers will need to do some serious work to relate this particular lection to its immediate Markan literary and theological context, which is conflict in Jerusalem.

The text helps the preacher with the introduction in 12:28. First of all, the lead character is a scribe. Scribes are some of the most consistent opponents of Jesus throughout the Markan narrative. As experts in the law, they are in conflict with Jesus both in his Galilee phase and now here in Jerusalem. The introductory verse also helps the preacher by reminding that this particular text's question results because the scribe overheard the previous dispute, thus referring back to the questions of Jesus authority (11:27-33), the parable of the Vineyard (12:1-12), the question about imperial taxes (12:13-17), and the dispute about resurrection and marriage (12:18-27). By highlighting this, the preacher can give a much deeper sense of what is at stake. If the preacher also takes time to mention that Mark's Gospel was written around the time of the temple's destruction, the whole conversation in this pericope will deepen considerably, especially as 12:33 comes into view.

Yet it is just as important to note that this is not your typical Markan scribe either. They are consistent opponents of Jesus in the Markan narrative, yet this particular scribe is described as "seeing that he [Jesus] answered them [the Sadducees] well." The narrator signals that *this* scribe is a bit more well-disposed to what Jesus might say. While the other texts in Mark 11–12 give notice of intent of entrapment or indicate a desire to ridicule Jesus (12:18-27), this final conversation highlights a different possibility.

Out of this, the scribe poses his question: "Which commandment is the first of all?" Clearly here the word first is not about mere sequence, but priority. It may reflect a concern common among interpreters to identify some way to organize and prioritize the Torah's 613 commands. Jesus is asked to weigh in on the matter.

His response in vv. 29-31 is noteworthy for its distinction. Jesus' response is not to choose a single commandment, but to join two. The first has to do with God and God's oneness: the Shema (Deut. 6:4). The Shema had the added power of being something that pious Jews would have recited twice a day. Its emphasis is on the love of God with one's heart, soul, and strength, to which Jesus adds in v. 30 loving God with "all your mind." The point has to do with loving God with all you've got. The second command, which Jesus quickly links to the first as equally important, is the love of neighbor in Lev. 19:18. These two for Jesus represent the law as a whole. Adela Yarbro Collins notes that Jesus' reply was not original in the sense of connecting love of God and neighbor—noting in particular that this was a combination found also in the *Testaments of the Twelve Patriarchs* and in other respects in *Jubilees* and Philo.[11]

However, Jesus' linking of these two particular commandments seems to have been distinctive.

The real surprise of this text commences with v. 32. The scribe commends Jesus as a teacher for his answer! In vv. 32b-33, the scribe then goes on to summarize Jesus' answer and to make a crucial addition for our text. The summary is not merely a rote one. The scribe uses language reminiscent of other biblical texts to indicate his agreement with Jesus: Exod. 20:3; Deut. 4:35; and Isa. 45:21. What he adds, however, is even more important. He compares the weight of this two-sided command to burnt offerings and sacrifices. This is not an utterly new notion. Texts like 1 Sam. 15:22 and Hosea 6:6 show similar tendencies. However, in doing so, the scribe suddenly gives this conversation a weight that is peculiar not so much to Jesus' time as Mark's readers' context. The issue of what really matters in the tradition becomes important precisely in the moment of historical crisis that the temple's destruction represents. What does faithfulness look like when there is no further possibility of making sacrifice in the temple? This is in fact a problem *in* common between the Markan community and communities that this scribe represents. In this odd way, the lection here opens up to the readers' present—and not in opposition to others' views but with an odd sense of solidarity. Preachers should take note.

After this, Jesus returns the favor and commends the scribe for his response. He sees him answering with discernment and says moreover that he is not far from the kingdom of God—a central component of Jesus' gospel ministry. And yet, paradoxically, it is in this strange exchange, with near agreement between two figures who elsewhere in Mark's Gospel would have been adversaries, that the door seems to shut. From here on out, not one of Jesus' opponents dares to ask him any more questions. After this unusual exchange, the confrontational questions from the religious leaders in 11:27—12:34 cease.

Two insights can be carried forward from this for today's homiletical theologian committed to wrestling with this puzzling lection. First, Mark goes out of his way to portray this scribe as sympathetic to Jesus. There is an unusual sense at the end of these conflict dialogues that conflict itself is not unremitting. This text resists the trend to turn all the scribes or all the religious leaders—let alone all of the Jews—into a foil for Jesus and his ministry. Second, the questioners here eventually do cease posing questions (12:34). But here we can see it is not because of simple antagonism. Jesus mentions that this scribe is not far from the kingdom. There is a sense in which even dialogue is called forward into God's ultimate purposes. All of our struggles must be

11. Yarbro Collins, *Mark*, 569.

seen in connection to that. The former gives us pause to write off anyone who disagrees. Christianity cannot use its own struggles with opponents as a way to demonize or dehumanize anyone. The latter, Jesus's statement about his proximity to the kingdom, helps us see dialogue's purpose in relation to God's ultimate desire for a reign of healing, reconciliation, and bread with others.

LECTION: THE DENOUNCING OF THE SCRIBES AND THE WIDOW'S OFFERING
12:38-44; PROPER 27

The grouping of these two units together has an impact on their interpretation. At the very least the prominence of the key word "widow" would seem to link them together. If so, then the two units also need to be understood within the unfolding narrative of Jesus' relation to the temple and temple leadership in 11:1—12:44, as well as the important speech about the temple's destruction that will take place in Mark 13.

One view of these two texts is to see them as the final indictment of the temple. The alleged rapaciousness of the scribes in 12:39-40 and the lamentable action of a poor widow throwing her paltry remaining savings into the temple treasury are therefore twin examples of the corruption of the temple.[12] If so, they would stand as a crucial indictment of the temple before Jesus' prediction of its destiny in the subsequent chapter.

Along the way, however, we have seen a more nuanced reading of the temple. Jesus' prediction is coming in Mark 13 and it will not look good for the temple—no surprise to Mark's late first-century audience either. At the same time, however, our readings this chapter have shown that the temple is still an area of Jesus' concern, even if its leadership comes under withering rebuke and is silenced in conflicted dialogues (12:34). In light of this, it is probably better to venture an interpretation that accounts for all the elements of this context. With the end of chapter 12, Jesus offers two examples of faithfulness, one negative and one positive. In the first, the religious leaders come up short yet again; in the other, the widow, we have one of the most powerful visions of the kind of discipleship that Jesus has been calling for all along.

Jesus sets it up in v. 38 with a word of warning: beware. The word for beware has been used with religious leaders elsewhere in the Gospel (8:15) and

---

12. Similar readings can be found in Addison Wright, "The Widow's Mites: Praise or Lament?—A Matter of Context," *Catholic Biblical Quarterly* 44 (1982): 256–65 and Ched Myers, *Binding the Strong Man: A Political Reading of Mark's Story of Jesus* (Maryknoll, NY: Orbis Books, 1988), 320–22.

will be used again shortly in Jesus' speech in the next chapter (13:9, 23, 33). Its presence here may be an indicator that Jesus is speaking to readers in Mark's time. Of course, we know from the text about the greatest commandment that Jesus does not likely mean "all" scribes (12:34), but the indictment is nonetheless strong. Jesus describes their clothing and their practices in social settings to remind his interlocutors of their privilege. In v. 40, however, Jesus accuses them of engaging in practices that deplete the resources of widows in connection with their public prayer leadership. Widows, of course, have an important place in the life of the people. They were a special concern of God's and therefore of the entire community in the Hebrew Bible as demonstrated by the law itself (Exod. 22:22; Deut. 14:29; 27:19). As a result, the accusation that an interpreter of the law is responsible for such actions in the context of the practice of piety is a serious one that represents a perversion of what should be. A difficulty scholars have with this verse is in figuring out the nature of the practices Jesus speaks about in this context. It is not easy to reconstruct the circumstances in which scribes could so piously exploit widows, although a few commentators have tried. Suffice it for us to say that the accusation is there to describe the depth of corruption of the leadership and to show how far short it falls of what God has a right to expect.

Jesus then changes his location in v. 41 and is described as observing the giving practices of the people who approach the treasury opposite him. This vantage point allows him to see two contrasting ways of giving: many rich people and a certain poor widow. The contrast allows Jesus then to set up a positive example for what was sorely lacking among the religious leaders. The rich people put more in, although Jesus quickly characterizes them as doing so out of their "abundance" (12:44). Jesus, however, values the widow's comparatively modest contribution of two *lepta*, the smallest coins available, for her contribution. In fact, Jesus says counter-intuitively, that she "has put in more than all those who are contributing to the treasury" (12:43)!

Two things help to make sense of Jesus' strange math. First, Jesus calls together the *disciples*, of all people, to communicate this insight—and with solemn language ("truly . . ." 12:43). She is thus an example of discipleship that Jesus wishes to uphold. Second, she is described as casting in "all she had to live on" (12:44), that is, in the Greek, her whole livelihood. For all the bad examples of leadership and the inadequacies of Jesus' own disciples, she represents a positive example of what Jesus hopes to see in the temple.

It is precisely these elements that are important for the lectionary preacher. Proper 27 is a long way away from the strained context of conflict in Mark 11–12. These texts are prelude to Jesus' announcement of the destruction of the temple and his own passion. These themes seem far away, except for one fact. In the liturgical year, the end of the year is also its beginning. While Mark's eschatological discourse of Jesus returning on the clouds is a distant memory from Advent 1, the temple's prediction, which sets the stage for it, comes up in Proper 28. Preachers may wish to supplement the memory of those other texts in Mark 13 and 11 from the sweep of the liturgical year (Advent 1, Palm/Passion Sunday alt.) to place it all in context. For Mark, Jesus' entry to Jerusalem, prediction of the temple's destruction, and eschatology are all of a piece. Preachers need to bundle them back together—and with Proper 28 in the offing, this is still possible for the discerning preacher.

The result of such bundling will be to make sense in a deeper way of the two texts for Proper 27. As Joel Marcus points out, the rich persons and the widow represent not just a moral contrast of two examples, but offer rhetorically an eschatological reversal.[13] I would like to expand this insight out to both texts. With the condemnation of certain scribes in relation to widows and with seeing a certain widow exalted for her generosity in the same way Jesus does—by giving up his "livelihood"—we experience the first being last and the last being first. In a moment, the text points beyond itself to the coordinates of the whole Markan Gospel: a gospel of Jesus' identity, the coming reign of God, and what that means for disciples living in the midst of a ruined temple.

13. Marcus, *Mark 8-16*, 859–60.

8

An Apocalyptic Farewell Address (13:1-37)

INTRODUCTION

This is one of the briefest chapters of this commentary, comprised of a single chapter of Mark's Gospel. Yet it is also one of the most important. We have mentioned that much of this narrative of Jesus' life and ministry needs to be read in light of later first-century realities, especially the destruction of the temple. In this chapter, it is as if the narrated Jesus speaks *directly* to that late first-century context. After a brief narrated introduction with Jesus and some of the Twelve coming out of the temple, we have in essence one of Jesus' most extended speeches in Mark. Its directness as address must be observed.

The title of this chapter is called an Apocalyptic Farewell Address. This requires some comment. Both the apocalypse and the testament are genres of which we have several examples in intertestamental literature: for example most of *1 Enoch*, *4 Ezra*, *2 Baruch* for the former and the *Testament of Moses*, the *Epistle of Enoch* (one of the five books of *1 Enoch*) or the *Testaments of the Twelve Patriarchs* as examples of the latter. The genres of apocalypse and testament are both helpful with Mark 13 because many of them contain scenes with an apocalyptic revelation (*T. Levi* 3:9—4:1; *T. Mos.* 10:3-9; *1 En.* 91:5b-10 [Epistle], and *1 En.* 102:1-4 [Epistle]). In titling this chapter, however, we cannot say that Mark 13 is an apocalypse or a testament, but rather that it plays on apocalyptic, testament-like expectations. Jesus' speech has apocalyptic materials in it. Yet it is also spoken, as in the testament genre proper, as a speech by someone about to undergo death with a view to their future. Biblical commentator C. Clifton Black captures it nicely when he says this discourse in Mark 13 functions as an *Abschiedsrede*, a farewell address.[1] I use the language of apocalyptic and

---

1. C. Clifton Black, *Mark*, Abingdon New Testament Commentaries (Nashville: Abingdon, 2011), 264.

testament-like here not to signify its genre, but its mode—solely to illuminate the apocalyptic motifs woven into its testament-like function.[2] This chapter is, in fact, carefully integrated into Mark's Gospel as a whole, both drawing on the preceding material and pointing forward to chapters 14–16 as well.

The lead-up is important. We have seen Jesus step forward in the prologue as both the gospel's object (the gospel of Jesus Christ in 1:1) and subject (the gospel of God's proclaimer with his announcement of the kingdom in 1:14-15). This programmatic double-sense of gospel cued us in as readers that the Gospel of Mark would be about Jesus' mysterious identity as it unfolds in the narrative and about the reign of God that he proclaims in word and deed. The subsequent narrative, as we have seen, points to both sides of this gospel: sometimes focusing on the strange apocalyptic disclosure of who Jesus was in his miracles, exorcisms, and teachings; and sometimes focusing on the eschatological kingdom that he proclaims and enacts. This issue then becomes sharpened after Jesus' arrival in Jerusalem and the conflict we have seen escalate in chapter 12—now focused more than ever on Jesus' identity in the temple itself. But here the attention turns to the future and the community after Jesus' death and the temple's destruction. At one important point in this chapter, Jesus actually speaks about the necessity that the gospel first be proclaimed to all nations (13:10). In this way, chapter 13 embodies both the disclosure of who Jesus is and the kingdom he proclaims in connection to the apocalyptic gospel—just now spoken in the present tense to the readers and hearers of this late first-century narrative who have their own struggles with temple destruction and a new situation with Jewish religious leaders.

It may seem odd to note that a text that deals with apocalyptic futures may also connect to the immediate narrative to follow in Mark 14–16, but it most emphatically does. The speech talks about the importance of waiting and watching in 13:24-37, but Jesus' companions fail to do so as early as the Gethsemane scene in 14:32-52. The speech talks about cosmic disturbances like the darkening sun in 13:24, but Jesus' own death on the cross is marked by an

---

2. The language of genre and mode comes from literary critic Alastair Fowler's theory of genres and modes in *Kinds of Literature: An Introduction to the Theory of Genres and Modes* (Cambridge, MA: Harvard University Press, 1982). Genres refer to the cluster of formal and material features that communicate a genre and its expectations for the reader. Modes refer to a kind of afterlife of a genre in another genre through the presence of certain motifs in a new genre. I think Mark's narration of Jesus' speech plays with certain motifs of apocalyptic and testamentary literature here. For a more detailed treatment of Fowler's work as it pertains to those relationships in Mark 13, see my book *Preaching in the New Creation: The Promise of New Testament Apocalyptic Texts* (Louisville: Westminster John Knox, 1999), especially chapter 3. In emphasizing the testamentary function in this commentary, I am amplifying an element that was only implicit in my earlier work on apocalyptic forms in Mark 13.

apocalyptic-like darkening of the earth in the afternoon in 15:33. Finally, the speech reestablishes the apocalyptic frame of the whole Gospel, which leads to the strange resurrection scene of Mark 16:1-8. And as for the temple, the speech itself ends with the temple figure of a fig tree sprouting leaves. We know that the temple's destruction has been shaping so much of this narrative, including Jesus' own cursing of the fig tree in Mark 11. While the figure does not undo the temple's fate, it does seek to place its catastrophic loss in a wider horizon of God's good eschatological purposes. Again, it is a future that has to do with Jesus' identity and the reign he proclaims—in short, the gospel promise itself. But it is also only a promise that he can give just as he does in his apocalyptic, testament-like farewell address.

The internal structure of this section is fairly straightforward. The narrative context for the address is set with Mark 13:1-8. The disciples' confusion about the temple leads to questions about when this will be and what its accompanying signs will entail. Jesus responds with the beginning of his speech (13:5b-8), thus reframing their question that equates such signs with the end. In contrast, Jesus calls in the first half of his farewell address for a praxis of watching out (Mark 13:[5b-8], 9-23) for false signs (13:5b-8) and "for yourselves" (13:9-22), that is, for events that should not be confused with the end. In the second half of his speech, he focuses on the promise of seeing (the apocalyptic theophany of the Son of the human in 13:24-27 and the sprouting fig tree in 13:28-32) and God's ultimate purposes in connection with a praxis of "watching" (for the coming Lord in 13:33-37).

From a lectionary preaching point of view, the struggle with the texts of Mark 13 will be one of continuity. Mark 13:1-8, which is read on one of the last Sundays of the church year in Year B, follows nicely on some of the conflict stories of Mark 12 in the lead up to Proper 28. However, Mark 13:24-37 is the only part of the farewell address from the same chapter that is read—and that takes place almost a year prior on the *first* Sunday of Advent in Year B! Preachers will need to supply context for both occasions so that the prediction of the temple's destruction is seen as more than a fit of pique emerging from the conflict and is set in relation to God's eschatological purposes and in light of the apocalyptic gospel. Conversely, when Mark 13:24-37 is preached, the immediately preceding conflict in Jerusalem only deepens and offers historical rootage for the apocalyptic events that Jesus speaks of in this text. Our culture tends to hear apocalyptic language and *detach* it from context, treating it a little like one of Nostradamus's predictions or tabloid fodder. The connection back to Mark 12 highlights the meaning of the catastrophe that was the destruction of the temple, the difficulty of religious conflict thereafter, and the very importance of the gospel itself as it emerges in Mark 1–12 as a whole. Preachers will want to find a way to bring together what the lectionary has structurally pulled apart. Yet preachers will also find some help in the structure of the church year to do so. The end of one cycle and the beginning of the next cycle do share an eschatological interest. Preachers who sense this, and take advantage of it as a teaching opportunity, will find the narrative split just a little less problematic and may discover there a hidden opportunity for reclaiming eschatology as part of their working homiletical theologies as we struggle to make sense of God's purposes in our own situations of crisis and grief and interreligious relationships today.

PASSAGES OMITTED FROM THE LECTIONARY

The omission of Mark 13:9-23 is problematic in the sense that elements of the "watch out" parenesis (exhortation) that take place here are not given their full due. Although Jesus' apocalyptic, testament-like farewell address seems to reframe the disciples' questions about the end, there is a richness to this material that is nonetheless important. Here, for example, Mark's use of Danielic apocalyptic traditions comes closer to the surface. Moreover, its rich contextual connections historically help to ground a discourse that otherwise is easily misunderstood (let the reader understand!). Preachers who wish to preach one of the two lections from this chapter would also be wise to understand this pericope in connection to them, even if it is not the focus of preaching by itself.

PERSECUTION FORETOLD AND THE DESOLATING SACRILEGE (13:9-23): OMITTED FROM LECTIONARY

With this pericope, Jesus' apocalyptic farewell address continues. While vv. 5b-8 focused on watching out for false signs and being misled, here the focus shifts beginning with v. 9 to "watching out for yourselves." Here the promise is being brought to bear even more personally for the readers' situation. The address thus turns even more directly toward the Markan community. Indeed, what follows sounds like words for a community under duress. The parenesis covers three specific areas:

1. When they hand you over, don't worry (vv. 11ff.).
2. When you see the abomination of desolation, flee (vv. 14ff.).

3. When one says, "look, here is the messiah" don't believe it (vv. 21f.).

The focus throughout this first half of the speech is about "watching out." Here Jesus describes the signs to watch out for, even if they are not yet "the end."

In vv. 11-13, Jesus draws the hearers' attention to what they are likely experiencing in the chaotic context of the temple's destruction. The list of circumstances in the lead up in vv. 9-10 is dire—handing over to officials, beatings, standing before governors and kings. The term "handed over" is the same used for Jesus both in the passion predictions and in the passion narrative to come—thus, in this sense, Jesus' community will share in his fate. Yet they are characterized as moments of testimony and witness. Mark is clear to understand these moments as connected deeply with gospel proclamation. In fact, the timetable, the eschatological scenario that was implied by the disciples' question in the 13:1-8, is itself subjected to the divine necessity that the gospel be proclaimed to all nations first. The community therefore is invited in the midst of this chaos in vv. 11ff. not to worry about what to say. Indeed, the hearers are reminded that the Holy Spirit will be with them. But such calm amidst the storm is quickly broken yet again. In v. 13, the stock apocalyptic motifs continue with familial betrayals, death plots, and hatred for Jesus' name (*1 En.* 100:2, *4 Ezra* 5:9; 6:24). Yet, through all the admonition and chaos, a promise concludes the section in v. 13: "But the one who endures to the end will be saved." Mark's Jesus does not spare them with this difficult warning, and yet he does not leave his contemporary hearers without hope either.

The second section that warns of the abomination of desolation in vv. 14ff. poses difficult historical questions. Was Mark's material here first written in response to a historical event concerning Caligula's effigy in the temple decades prior? Was there some catastrophic event in the Jewish War in Mark's own time when certain revolutionaries or the general Titus violated temple space or a political figure set up some pagan altar or image? These questions are exceedingly important, but also exceedingly difficult to pin down decisively. Part of this is due to the allusive nature of apocalyptic language itself and the way its typologies play out over multiple historical periods. The language of the abomination of desolation appears in the book of Dan. 9:27, 11:31, and 12:11, where it speaks of an altar set up by Antiochus IV Epiphanes in a signal period of Jewish persecution. Its use here likely plays off that type, even if the language is so allusive that it makes our normal historical precision so difficult. Whatever the event, Mark wants to be sure that the reader understands. For us, the picture is a bit more difficult to understand except to say that Mark's

Jesus encourages his hearers to flee and realize their safety and ultimate destiny lies elsewhere. This fleeing does not include avoiding the pain of the historical moment: they are not fleeing suffering, but instead are to pity the pregnant or nursing and pray that the time of year will not make their egress difficult (vv. 18-19). Their only hope is in the idea that God can keep the suffering to a minimum by foreshortening the time for the sake of the elect. The warnings are mysterious, but not sensational. They are sobering, yet placed within the arc of divine action and purpose. In that sense, they actually point to the promise.

The final subsection in this first half of Jesus' apocalyptic farewell address concerns another round of messianic warnings in vv. 21f. Are these the same figures the Markan Jesus warned about in v. 6? Do they represent more false prophets who link certain persons or events to Christ's return? Again, the historical context admits several interpretive possibilities, none of which can claim to be nearly as obvious to us as the warnings may have been to Mark's community. Whatever it is, the advice from the Markan Jesus is the same: don't believe it. Consistent with the overall frame, these tribulations are not an immediate sign of the end. Therefore in 13:22b-23, Jesus returns to his opening theme: don't be led astray, but watch out.

LECTIONS

In an odd way, the reading of these two separated texts does serve the overall shape of the chapter. The omitted section is precisely what is downplayed in favor of what follows in 13:24-37. Still, the discerning preacher will want to provide context that will give a deeper meaning to the eschatological fireworks of this chapter. The reality of the temporal distance between the reading of Mark 13:1-8 at the end of Year B and the reading of 13:24-37 at its beginning, will require some work on the part of the preacher. For suggestions about the promise and struggles of doing so, see the chapter introduction above.

LECTION: THE DESTRUCTION OF THE TEMPLE FORETOLD
13:1-8; PROPER 28

The text begins with an important change of location and shifts early on to yet another one. After several scenes in chapters 11 and 12 where Jesus comes repeatedly to the temple and gets involved in a series of conflicts with religious leaders, eventually leaving them silent, Jesus now "comes out" of the temple. The moment occasions yet another misunderstanding from one of his disciples who remarks about the temple's grandeur. Jesus responds in v. 2 with a prediction of the temple's destruction. Given the significance of the temple as a sign of God's presence, the prediction is culturally, politically, and theologically problematic. It explains on the narrative level some of the reaction against Jesus to come. It also explains at the level of the text's late first-century readers why the words to follow matter so very much.

Yet because of his disciple's misunderstanding, the Markan Jesus is not through with this moment. The narrator places Jesus now *opposite* the temple, on the Mount of Olives, and in a seated position as teacher. This location seems to highlight the distance here—especially since the Mount of Olives is understood as a place of revelation and judgment.[3] It signals to the reader that what follows is again of revelatory and apocalyptic import. It is an important frame for the speech and undoes the disciple's misunderstanding of the moment.

The narrator thus lets us know that the misunderstanding is broader than one disciple's effusive comment. In v. 3b, four leaders of the Twelve ask Jesus privately about this—recalling how such private moments become occasions for Jesus clarifying his otherwise mysterious apocalyptic statements, parables, and revelations (including Mark 9:2). Because we as readers are present to overhear it, we, too, are privy to any revelation to follow. The four disciples present then ask two questions that will in turn shape Jesus' apocalyptic farewell address in 13:5b-37. The disciples wonder when this will be and the sign of their accomplishment. They wonder how this predicted event of temple destruction (13:1-2) relates to "all these things," namely, apocalyptic scenarios of the end.

In response, Jesus opens his nearly chapter long speech by telling his disciples to beware of being led astray. The word beware is actually a word meaning "watch out." Jesus is concerned that they are "looking for" the wrong thing with their question. His concern is that they might be misled if they are fixated on such signs. While he later in the speech gives them something to "see" in 13:24-27 and in 13:28-31 and something positive to watch for in 13:32-37, for now he wants in the first part of his speech to disabuse the disciples of their sign fixation. To do so, he speaks of several stock apocalyptic motifs: wars, earthquakes, famines. Yet he just as quickly reframes their importance. They are not the signs to focus on, nor are they even signs of the accomplishment of the end. They are the beginning of the birth pangs. This figure, too, is common in apocalyptic literature. In the prophetic literature of

---

3. D. E. Nineham notes the connection of apocalyptic judgment to Zech. 14:4 in particular in *The Gospel of Saint Mark* (Harmondsworth: Penguin, 1963), 342.

the Hebrew Bible (Isa. 13:8, Jer. 4:31, Hosea 13:13, Mic. 4:9, among others), the birth pangs are usually a figure of the suddenness and surety of divine judgment. In intertestamental apocalyptic literature (*1 En.* 62:4 and *4 Ezra* 4:40–42), however, it is often a figure of painful new birth.[4] The image is a common stock element in the messianic woes and functions to reframe the disciples' question here.

At the same time, all this apocalyptic language is not solely about events, but it is also about identity. In 13:6, the text mentions that part of the problem with being misled is believing in persons who make claims for themselves such as, "I am he!" The Markan Jesus seems to be concerned that those caught in the throes of such events might not just misread signs but be misled by false prophets or leaders, perhaps even confusing them for messianic figures. Not a few commentators note here the connection to the situation of the Jewish War when many such pretenders arose. At any rate, in this part of the text, Jesus wants to ensure that the disciples understand. The chaos of events around the temple's destruction and the questions of identity that ensue should not lead them astray. All these things are prefatory to the central eschatological revelation that is to come in 13:24ff.

Preachers dealing with this text will have an opportunity to counter some of the more speculative cultural interpretations of apocalyptic literature. While most of this text consists of dire predictions and misunderstanding, Jesus' own reframing of the birth pangs gives preachers a platform for articulating gospel in the midst of crisis and grief. A rich reading of the birth pangs tradition would likely yield a powerful sermon and a counterpoint to a wayward apocalyptic voyeurism in contemporary life.

LECTION: THE COMING OF THE SON OF MAN, THE LESSON OF THE FIG TREE, AND THE NECESSITY FOR WATCHFULNESS
MARK 13:24–37; ADVENT 1

After leaving the temple and surprising the disciples with both a prediction about its future and a series of warnings and exhortations about the tribulations to come, Jesus shifts his focus in the middle of his long apocalyptic farewell address. In 13:5b–23, he kept reminding the disciples (and the Markan community whose situation he was describing) to "watch out." In the second

---

4. I treat this figure as an apocalyptic motif in much greater detail in *Preaching in the New Creation,* 100–1.

half of the speech, however, Jesus wants them to "see" (13:26) and "learn" (13:28) so that they can now "watch" (13:33-37) in new ways by keeping "alert" and "awake." Although the disciples begin the speech by wondering whether the temple's destruction is the definitive sign of the end, Jesus' reframes their concern by redirecting their gaze from penultimate signs of tribulation to something really worth seeing and watching for: the coming of the Son of the human.

The structure of the second half of the speech helps us along. After so much "watching out" in 13:5b-23 with the verb *blepete* in Greek, the verbs of seeing suddenly shift in 13:26ff to "they will see" (*opsontai*) and "keep alert" (*agrypneite*) and "keep awake" (*grēgoreite*). Along the way, the Markan Jesus also gives us figures to look at as a way of understanding just what we are seeing: the shooting leaves of the fig tree in season and the analogy of the doorkeeper. These words of seeing and imagery help to organize the speech for hearers and readers:

13:24-27	Then they will see (v. 26)	Cosmic disturbances and Son of the human's arrival
13:28-32	Learn from the fig tree (v. 28)	Parable from nature
13:33-36	Watch/keep alert (v. 33)	Parable from everyday life
13:37	Keep Awake (v. 37)	Final Exhortation given "to all"

The apocalyptic farewell address thus gives a unified effect by altering the words of watching and seeing and postponing the most important thing to see toward the end of the speech. This structure reinforces the Markan Jesus' strategy of not assuming that signs of tribulation or even the temple's destruction are themselves "the end" but looking ahead to God's ultimate purposes with the return of the Son of the human and the praxis of watching that his coming sustains. This is the vision he wishes to leave the Markan community with his apocalyptic farewell address.

It begins in the first section by refocusing hearers' attention in vv. 24-27 with a visually arresting apocalyptic type scene called a theophany. The speech first tries to orient the readers to what they will see. In v. 24, the description begins with "in those days." This is eschatological language. It is then further separated from the preceding events of tribulation by referring to this new vision as "after that suffering." Once the Markan Jesus has indicated that this is now something qualitatively new in the speech, the theophany itself begins. In the Hebrew Bible, theophanies start with (A) God coming, speaking, or going forth and (B) as a result, nature being shaken or disrupted (Judg. 5:4-5; Amos 1:2; Isa. 13:9-10). In intertestamental apocalypses, the form takes a new shape by adding a third part to the form: (C) eschatological judgment and/or salvation. This threefold form of the *apocalyptic* theophany typically starts with (A) God coming/speaking/going out, moves to (B) cosmic disturbances, and ends with (C) a description of eschatological outcomes, usually salvation and judgment (*1 En.* 1:8-9; 60:6; 90:19; *T. Levi* 4:1; *4 Ezra* 7:36-38; 9:7-9; and 13:9-13).[5] In this *apocalyptic* farewell address, the Markan Jesus is not giving a full apocalypse, but is playing on the expectations of typical apocalyptic scenes to make his point. As a result, we need to pay attention to how the Markan Jesus both meets and thwarts the expectations of the apocalyptic theophany. First, we must acknowledge that all three elements are present here: coming of a divine figure cosmic convulsions eschatological outcomes. Where the Markan Jesus differs, however, is equally important. The theophany here begins with cosmic convulsions (sun, moon, and stars in vv. 24-25) and only afterward shows the Son of the human coming (with clouds in v. 26). If nothing else, this builds suspense—not a bad idea if your conception of the Son of the human is connected to his mysterious hiddenness as we have seen in the unfolding Markan narrative. The second change is, however, even more important. When it comes time for the eschatological outcomes in v. 27, the picture described is one of gathering in salvation—here, at least, divine punishment is absent. The angels are sent to "gather" the elect from the four winds and corners of the earth. Again, the Markan Jesus asks us to look beyond the signs of tribulation to the focal sign of the end: the arrival of the Son of the human to gather the elect.

Why the Son of the human? Many eschatological scenarios can be traced back to the mysterious Son of the human in Dan. 7:13. This text and this figure become central in many apocalyptic visions. Jesus himself draws on this tradition, although he is quick to contrast his notion of the hidden Son of the human to explain his mysterious, apocalyptic identity that is all tied up with suffering, death, and resurrection. Again, Jesus' variations on this tradition may be important here. In Dan. 7:13, the Son of the human ascends to rule; this Son

---

5. The nuances and variations of the apocalyptic theophany are explored in greater detail in *Preaching in the New Creation*, 41–44.

of the human arrives on Exodus-like clouds with the help of angels to gather and thus usher in God's reign.

Once the vision has been set out, the Markan Jesus continues to help his disciples understand its importance for discernment. The disciples asked to know when the end would be. Jesus uses a lesson from the fig tree (vv. 28-32) to help them understand. As in chapter 4 with the parable of the Sower, Jesus makes a case from nature. The fig tree, of course, was a symbol in chapter 11 of Jesus' curse because of the fruitlessness of temple leadership. Here, however, the fig tree helps to discern the times. When it sprouts leaves, summer is near. Likewise, you will know that he is near—just look for the sprouting leaves. Jesus then ties this notion with a prophetic statement in v. 30 that he gives with solemn words of assurance. Its promise that "this generation will not pass away" poses problems for interpreters, just as a similar promise did in 9:1. The subsequent statement in v. 31, however, may be relativizing the timeframe a bit. Even if everything does "pass away," Jesus' words will abide. Here the Markan Jesus is also rooting the claim in Jesus' reliability as prophet, which has been demonstrated time and again throughout the unfolding Markan narrative. At the very least, Jesus' own life, which includes so much of the apocalyptic stock materials (imploring his disciples to watch with him at Gethsemane, his handing over to the authorities, the crucial role of Judas in his disciple "family," or even the darkening of the sun as his crucifixion draws toward death), would seem to indicate one sense in which the promise is good. They will see these things come to pass—if not in an absolute sense, in a more imminent, parabolic, and mysterious one—in his path and theirs. If that is not clear, then v. 32 drives the point home. No one knows the *exact* day or hour: not angels, nor even the son—just the Father. The rest is speculation. In the meantime, the point of the parable is to reinforce hearers in how it shapes them here and now in their praxis of watching, to which we now turn.

In vv. 33-37, Jesus finishes his apocalyptic farewell address with another parable and a call to watch by keeping alert and awake. In v. 33, the familiar verb for watch reappears but now is paired with *agrypneite*, keep alert. In this section, Jesus turns to positive exhortation. Since one does not know the hour (an affirmation of v. 32) one should be at all times alert. Here the word for hour is *kairos*, which keeps the eschatological horizon of the figure in view. With v. 34 the parable itself ensues. A man goes on a journey and makes sure the slaves have tasks to do while instructing the doorkeeper to keep watch (*grēgore*). Everyone, in other words, should keep at their appointed tasks because no one knows when the householder returns—lest one be found asleep on the job when he does. In light of this, Jesus concludes the speech with one final appeal both to the four disciples hearing the speech and to any like us who read or hear it: with a word of watching for one and all—keep awake (*grēgoreite*). The figure is down to earth and thus transposes the cosmic discourse of apocalyptic eschatology into a more quotidian key. The question for those expecting signs is never about intellectual speculation or the management of timelines and scenarios but rather faithful living in indefinite expectation amidst the ordinary. This will be underlined by the subsequent narrative to come in Mark. Jesus' own passion is nigh. Will his disciples stay awake in that concrete moment? At which watch in the night will the crucial moment come? The Markan narrative draws us more deeply into the eschatological parable by placing Jesus' own disciples into just such a moment of discernment in Mark 14.

Preachers will find this relationship between Jesus' apocalyptic farewell address and the struggles of the disciples a helpful way to express eschatology. Eschatology is not some speculative enterprise. It is rather a future vision whose power is the way it impacts us in the present. Learning how to read apocalyptic material as we find in this speech of Jesus requires just such a homiletical-theological juxtaposition. Homiletician Martha Simmons puts it this way: "eschatology is where the sweet bye and bye meets the nasty here and now."[6] Mark's Jesus, who has been trying to teach his often-misunderstanding disciples the "way," might just concur. In the midst of struggle and suffering, eschatology is itself not a gift for the future, but for the present time.

---

6. Martha Simmons, introduction to *9.11.01: African American Leaders Respond to an American Tragedy*, eds. M. Simmons and F. Thomas (Valley Forge, PA: Judson, 2001), x.

9

The Passion of Mark's Gospel (14:1—15:47)

INTRODUCTION

Until this point we have been careful to place individual lectionary pericopes in close relationship to Mark's theologically driven narrative. While the section introductions were careful to integrate every pericope, whether it appears in the lectionary or not, into the overall Markan vision, here in this centrally important section of Mark, we step back from the trees just a bit to glimpse the forest. Mark 14:1—15:47 represents an important macro unit of Mark: the passion narrative. Here, more than any other place in Mark, it makes sense to stand back and appreciate the "whole." Much as one might step back just a bit when appreciating a major work of art hanging in a museum, Mark's passion narrative provides the kind of integrated theological artistry that should give us pause and maybe even invite us to try to see it whole. Our text is that important.

One reason we know this to be the case is the tradition itself. Although the four Gospels do not agree in every detail, the architecture of the passion narrative is fairly consistent across the four canonical Gospels. Since John is not normally reckoned as dependent on Mark in the way its synoptic cousins are, it may be that the reason for this is a preexisting passion narrative tradition, to which all four Gospel writers must rightly bow. However, it is also true that Matthew and Luke have very carefully taken up Mark's version for their own purposes. Although they do indeed redact what Mark has offered, the fact that they stay as close as they do to Mark's carefully wrought theological vision speaks volumes. Mark may offer us an unfinished theology (see Introduction), but the theology it does offer is profound and, through subsequent redaction of that tradition, clearly one that must be reckoned with.

The centrality of this narrative is also evidenced by its importance for Mark as a whole. We mentioned in the introduction that NT scholar Martin Kähler thought Mark represented a passion narrative with an extended introduction.[1]

While this statement does not actually sound like a compliment to Mark's narrative art, its backhanded nature does indicate at the least that Mark's passion story is clearly the highpoint of his narrative. Here so much of his artistry and thematic richness converges in a central moment. We have seen that Mark can indeed be a bit "stumpy-fingered" in his work, but here his narrative shines. We would be wise to attend to it in a special way.

We are aided in this move by the calendar and the lectionary. Much as the Markan narrative slows down from its breathtaking pace from the early Galilean ministry to the excursion to Caesarea Phillipi and then all the way up to Jerusalem, this part of the church year slows down the action to a crawl. Mark does not note just "days," but "hours" as they pass. We experience these two chapters of Mark in particular in a kind of narrated slow motion. The calendar, fortunately, has a similar intention in mind. The calendar is not content in this high season with touching lightly on texts from week to week, but invites us to slow down the action with a long reading on Palm/Passion Sunday and the carefully wrought days of Holy Week.[2] The calendar wants us to linger with these events and gives us liturgical room to do so. At the level of the lectionary itself, which depends on the structure of the calendar, this becomes clear. Palm/Passion Sunday includes generous options for reading all the passion narrative (Mark 14:1—15:47) or a major section (Mark 15:1-39 [40-47]) as an alternative reading for the day. Worship leaders will want to take advantage of this opportunity and avail themselves of it, especially if they intend to read the Markan resurrection narrative (16:1-8) as an alternative on Easter itself (Mark 16:1-8 is a regular reading for those congregations that observe the Easter Vigil).

The way in which Palm/Passion Sunday is itself celebrated is largely a help to the preacher who wishes to take the Markan passion narrative seriously. I can remember as a child our old Palm Sunday celebrations. While the idea of waving palm fronds and singing rousing Palm Sunday hymns was beautiful in its own right, the juxtaposition of the liturgy of the palms with that of the passion not only deepened the celebration, but gave it a tone much more resonant with Markan theology. But what I experienced as a change from older practice was actually a reclaiming of an ancient practice of observing the two together. If my childhood Palm Sunday sometimes tended toward

1. M. Kähler, *The So-called Historical Jesus and the Historic Biblical Christ*, trans. C. Braaten (Philadelphia: Fortress Press, 1964), 80, n. 11.

2. In Year B, Mark is the primary focus for Palm/Passion Sunday and the Easter Vigil that follows. The Johannine materials, which complement Mark's Gospel for parts of Year B, are the focus for Holy Week, with the Johannine passion narrative taking the lead on Good Friday itself.

simple triumphalism, the inclusion of the extended passion narrative as part of liturgical renewal helped to bring out ironic elements of the entrance to Jerusalem and Jesus' suffering and death in much more profound ways. We have noted throughout this Gospel that Mark offers a kind of theology of the cross, not in the sense of some finished atonement theory, but in the thought that the gospel itself is revealed mysteriously in its opposite, in weakness, rather than in triumphant power. This structural relationship in the day that is Palm/Passion Sunday helps us all to appreciate much more correctly the irony that attends Jesus' entry into Jerusalem (Mark 11:1-12) and strange testimony to gospel truth that attends Jesus even in his suffering and death on a cross. To this extent, the calendar and lectionary are friends to Mark's narrative theological vision.

What is neglected, of course, is the intervening material between the entry into Jerusalem and the passion itself: mostly Mark 11–13. Much of this material in Mark is omitted from the lectionary altogether. In part, its parallel versions are picked up in Year A when Matthew treats them. In other cases, especially parts of chapters 12 and 13, they show up either as Advent texts at the beginning of Year B or late Proper texts at the end. We know from our careful reading that the conflict with the religious authorities that comes out in the open in chapters 11 and 12 lays the groundwork for the unfolding action in the passion narrative. Jesus' relationship with the religious authorities there is one of the major drivers of the events described in 14–15. Without this, Sunday worshippers might not easily understand why the Galilean miracle worker whom Year B worshippers met in Epiphany is suddenly so strongly opposed when worshippers begin hearing more of the Markan narrative again after a several week Johannine stretch in Lent. When Mark 13 is not understood in relation to the passion narrative, some of its apocalyptic and eschatological character is lost. The commentary chapter on Mark 13 was careful to lift up and foreshadow the ways in which Jesus' apocalyptic exhortations were not solely matters of a distant concern, but took immediate shape in the passion narrative itself. In other words, in Mark's eyes Jesus' death is itself an eschatological moment. For hearers who fail to understand this, Mark's apocalyptic mystery of the gospel of Jesus' identity and reign-of-God announcement will become detached from these events. The risk is a loss of depth of Mark's vision. This loss requires careful work by the preacher who wishes, above all, to let the Markan passion narrative also connect up with the strange resurrection good news of Jesus' promise amidst the disciples' failure in Mark 16:1-8. In the end, care to such matters will aid in celebrating the gospel message that Mark is offering in all of its apocalyptic mystery.

While we can applaud the very focused use of Mark's passion narrative in this way, it also poses challenges for the preacher. The most obvious one is that few liturgies that include both a service of the Palms and the extended passion readings presuppose a full sermon. In fact, on such days, the sermon is most likely to be omitted altogether. This represents, of course, a hidden strength in allowing a full text to speak in its own voice. In an age of biblical illiteracy, this cannot be gainsaid. It is an opportunity for hearers to get a more ample grasp of Scripture through a very generous lection. The flip side, of course, is that these same texts also harbor some problems that we should be loath to leave unaddressed. Imagine reading a passion narrative, for example, where Jewish religious leaders receive the bulk of the blame for Jesus' death and the crowds in Jerusalem call for Jesus' crucifixion. It is not hard to imagine because this is precisely what we hear year after year: elements that reflect an intra-Jewish conflict in the first century and appropriated through a long history of pogroms and violence against Jews leading to the modern phenomenon of anti-Semitism. Scholars can argue whether anti-Jewish elements are present in one or more of the Gospel passion narratives, but it is hard to imagine that the problematic way we moderns hear such texts after centuries of Christian persecution of Jews would suddenly magically delete from our perceptions. Even on days when preachers do not preach a sermon, it may well become necessary to say in some capacity a word about the struggles of the first-century world that doesn't reactivate the anti-Semitism of the modern world. This is a profound ethical issue for contemporary Christian proclamation in a religiously pluralistic world.

Something similar could also be said about how we hear such narratives generally. It is sometimes hard for us to hear a passion narrative and not think in terms of Mel Gibson movies or rigid doctrinal formulations that make atonement almost sound something akin to child abuse. Each Gospel deserves an individual hearing on that account, if nothing else because they do not see all such things in the same way. Here preaching is valuable for clarifying what a text is *not* saying so we can clear away the clutter. Mark, for example, does not go into great grisly detail about Jesus' experience of suffering in the same graphic terms or contemporary cinematic tendencies toward the pornography of violence. Mark also makes only the most modest theological claims for Jesus' death and does so without the full benefit of anything like a doctrine of the Trinity either (which was much later developed). Preachers can help in such moments to let the otherness of Mark speak even while we come to terms with our own theological perspectives on such matters.

One of the most significant problems in this light is the break that happens in the reading of the Markan narrative over Year B. The problem of the disciples' emerging misunderstanding receives its fullest treatment in the middle of Mark—after his early Galilean ministry and before his entry into Jerusalem at 11:1. Many of these texts, if they do appear, show up in their most convicting form in the Season after Pentecost. In order for the longer text of Jesus' passion to be heard aright, something must also be noted about this important shift in Mark. Matthew, of course, softens this theme and gives Peter and the other disciples a much more constructive place in the narrative overall than Mark does (e.g., compare Peter's confession and response to the first passion prediction in 8:27-33 with the version in Matt. 16:13-23 as well as the disciples' general rehabilitation in Matthew's resurrection appearance in 28:16-20!).

Nonetheless, the structure of the lectionary also offers homiletical opportunities for preachers who wish to see the passion narrative whole. We will look first at how the lectionary sets up some important features of a holistic reading of Mark and then turn to some strategies for carrying them out given the shape of the liturgical day and the length of the Scripture reading prescribed.

Bracketing the epiphany readings—which focus so much on Jesus' Galilean reign-of-God ministry in all its wonder-working acclamation—are some crucial texts that together with the Epiphany readings can lay the groundwork for a more holistic celebration on Palm/Passion Sunday. In Advent 2, toward the very beginning of the Markan liturgical year, we benefit from reading Mark 1:1-8, the proclamation of John the Baptist, in two significant ways. First, the story of Jesus is set in close relation to that of John the Baptist as an Elijah-like figure. The imagery of Elijah preoccupies several sections of the passion narrative, thus calling to mind that Jesus' death is not some outlier. As a result, the Elijah imagery finds resonance not only in John's ministry, but in Jesus' own fate at the hands of the powerful (6:14-29, though read later in the year, could profitably be mentioned at this point). Second, this text lays down the important thematic that we have been highlighting throughout our close reading of Mark: the gospel of Jesus Christ [Son of God] in the title of 1:1. This theme is likewise taken up again at the Markan Gospel's passion narrative with the anointing at Bethany (14:9) at the beginning of our passion reading. This connection with Jesus' death will also be important for establishing Mark's unique concern for a theology of the cross, too.

After Jesus' early reign-of-God ministry, some of these same key elements of Mark's theologically-driven narrative are taken up again at the transfiguration and the beginning of the Sundays in Lent. In the Transfiguration (or alternate Lent 2) text, Mark 9:2-9, the gospel of Jesus' identity first disclosed to the reader in 1:1, together with its resonant text at Jesus' baptism in Mark 1:9, is reiterated in an apocalyptic-like revelatory moment on the mountain where the divine voice speaks: "This is my son." Again, this helps to carry forward central Markan themes that will aid in grounding the passion narrative's profound concern and ironic treatment of Jesus' identity. On Lent 2 this is also helpfully joined with a reading from Mark 8:31-38 as an alternate reading. Preachers who plan this process can thereby introduce key elements of Jesus' suffering, hidden Son of the human Christology, which so critically qualifies his identity in Mark; at the same time, through Peter's rejection of Jesus' passion prediction of suffering and death, preachers can also focus significantly on the disciples' misunderstanding. Again, this will have an impact on how Mark's theology of the cross helps shape the important passion narrative. Although the sequencing of many texts in Mark in the lectionary leaves something to be desired, there are indeed options in the Year B sequence that help to repair some of those holes and lay a groundwork for a powerful, holistic hearing of Mark 14–15 on Palm/Passion Sunday.

All of this, however, does not deal fully with the homiletical problem of a day with a long Scripture reading of the Markan passion. Many congregations on such days will heed the rubrics that advise letting the narrative itself be the focus for proclamation on that day. Time constraints in some communities may also make it less likely that preachers will have the latitude to develop a full sermon in conjunction with a liturgical day that already has two major parts: the liturgy of the Palms and that of the Passion. What are preachers to do?

One helpful thing to remember is that proclamation is neither limited to sermons nor to Scripture. In a sense, much of the liturgy is concerned with proclamation. Therefore preachers should not feel that proclamation on such days has to be a zero sum game. Careful planning can both anticipate the challenges we have identified above while also realizing the opportunities that we have begun to sketch here.

Earlier we identified that certain theological problems with the Markan narrative (anti-Judaism, concerns with the portrayal or understanding of suffering or violence, theological misunderstandings) and opportunities (ways of bringing in Mark's focus on his understanding of the gospel, its revelatory apocalyptic character, and the disciples' misunderstanding from Advent 2, Transfiguration, and Lent 2 texts) ought really be addressed at a time when we focus on the passion narrative. Both the challenges and the opportunities can be done in several ways.

Sometimes Scripture readings can be introduced with brief comments that frame the text for the hearers. With just a few sentences, the reader can prepare the hearers to engage fully with the text. This requires great economy of speech on the part of the pastor or other worship planner. When done well, however, it will at least place issues before the congregation so it can hear the texts with deeper discernment.

Another option might be for a preacher to do a short homily that frames up a special concern or thematic focus. In congregations where there are specific histories with violence, abuse, or theological misunderstanding, this could be particularly useful. That being said, the brevity of such an option will prove challenging to pull off in other circumstances. The length of the reading will probably force preachers to engage in some homiletical triage! Whether one wants to link up earlier understandings from the lectionary readings or head off problematic interpretations, the preacher will likely need to make careful, limited choices here.

Yet another option is to consider how other parts of the liturgy might aid in deepening understanding, particularly around the problematic portions of the passion narrative. Imagine, for example, that the Prayers of the People include opportunities for congregants to pray for victims of violence or religious prejudice. One could also think of how such prayers might build on themes of the passion narrative so that Jesus' gospel of the suffering, hidden Son of the human and the reign of God might open up new venues for God's work among us broken disciples, again, including standing up for victims of violence or religious intolerance. In such cases, the prayers might also lift up Markan counter-narratives that work against the way some of these texts have been *misused* in Christian history.

Finally, while teaching adult education courses on the Markan passion narrative takes us outside of the realm of worship, such work can also aid the preacher on a Sunday where a full sermon may not be feasible. In this case, it is important to note that the functions of teaching and proclamation, while not always identical, are indeed both central to the gospel in its fullness. Such a move will also serve to deepen worship and the general participation of the laity, especially if it opens to wider conversation about the Markan text in light of our own context today. For that matter, opportunities to deepen relationships with groups working against violence in a community or those working for interreligious understanding will give hands and feet to these concerns whether the passion narrative texts are read in worship or studied in a classroom. A whole ministry approach to this problem can help all around for this central season of the church year.

Lection: The Markan Passion Narrative
14:1—15:47: Palm/Passion Sunday

The outline of this section is somewhat different from the other chapters of this commentary. Our focus here will be on the structure of the whole Markan passion narrative; its individual pericopes will fade a bit from view. Yet while we focus on the plot structure of the whole two chapters, we will also be trying to grasp Mark's unique way of helping us understand this story in terms of its plot structure, narrative rhetoric, setting, and characterization. Throughout, we will try to draw some conclusions about Mark's narrative theology in 14–15 and then shift to our own homiletical-theological task in interpreting Mark's passion narrative in today's contexts.

Plot Structure

The structure of Mark's passion narrative is, for many of us, second nature. We are so accustomed to hearing it unfold during this season that it helps to slow it down to see it whole.

Chapter 14 has a distinctive shape that is worth noting. This chapter begins and ends with two "intercalations," Markan narrative sandwiches, that are designed to frame our reading and hearing of this narrative. I outline chapter 14 this way:

- Intercalation
  − The chief priests and scribes plot to kill Jesus, but not during the feast (14:1-2).
      · The woman's anoints Jesus for burial at Bethany, evoking an instantiation of the gospel (14:3-9).
  − Judas plots with chief priests against Jesus at the "right time." (14:10-11)

- Jesus' foresees the preparations and provisions for Passover (14:12-16).

- Jesus predicts his "handing over" while sharing Last Supper with disciples (14:17-22).

- Jesus predicts scattering of disciples, resurrected leadership to Galilee, and Peter's denial on the way to the Mount of Olives, though disciples reject the predictions (14:27-31).

- Jesus prays at Gethsemane, struggles with God, resigns himself to God's will, but finds disciples unable to support him through the night to face this "hour" (14:32-42).

- Jesus is arrested at Gethsemane and the disciples flee (14:43-52).

- Intercalation
  - Peter follows from afar to the courtyard outside Jesus' interrogation at the High Priest's place (14:53-54).
    - The religious leaders accuse Jesus in vain, but in response to the High Priest's question, Jesus reveals himself and brings their judgment upon him (14:55-65).
  - Peter conceals himself and denies Jesus three times (14:66-72).

The intercalated stories at the beginning and end of chapter 14 help to frame this most difficult part of the narrative. Two central issues about this structure help to focus our attention.

First, one of the chief problems with the unfolding story has to do with awful events that happen to Jesus and their connection with the story's characters. The first intercalation frames the story by helping us to see a narrative that has human agents who are responsible for their actions as well as a divine purpose that works both through and despite them. At the very beginning, the chief priests and the scribes indicate their desire to see Jesus die—although they do not wish to do it during the feast. At the end of the intercalation, we learn that Judas has decided to work with them to hand over Jesus "at the right time." We learn, of course, in the unfolding of the narrative that the religious leaders' earlier stated desire not to do so "during the feast" is thwarted. The chief priests and the scribes may perceive themselves as the agents in this situation, but they fail to understand the deeper divine purpose in the whole. This is revealed in the intercalated story of the anointing at Bethany in between. Even though some present at the dinner at Simon the leper's fail to see the significance of the moment when the woman lavishly anoints Jesus, Jesus understands it in two key ways: as his anointing for burial *and* as an instantiation of the gospel, for which he solemnly predicts she will be remembered. Jesus' death is coming. Some people think they alone are engineering it. Underneath, however, is a lurking divine purpose in the gospel. From here on out in the passion narrative, we must be aware both of human responsibility *and* divine purpose. As an example from later in the narrative, Judas will betray Jesus, yet the verb used in Greek, *paradidōmi*, also means to "hand over," which is the mysterious word used for divine action concerning the handing over of the suffering servant in the LXX. Such is the mystery of human and divine agency in the Markan passion. This intercalated story at the beginning of Mark 14 provides a frame for the upcoming passion as a whole. Jesus is sovereign, but many others think they are in charge. Jesus is passive after his arrest, but only because he is resigned to the divine will. This drives a lot of the irony going forward where characters do not understand why Jesus does not save himself if he can save others. He won't because he can. Although Mark never really explains it explicitly, he views Jesus' death as a ransom (10:45), a serving and suffering for setting free.

Second, the intercalated stories of Mark 14 also set up the diverging paths of Jesus and his disciples. As the narrative of chapter 14 unfolds, these divergences become clearer through several predictions that Jesus makes about himself, his disciples generally, and Peter specifically. All this comes to a head in the other bookended intercalation of chapter 14: the story of Jesus' confession embedded in Peter's denial (14:53-72). The way Mark tells the story is not just of Jesus' trial, but a double trial in which Jesus makes the good confession and Peter retreats crying into the night with nothing but his own denials ringing in his ears. The intercalated story seals their fates. Going forward, the disciples are absent from the story. After this scene, Jesus is no longer the same agent as before—in fact, he hardly even speaks in chapter 15. But in between the two intercalated bookends of chapter 14, Jesus does reliably predict many things about the disciples and himself and thus shows he is not the fated victim. He knows full well what comes and he submits to it willingly. What is more, even amidst all the predictions of failure about his disciples, the promise still comes. It comes in Bethany when he predicts that wherever the gospel is preached, the woman who anointed him for burial will be remembered. The gospel, even as it embraces Jesus' anointing for death, moves out ahead. We discover as well in 14:28, that even amidst all the predictions of falling away and fleeing of his disciples, Jesus embeds yet another promise: "But after I am raised up, I will go before you to Galilee." At the moment the disciples do not even seem to hear it, but there it is. Human failure does not mean divine failure. The promise moves ahead. Perhaps, as Donald Juel puts it, Jesus' resurrection after our passion narrative means he is "on the loose."[3]

All this is important as we turn now to chapter 15. From this point we turn away from the Jewish world of chapter 14 to the gentile context of the Roman imperium in chapter 15. Jesus is sent now bound to Pilate, who pursues his own investigation and takes his own course of action. The events that follow now juxtapose Rome's purposes and those of God. Because the intercalations of chapter 14 have helped to set up this dynamic of human and divine agency, the events surrounding Jesus here take on power both for what they are and the ironic truth to which they bear witness.

- Trial before Pilate as "King of the Jews" and the release of Barabbas to the crowd (15:1-15)

- Soldiers mock Jesus as King (15:16-20)

- Jesus goes to Golgotha (15:21-24)

- Jesus is crucified as "King of the Jews" (15:25-32)

- Cosmic events at the death of Jesus (15:33-41)

- The burial of Jesus' body before the Sabbath (15:42-47)

The first thing to note is the change of terms. Although the trial before Pilate has many of the same features of the trial at the High Priest's place in the previous chapter, the charges are different. The careful use of traditional language in the Jewish context has now given way to a Roman perspective: the concern whether Jesus is "King of the Jews" or not. From the Roman perspective, the idea that Jesus was a political rival to Rome was all that

3. Donald Juel, *A Master of Surprise: Mark Interpreted* (Minneapolis: Fortress Press, 1994), 120.

mattered. Never mind that a Jewish messianist would never use the title "King of the Jews"! The issue in chapter 15 is Roman power. Yet, in his way, Jesus deals with imperial claims by holding to the divine purpose that has claimed his will from the beginning. Along the way, there are a few surprises. Jesus' death is not simply just one more under Roman management. From the sixth to the ninth hours, the sun is darkened, a sign of theophany that turns this from just one more Roman execution to a death of eschatological significance. At the point of his death, the curtain of the temple is ripped in two—the same verb that describes how the skies were "ripped open" at his public baptism in chapter 1! What is more, whether in truth or in biting irony, even the Roman centurion makes a confession in 15:39: "Truly this man was God's Son." This death is more than just another imperial execution—it is an eschatological event. In the narration, both elements come through: human plotting and divine purposes, the disciples' failure and Jesus' eschatological promise. Structurally, the Markan passion narrative invites us more deeply into the mystery of the gospel that is Jesus' identity and the reign of God to which he looks forward.

NARRATIVE RHETORIC

Here we consider how Mark narrates his story and the rhetorical effect of it. It is this juxtaposition of human agency and divine purpose and the disciples' failure and Jesus' eschatological promise that shapes our perception as readers. The narrator portrays Jesus as offering a reliable point of view for the unfolding events. Time and again, Jesus uses the solemn language of prophetic speech ("Truly I tell you . . .") to introduce elements of the story going forward: both the promise of the gospel (14:9, 25) and the failure of the disciples (14:18, 30). The latter in particular add to the authority of Jesus' point of view by coming to pass within the scope of the narrative itself. Jesus' prophetic predictions are reliable and show he is prescient and no victim of circumstance, let alone someone else's machinations. The same point of view is also born out in some of the other less solemn details. Jesus correctly predicts how the disciples will find a place to celebrate the Passover. They "found it just as he told them!"

Often this point of view is bolstered by Scripture, whether explicitly quoted or implied. If there is a divine necessity (*dei*) that governs the plot of this Gospel as a whole, it receives much of its characteristic shape by being grounded in Scripture. In the passion narrative, four texts in particular come most clearly into play: Zechariah, Daniel, the Psalms, and Isaiah. The first two texts Jesus essentially quotes to bolster what he says. As he announces on the way to the Mount of Olives that the disciples will fall away, he roughly quotes

Zech. 13:7 to describe what will shortly happen at the end of Gethsemane: "I will strike the shepherd, and the sheep will be scattered." The disciples object, but in a scant few verses, they do in fact scatter into the night. Daniel 7 and Psa. 110 are also quoted directly in Jesus' revelation before the High Priest at his interrogation. While agreeing with the High Priest that he was "the Messiah, the Son of the Blessed One," he goes on to quote pieces of Dan. 7:13-14 and Ps. 110:1 to qualify the sense in which he understands himself messianically: that is, Jesus is Son of God in that he is the hidden, Son of the human at God's right hand, whose vindication is coming together with the clouds. While this language takes us beyond the narrative itself to the future, it lends its own hidden, eschatological authority to Jesus' claim to be who he claims to be even as he faces conflicting charges and accusations before the High Priest. Many other psalms also give credence to the difficult story of Jesus' passion in Mark. Most do so, however, with the faintness of allusion rather than in recognizable quotes. Here two sets of texts stand in a special relationship to Mark 14 and 15: the psalms of the righteous sufferer and Isaiah's suffering servant. Although several Psalms play important roles in Mark 14–15, two in particular are repeatedly sources of allusions: Psalms 22 and 38.[4] Psalm 22 is practically a subtext and sometimes roughly quoted for the events around Jesus' mockery, crucifixion, and death in 15:24-38, including the important cry of abandonment in 15:34. Psalm 38 shows up more than once in connection with Jesus' silence before his accusers. The effect, whether as allusion or near quote, is to saturate the claims of divine purpose in this narrative with familiar texts and images of Scripture, thus rendering Jesus' point of view about his plotted death theologically plausible and even compelling. The same holds for Second Isaiah's suffering servant. In Mark 14:65, the description of Jesus' physical treatment after his confession in 14:6 and the High Priest's charge of blasphemy, certainly is reminiscent of Isa. 50:6. Again, so much of what happens here gains plausibility as part of the divine purpose by virtue of its resonance with traditions from Isaiah.

The effect of the narrator's art is to make it possible for us as readers to see and understand what many of the characters within the narrative cannot. Jesus' claims about God's purpose are not simply absurd or blasphemous but cohere with the Scriptures themselves. This gives us as readers some ironic distance that characters in the story do not seem to possess. That for which Jesus is mocked, ridiculed, and even executed, he truly is. It is as a matter of narrative rhetoric

---

4. Joel Marcus offers a helpful table cataloging the relationships between several psalms of the righteous sufferer and Mark's passion narrative in *Mark 8-16*, Yale Anchor Bible (New Haven, CT: Yale University Press, 2009), 984.

an embodiment of the very theology of the cross we have been mentioning through these pages. This becomes important for the way in which the Markan narrator deals with these events and the resurrection to come. The disciples in Mark fall away and disappear from the narrative. And yet the promise is still given: both here in the passion narrative and in chapter 16. The relationship to the reader as someone who has an understanding of these events *different* from Jesus' own disciples is absolutely crucial to what happens after the story. The reader plays a key role in this part of the Markan narration and in the events that unfold out of it.

SETTING

Through much of the commentary, we have noted how elements of the Exodus story have influenced Mark's narration of the Gospel. With the passion narrative this comes even more to the fore.

The plotting revealed that the religious leaders wished to see Jesus killed, but not so as to disturb the feast (14:2), lest the people riot. This is one of the first expectations overturned by the Markan passion. The events of the narrative are closely related, day by day, almost hour by hour, to observances around Passover and the Feast of Unleavened Bread. This Mark notes by important day and time references that occur at several points in the narrative: 14:1, 12, 17 and 15:1, 25, 33, and 42. They help to mark the passing of significant times for the narrative: the beginning of the feast, the time for the Passover celebration, the crucial hours of Jesus' passion, and even as indicators of a coming Sabbath. Though the leaders wished to avoid doing things during the feast, the story is saturated by Passover.

The observance, of course, recalls the Exodus itself, Israel's primal story of slavery and freedom. It offers a profound sense of God's liberative purposes to the moment. In the time of Jesus, the feast had gathered to it a strong eschatological sense. At a time of imperial oppression and colonial power, the Passover pointed to God's intentions for Israel: not slavery, but freedom. This connected deeply to Jesus' ministry both here and elsewhere in the Gospel, as we have noted. We recall, for example, the profound Exodus imagery that surrounded the feedings of the five thousand and the four thousand in Mark 6:30-44 and 8:1-10 respectively. Here, during the Passover, we witness Jesus celebrating the paschal meal with his disciples. Later and with frankly sparse description of anything that looks like a Passover rite, he uses the familiar pattern we saw in the feeding stories. Jesus takes, blesses, breaks, and gives. While this Passover meal, as Mark portrays it, lacks several of the distinguishing marks we would expect, Mark's Jesus clearly celebrates it to make a point about what God has done and what God is doing as Jesus shares the meal with the very disciples about to fail him. Jesus uses the context to make a Christological point about his body and blood, his coming suffering and death. What is more, Jesus joins this to one of his prophetic sayings in 14:26: "Truly I tell you, I will never again drink of the fruit of the vine until that day when I drink it new in the kingdom of God." In doing so, he underlines the eschatological focus both of the Passover setting and the meanings he imbues it with in the Last Supper. He orients this night, where he shares Passover and offers his body and blood as signs, toward God's eschatological purposes.

All of this has a secondary effect in the unfolding narrative. The importance of the feast and times around it also highlight the strangeness of the action of Jesus' trial. That such an event should happen during the feast only underlines its injustice. From sundown on the Passover to sundown the next day Jesus celebrates the paschal meal with his disciples, prays in Gethsemane while his friends fade and flee, gets arrested, interrogated, and accused before the High Priest and religious leaders, is sent off to Pilate for judgment, is mocked, marched off to Golgotha, is crucified, died, and is buried. Mark wishes to link these events closely to Passover. John, by contrast links Jesus death to the day of Preparation. Mark is precisely making his point about these events by narrating the setting of the story as he does.

Yet, this eschatological sense of Passover is not all that is at stake. This story comes on the heels of Jesus' apocalyptic farewell speech in Mark 13. As we have noted, it carries forward many of the same notions of waiting, watching, apocalyptic theophany, and other cosmic signs. Mark helps elaborate this not only by repeating those themes in Gethsemane's scene of keeping awake and eschatological testing/temptation in 14:32-42, Jesus' confession as the Son of the human coming with the clouds at 14:62, and the cosmic portents that attend Jesus' death in 15:33-37. Mark also reminds us of "the hour" that is coming and indeed has come. All this is to say, again, that the sequence of events leading to Jesus' death is not just one thing after another. It represents eschatological time. It is God's future impinging on the present. To the degree we readers grasp the setting Mark gives to the narrative, we make ourselves available to Mark's Gospel of the gospel. The good news is Jesus Christ, Son of God, understood as the hidden Son of the human in the midst of suffering, death and resurrection. Yet it also points to the gospel of God he announces: God's kingdom purposes that even now are drawing near.

CHARACTERS

Finally, we turn to the characters as they are portrayed in the Markan narrative. We look chiefly, of course, at Jesus and the disciples, but we must also make note of Jesus' opponents and even the lesser-known characters and the crowds. We noted earlier in this chapter the history of anti-Judaism that attends Christian abuse of these stories. We need to read the development of characters critically in order to see what Mark is really writing. They will all help us understand the gospel that Mark is intending to proclaim.

JESUS

Jesus is the center of this narrative. We have mentioned the shift in how his character functions in chapters 14 and 15. In chapter 14, Jesus is disclosed as having insight into the unfolding events. He uses prophetic speech to make announcements of what will be happening concerning the gospel remembrance of the woman and her alabaster jar at his anointing for death, his handing over/betrayal by one of his disciples, his future enjoyment of wine in the kingdom, and Peter's threefold denial. Chapter 14 helps us see the complex relationship between his opponents' plotting and the divine plot of his passion and resurrection. It does not turn Jesus into a victim of those events. He goes knowingly to his death, even if it grieves him deeply. In chapter 15, however, Jesus is no longer active, but passive. He remains silent through most of the events around his trial, mockery, crucifixion, and death. Yet this grows also out of his obedience to God's purposes. It is "necessary" that the Son of the human suffers and dies and after three days is raised—Jesus has been saying this since Caesarea Philippi in chapter 8. In fact, when he is arrested, he disputes the tactics of those coming with weapons by night to Gethsemane. After all, he had been teaching in the temple openly and peacefully. Still, he reasons, the Scriptures ought to be fulfilled (15:49). But this statement is no exercise in exegesis. For Jesus, it is about acknowledging the divine will.

This does not negate, however, the profound humanness of his portrayal in Mark's passion. Jesus is no automaton here. He is dining with Simon the leper when he praises a woman for anointing him for burial. He is dismayed and distressed in Gethsemane and describes his soul as grieved unto death. He falls down on the earth to pray that the hour might pass him by and even asks God to take this cup away, before reaffirming the divine will. Who can forget his cry of abandonment on the cross or his loud cry when he breathed his last? Jesus is resolved to living out God's will, but he does not do so stoically. This Jesus dies no antiseptic noble death of the hero. He dies in solidarity with a fearful, suffering humanity. In doing so, Mark does not resolve mysteries of suffering, but sets them out for us to see in struggle. Mark does not benefit from a later theology of the Trinity that tries to explain that suffering in light of the relationships of the persons of the Trinity. Jesus offers something less finished and more paradoxical. Mark as narrator leaves us room to continue the struggle even while we hold to the promise that animates Jesus to the end.

And yet in this story, Jesus is ultimately defined theologically by the disclosure of his identity that happens before the High Priest—a revelation toward which the whole story of a hidden, suffering, messianic Son of the human has been pointing pretty much in secret until now. When questioned repeatedly either here or at Pilate's, Jesus is largely unresponsive. Yet when the High Priest asks if he is the "Son of the Blessed One," Jesus says "I am." He then goes on to speak publicly of what he understands by that, recapitulating much of the mysterious disclosure that Mark's Gospel has rehearsed over fifteen chapters about the Son of the human. Yet here in 14:62, Jesus also claims the identity of God's Son or Messiah that the Markan narrator has disclosed only piecemeal until now, especially in Mark 1:1, 1:11, 8:29, and 9:2. The revelation is a crucial one and occurs in a kind of theophanic and epiphanic shape. It is a crucial, disclosive moment of Jesus' character.

THE DISCIPLES

We have already noted that the plotting and the narrative rhetoric place the readers in a strange relationship with the disciples. We tend to understand better than those ostensibly closest to Jesus. This is nothing new. We noted earlier in Mark's Gospel that the disciples often failed to understand Jesus' identity and what it meant for discipleship in particular. It was Peter who rebuked Jesus at the first prediction of the passion in chapter 8. It was the disciples who struggled to understand not only parables and teachings, but miracles of feeding as in Mark 6 and 8. But the narrative never really gave up on them. Blind Bartimaeus reminded us as readers that blindness can also be a halfway state of seeing, while not seeing fully. Yet in the passion narrative, the disciples fall away at Jesus' arrest and do not reappear again.

Yet two disciples stand out for individual treatment. Judas is portrayed as plotting with Jesus' opponents and at Jesus' arrest uses a kiss as a signal to hand him over. Mark is not terribly interested, however, in developing Judas as a character. His portrayal is fairly flat in Mark's passion narrative and helps mostly to carry out his function in the plot. By contrast, Peter is developed somewhat more as a full character. Jesus' prediction about his denial causes Peter to protest in 14:29. Peter continues in Jesus' favored company with James and John (as at the transfiguration in 9:2) during Jesus' difficult night in Gethsemane in 14:33ff. Still, Peter fails the test so dismally that Jesus reverts to calling him Simon (14:37), his name before his call. To his credit, after the other disciples flee, Peter still manages to follow from afar to the High Priest's courtyard, but even there, as Jesus confesses his identity, Peter denies three times. Peter is a conflicted character and helps to highlight both the possibility and the distance between Jesus and those who follow. Although the disciples get rough treatment in Mark, especially compared to the other Gospels, even the Markan narrator has not given up on Peter altogether. In chapter 16, the young man in white at the tomb will urge the women to share news of resurrection with the disciples and, yes, Peter, too.

In this context it is probably best to mention the other young man in Mark's passion narrative. In 14:51–52, he makes a brief cameo appearance at Jesus' arrest. This odd, mysterious story has unleashed a lot of speculation and a few scholarly surprises. Suffice it to say that the young man is a further representative of the disciples (he is said to be "following him" in 14:51), whose naked state describes nicely the fleeing vulnerability they all embody. Perhaps the murky circumstances of his mention helps to underline the mystery of the gospel itself!

THE RELIGIOUS LEADERS: CHIEF PRIESTS, SCRIBES, ELDERS, AND THE SANHEDRIN

The opponents tend to function more as a group and Mark does not always differentiate well between them. One gets the impression from Mark's narrative that the chief priests and the High Priest in particular play a more central role—especially at the high point of the narrative when Jesus is being interrogated by him. The scribes, elders, and the rest of the Sanhedrin tend to function in relation to whatever the chief priests are doing. When they appear, they tend to be listed as part of a series of agents and in relation to the chief priests. Mark does not identify the High Priest by name, although historians believe it would have been Caiaphas. This may be because Mark's interest is not in developing them as characters, but in letting them play a function in the plot. Because of the history of Christian anti-Judaism, Christian preachers may want to resist flattened characterizations that tend to reinforce ancient hatreds. Perhaps some insight into the role of the chief priests in the society and politics of the time would at least allow preachers to represent the situation with greater nuance and complexity. Mark also helps us by portraying one such leader, a respected council member by the name of Joseph of Arimathea, as "waiting expectantly for the kingdom of God" (15:42) and therefore ready to see to it that Jesus receives a proper burial before the Sabbath. This brief character cameo stands against any attempt to paint all Jewish religious leaders with a single brush. Preachers today might want to follow Mark's lead here.

THE CROWDS

The same could also be said for the crowds in Mark's passion. The crowd in the Gospel has tended to favor Jesus, which posed a *problem* for religious leaders when they sought to oppose Jesus. The scene with Barabbas, however, is one where the leaders seem to succeed in turning the crowds against Jesus (15:11-15). It is important to remember here as well that flattened portrayals of Jewish persons are not even consistent with Mark's Gospel as a whole. Preachers should always read such texts with discernment.

INDIVIDUAL CHARACTERS IN CAMEO

Perhaps the strongest characters alongside Jesus in the Markan passion narrative are the women who are portrayed. The woman who anointed Jesus in 14:3-9 comes off best of all among all those around Jesus. She correctly perceives the situation and Jesus' coming absence and embodies the gospel with her actions—which Jesus himself predicts will be remembered. In the shadow of difficult stories of rejection, suffering, and death, she finds a way for the gospel to be heard. Some of the other women around Jesus show constancy—even if from a distance (15:40)—that the male disciples do not after they scatter at Jesus' arrest. Women are mentioned toward the end of the passion narrative as witnesses both to Jesus' death and burial. Since they are mentioned by name, "Mary Magdalene, and Mary the mother of James the younger and of Joses, and Salome" (15:40), clearly their witness is of value and importance to the tradition, especially in terms of the empty tomb of Mark 16.

There are other characters that could be mentioned. Like the women, they often tend to be faithful or at least promising when the male disciples are not. Such characters tend to appear almost elliptically in passing: Simon the leper; Simon of Cyrene, the father of Alexander and Rufus; servants; attendants; the centurion and other soldiers. But what Mark paints chiefly in the passion narrative is a riveting, well-peopled scene rich with humanity and seemingly graced above all with Jesus' own vulnerability tilted mysteriously toward God's eschatological promise of the kingdom.

HOMILETICAL THEOLOGY

With this section we move from a close reading of the passion narrative itself to an interpretation of Mark's narrative theology of the gospel. The goal here is a proximate one. While no interpreter can interpret without leaving at least a few fingerprints on the object of study, the goal here is to try to let Mark's theology speak in its otherness even while dialoging with it today. Along the way, this requires critical judgments and weighing options: what should be foregrounded, what should remain in the background? The result will be, of course, a partial one. But the goal is worthy: to try to let Mark's theology come through in its own terms, consistent with what has been narrated, but also to engage it for today as an act of contemporary theological understanding. Because the passion narrative does not deal with the whole of theology, what results here is piecemeal. These represent some key elements of a Markan narrative theology and not anything like what we would consider a full systematic treatment. Mark, we now realize, wrote a Gospel on the move linked together with adverbs like "immediately" and more *kai* conjunctions than you can shake a stick at. If we want a more finished Gospel, we might turn to Matthew, Luke, or John—all of whom probably wrote later. I would also like to contend, however, that Mark's *theology* is also unfinished because it was written at a time of crisis, perhaps even trauma. It offers opportunities for reframing and reorienting our own settled perspectives—and that is good. At the same time, it struggles at points to deal with theological problems and work them through, in part because it is likely written at a time of grief. We need to let Mark be Mark, but his theology does not exist solely for us to accept it uncritically. Therefore, we will conclude this chapter with our own homiletical theology, an attempt not to think Mark's thoughts, but to think *with Mark* toward our own time and place, one marked by celebrating Palm/Passion Sunday in the twenty-first century.

ESCHATOLOGY

We begin, uncharacteristically, with eschatology. Most systematic treatments end with eschatology because of our embarrassment over "the last things." For most moderns it is best to tuck eschatology away in the attic and hope no one asks too many questions. Mark, however, seems thoroughly enamored with eschatology, occasionally shifting into an apocalyptic mode. Mark's Gospel, narratively speaking, is *not* an apocalypse, but like many literary genres, the

Gospel of Mark is capable of shifting into the apocalyptic mode, often with the use of apocalyptic symbols, motifs, and forms. To discuss the apocalyptic mode is not to reduce Mark's eschatology to this type, nor is it to assume that apocalypses are only about eschatology. In fact, apocalypses have keen concerns that overlap elsewhere in Mark's narrative: concerns for divine revelation, transcendent realities, otherworldly intermediaries, and sometimes even spatial interests in supernatural worlds, not just eschatological times.[5] Other students of apocalypses have noted that they are also interested in heavenly mysteries, not just future times.[6] In asserting that Mark narrates the Gospel in an apocalyptic mode, it is to say that Mark evidences concerns for features that are common in apocalypses and related literature from the time. Along the way we have been highlighting ways in which Mark's theology generally *and his eschatology specifically* have been given an apocalyptic cast. All this helps to show Mark's unique way of looking at things and narrating his Gospel of the gospel of Jesus Christ and the kingdom to which he points.

The apocalyptic side of his eschatology comes through in the way Mark narrates the significance of Jesus final days and hours. In fact, Mark's use of the word "hour" has an eschatological color that is reminiscent of the way Jesus uses the term in the apocalyptic farewell speech of Mark 13. We have mentioned along the way many other themes taken up from chapter 13 in Mark 14's Gethsemane episode: especially the idea of "staying awake" or "keeping alert," which was so prominent in 13:32-37. There is more to see here eschatologically. Joel Marcus argues that such thematics continue into the arrest scene featuring the "fleeing" of the disciples (Mark 13:14).[7] One could make similar arguments about 13:9-13, which warns about being bound, brought before councils and authorities, and having brother turn on brother—all of which become actual features of the unfolding passion narrative itself. Eugene Boring also notes that the language around Jesus' cup in Gethsemane link

5. The terms I am using in this description come from a definition of the literary genre apocalypse that was generated in the SBL Apocalypse Group devoted to a phenomenological study of the literature: "'Apocalypse' is a genre of revelatory literature with a narrative framework, in which a revelation is mediated by an otherworldly being to a human recipient, disclosing a transcendent reality which is both temporal, insofar as it envisages eschatological salvation, and spatial insofar as it involves another, supernatural world," in "Apocalypse Group"; John J. Collins, ed. *Semeia* 14 (1979): 9.

6. Christopher Rowland, *The Open Heaven: A Study of the Apocalyptic in Judaism and Early Christianity* (New York: Crossroad, 1982) and Michael Stone, "Lists of Revealed Things in the Apocalyptic Literature," in *Magnalia Dei, The Mighty Acts of God: Essays on the Bible and Archaeology in Memory of G. Ernest Wright*, ed. Frank M. Cross, William Lemke, and Patrick Miller (Garden City, NY: Doubleday, 1976), 443.

7. Marcus, *Mark 8-16*, 994.

this moment to the cup of the final judgment of God (as in Rev. 14:10 and 18:3).[8] I have also argued that elements of apocalyptic theophany are played out both in Jesus' confession before the High Priest and in the narrative of his death. The former is a reference to Dan. 7:13, but is given in the form of an apocalyptic promise akin to Mark 13:26: "and you shall see the Son of Man . . ." Even more interesting is the narrating of apocalyptic events around Jesus' death with the darkening of the sun (13:24 and 15:33) and effacing of the divine/human boundary in the ripping of the temple veil (15:38), which uses the same Greek verb as the one that marked the ripping of the heavens at Jesus' apocalyptic baptism (1:10). Mark wishes us to understand Jesus' identity and ministry as breaking things open and that means understanding even his death as an eschatological event.

This may seem odd to those of us who usually view the passion narrative in terms of guilt, forgiveness, substitutionary atonement, or forensics. Mark's view is different and marked by an eschatology that sometimes turns apocalyptic in that it sees a deep split between the ages and even now an irruption of the divine into a demonic world. But its importance will be borne out already in the events that follow. Mark's brief resurrection narrative in 16:1-8 is itself an apocalyptic notion. We would be wise to understand Mark's narrative eschatology in 14–15 in terms that will help us make sense of the astounding news to follow. Both may help us to crack open our too-often closed approaches to understanding God's purposes transactionally in atonement and instead to find ourselves drinking "new wine" even amidst the "old age." This is, after all, already emerging as the cross becomes the theophanic place where the sun strangely darkens even as God tears loose through the curtain toward humanity. Wrestling with Mark's apocalyptic take on Jesus' passion, may help transform our Palm/Passion observances from intrapersonal pieties to a more cosmic understanding of suffering and redemption.

GOD, SUFFERING, AND THE WAY OF THE CROSS

On this issue, Mark does not offer us a finished theology, nor even any fully coherent way of thinking about God and suffering in the passion narrative. When we read such a narrative, we are brought into what we described as the Markan paradox of human agency and divine will. The narrative tells a story and does not explain. We bump into theological limits with Mark's story.

---

8. Eugene Boring, *Mark: A Commentary*, New Testament Library (Louisville: Westminster John Knox, 2006), 397.

At the same time, there is some strong sense that suffering is necessary to the divine purpose. The rest of the Markan narrative prepares us for this, especially the three passion predictions in Mark 8, 9, and 10. Within the passion narrative itself, this sense of necessity is conveyed by Jesus' resolve to do God's will, the saturation of suffering in the language of Scripture (especially Zech. 13), the psalms of the righteous sufferer, and the suffering servant of Isaiah. Such a notion invites readers into a rich paradox of human and divine action. At the same time, it poses problems about how we relate God to suffering as a general category. In order to understand why Mark is willing to link God to suffering in this way, it would be even more helpful to have a clear understanding of what Mark's Gospel means by suffering itself. Is it only Jesus' suffering that is willed? Is the suffering of discipleship as "taking up one's cross" included in the same way? If so, is that suffering only limited to certain forms of engagement, or does it carry over to all forms of suffering in ordinary life?

The importance of a theology of the cross—again, not an atonement theory, but an understanding of divine revelation in places like suffering rather than "glory"—is its resistance to success thinking. This cannot be gainsaid in North American churches that too quickly succumb to such thinking and practices in our culture. Palm/Passion Sunday helps to stand as a bulwark to such thinking by placing the dangerous memory of Jesus' suffering and death before us. At the same time, the cross and suffering as symbols have also generated a pious complex that has also served to keep those who are suffering compliant. It can also render Christian faith into a kind of passive vision that turns discipleship and the call of the cross into mere self abnegation and complicity with abusers and the powerful. Somehow we must hold to the cross as that proper bulwark against success thinking even while dealing discerningly with the ways in which even this good thing can be abused and distorted. Worship leaders and preachers have unfinished theological work to do!

Perhaps the problem is when we view the cross purely as an object of faith rather than as belonging to the praxis of faith. As untethered object, the cross can be mystified and disconnected from the rest of life in such a way that it allows us to see our own lives *less* deeply and less real. By contrast, Martin Luther, one of the great advocates of a theology of the cross, argues that such a theology "calls a thing what it really is."[9] Perhaps for the cross to function for the doing of Christian theology on Palm/Passion Sunday it needs to operate more as a critical principle than as a detached object of devotion. As critical

9. Martin Luther, "Heidelberg Disputation," in *Martin Luther's Basic Theological Writings*, ed. T. Lull (Minneapolis: : Fortress Press, 1989), 31.

principle it does not so much prescribe suffering but helps to *describe* suffering, that is, to make sense of suffering in connection with the vocation of disciples. This way, the idea of suffering as a reified object or general principle is seen for what it is—as missing the point. "Take up your cross and follow me" is not a general call to embrace any suffering that happens to be out there, least of all that which someone lays upon us for their own benefit. Instead, because it is a calling on the way, it assumes that certain kinds of suffering or cross bearing are connected with the vocation of following. But if Jesus calls disciples to leave family behind, surely the cross is not a call to turn around and re-submit to a serial abuser. Yet perhaps there are places where to follow as disciples means coming to terms with the suffering that the following itself engenders. Like those committed to a "praxis of faith" in moments of profound social change like Civil Rights, it means reckoning with the suffering that comes with living out the new age even now in this place of darkness and separation.

Ched Myers argues that the cross in Mark functions as a kind of invitation to nonviolent resistance. He acknowledges that the same Jesus who engages in a radical reign-of-God ministry in Galilee in the first half of Mark is the same one who marches up to Jerusalem to die on the cross as an act of obedience to the divine will in the passion predictions and narrative in the second half of the Gospel. The cross as an act of nonviolent resistance helps him to hold the two parts of the story together. One does not have to share Meyers's politics to appreciate the notion. Martin Luther also assumes that the gospel generates opposition that itself leads to suffering. It is why Luther thinks that what makes a good theologian able to discern the gospel aright is wrestling with the Scriptures, prayer, and suffering (*meditatio, oratio, tentatio*).[10] Suffering comes *with* gospel engagement. Another reason for rethinking the reified cross comes from NT scholar Brian Blount. Blount is convinced that the cross in Mark must be read in terms of the resurrection.[11] Thus, he argues, whatever we say about the cross must also come to terms with the radical newness God is up to in this apocalyptic Gospel.

In either event, turning the cross into a critical principle for the praxis of faith makes it harder to associate the cross and suffering with either success on the one hand or a prescribed masochism for victims either. Jesus envisions, even in the midst of the description of so much suffering and failure in Mark 14–15, that he will still go ahead of his disciples to Galilee after the cross. Despite the failure and in the midst of suffering in relation to the gospel,

10. LW 34, 285; WA 50, 658–659.

11. Brian Blount, "Invasion of the Dead: : Preaching Mark," (Lyman Beecher Lecture, Yale Divinity School, New Haven, CT, October 12, 2011) at http://www.youtube.com/watch?v=5vq_GY31fJ4.

there is a resurrection promise. The cross does not exist to reify itself as a universal prescription for generic suffering. The cross reveals God in the midst of suffering and points to a promise that we hold on to even as we cry out like Jesus from the cross or hold it back up to God in the dark night of the soul. We cannot know everything there is to know in the midst of suffering and pain, but we can trust in the midst of suffering in our vocation that the promise is good and even now pries open our closed worlds. Like Jesus' cross in 15:33-39, it does not so much prescribe but describe the painful movement from the old age to the new.

If so, it may help us to celebrate as the woman did who proclaimed the gospel by anointing Jesus for burial in 14:3-9. There is indeed a mystery of the divine will in Jesus' suffering and death. But it cannot be interpreted apart from his unique mission of ransom (10:45) to which it mysteriously points amidst a feast of Passover liberation. Yet because it is a mystery, and not some reified object, it invites us in our own praxis of faith to reengage as theologians of the gospel.

Joel Marcus notes that Mark's Gospel does not just preach, but poses profound problems for faith that subsequent interpreters had to take up again and again. Marcus highlights some of these "embarrassing" elements for early Christian faith: "Jesus' despair in Gethsemane, his denial by Peter, his abandonment by other members of the Twelve, and his cry of dereliction from the cross. These embarrassing features are unlikely to have been invented by early Christian storytellers."[12] These same embarrassments help us to reengage the rough edges of our unfinished tradition as theologians. Perhaps around this issue of suffering we can in our time and place discern enough of the gospel promise in the midst of suffering to pick up the shards of truth and solder them together in light of our vocational cross, falling prey neither to the idolatries of success nor any generic mystifications of the suffering of the oppressed. If so, they will deepen our readings of the Markan passion narrative on Palm/Passion Sunday and deepen our participation in this Gospel of the gospel.

---

12. Marcus, *Mark 8-16*, 927.

Epilogue: Mark 16

With this final section, Mark's Gospel of the gospel comes to its apocalyptic conclusion. Consistent with the rest of Mark's text, it is not a full-blown apocalypse, but a Gospel in an apocalyptic mode. What Mark does differently, however, is to make sure there is at least some element of mystery here. Something important is indeed disclosed after Jesus' death, even as the narrative continues to point forward promisingly in ambiguity. While most of the Gospels we know end with resurrection appearances, Mark ends with quite a bit less: an empty tomb, a commission to tell and call the disciples and Peter to meet Jesus in Galilee, and a surprising reticence on the part of the women at the tomb to carry it out. In fact, 16:8 narrates their astounding response in my oddly-worded, wooden translation: "they said nothing to no one, for they were afraid."

That, however, is just one of the problems. To come to terms with Mark's curious ending we need first, however, to get past its *endings*. It seems Mark 16 has some extra mysteries of its own!

EPILOGUE: THE ENDS OF THE GOSPEL (16:1-20)

INTRODUCTION

The mysteries become clear to preachers who venture to the end of Mark's Gospel in their Bibles. One would think that the first Gospel would end as unambiguously as it began. We called Mark 1:1-15 a "prologue" as a way of describing its function relative to the rest of the narrative. The first verse reads like a title: The beginning of the Gospel of Jesus Christ [Son of God]. How wonderfully clear! Indeed, we saw that the prologue set the agenda for reading both by describing the gospel good news in terms of Jesus' identity (Mark 1:1, which was carried forward and elaborated in 1:11, 8:29, 9:2, and ultimately 14:62 with Jesus' confession before the High Priest) and in terms of the announcement of the kingdom that Jesus himself equates with the gospel of God (1:14-15) and becomes concrete in his subsequent ministry of teaching, healing, and exorcism. For all that clarity, however Mark's gospel ends in surprising ambiguity. The preacher who looks at the final chapter of the Gospel discovers not one ending, but three. There is the ending that most scholars agree on: the one that concludes with 16:8. There is the ending that appears, largely in brackets, in most Bible versions: 16:9-20, usually called the longer ending. Finally, there is the intermediate ending, which doesn't even merit a verse number. By the time you have sorted through them, you might think you had ended up in one of those mystery dinners where you participate in solving a detective story by choosing conclusions from the menu.

It is better, however, to consider the endings together. That way we can understand what is at stake theologically in the decisions that have been made. Along the way we will discover some greater theological clarity about what Mark is up to and what we are up to when we engage in our own act of theological interpretation in preaching the end of Mark for some Easter celebration.

I write "some Easter celebration" with great intentionality. The most likely ending of Mark, 16:1-8, appears as an alternate for Easter B and a common text for the Easter Vigil in years A, B, and C. While the alternative endings do not appear in the RCL, Mark 16:15-20 does appear in the Roman Catholic lectionary as an alternate for Ascension Day. The upshot for most of us is that we will not need to choose on Sunday morning which ending to observe, even while we can find a unique and powerful Easter witness even with Mark's most likely and yet troubling ending: 16:1-8.

PASSAGES OMITTED FROM THE LECTIONARY

Our goal here is not so much to exegete these texts in full. Not only do they not appear in the RCL, they are not even judged to be reliably part of the Markan text itself. At the same time, some appreciation for their theologies can help us sort through the choice that Mark's theologically-driven narrative *did* make and help us understand it in the context of the early church. This, in turn, will make us better homiletical theologians as we proclaim the Easter gospel with Mark and his strange, apocalyptic Gospel.

The Longer Ending (16:9-20):
Omitted from The Lectionary

This particular ending was for many years the most common ending of Mark. It became the normative one for Mark in a number of manuscript traditions. It featured themes from the rest of Mark's Gospel that gave it some resonance with that text and thus for some a plausible "ending" to the story: the mention of Mary Magdelene and the remaining disciples of the Twelve (vv. 9, 14), the problem of hardness of heart (v. 14), preaching the gospel (v. 15), healing the sick (v. 18), and the right hand of God (v. 19b). Such themes, however, do not suffice to make an authentic ending to a unified Markan text. Clearly, the vocabulary of the pericope has changed as evidenced by the very least of the importance of confirmation of "accompanying signs" (vv. 17, 20) such as handling serpents and drinking poison! The development of a section as well that focused on Jesus' exaltation to God's right hand (v. 19) did help to bridge a problem that Mark never really thought to solve in his narrative, but might also indicate that it, too, comes from a later period than Mark's own time.

In short, the longer ending reads like an attempt to fix Mark's ending in 16:8. It uses some important Markan themes but seems to supplement them in ways that seem quite alien to the rest of the Gospel. The fact that this ending does not appear in many of our oldest manuscripts lends credence to the notion that it is not likely an authentic ending. In fact, since Mark 16:8 is so difficult and so theologically problematic, it better explains why someone might try to offer an alternative to it—whether the longer ending, the shorter ending, or even Luke or Matthew! It may be that Mark's perceived problematic closure in 16:8 and his lack of resurrection appearances encouraged some to try to lay hands on Mark's Gospel itself.

The Intermediate Ending:
Omitted from The Lectionary

The intermediate ending is even more modest. It appears by itself in only one old manuscript. It is called the intermediate ending because it usually appears as a brief bridge between Mark 16:8 and the longer ending in 16:9-20. Although it is brief, the vocabulary is very much non-Markan. Again, it is easier to assume that it exists to smooth over the difficulties of Mark's admittedly awkward ending at 16:8.

Nonetheless, preachers have something to gain from these efforts. One could argue that every act of preaching is an attempt to carry forward the vision of the gospel. Indeed, every act of biblical interpretation in preaching is itself a *paradosis*, an act of handing over or traditioning—which, if you know Greek, is also the same word for betrayal! This means that there are no perfect interpretations that are faithful to some perfect original. What we have is Mark's own Gospel of a gospel with all its oddities and imperfections, which is now handed over to us. And so we turn now to this chapter's sole RCL lection to see how we might faithfully "hand over" Mark's ending one more time!

LECTIONS

This lection appears either on Easter Sunday B as an alternate or for any service of the Easter Vigil ABC. It is the capstone of the Markan narrative and carries forward in a uniquely apocalyptic way Mark's sense of the gospel that began with 1:1. Those preachers who used the Markan passion narrative on Passion/Palm Sunday will be aided by that. As we demonstrated above, the Markan passion narrative highlights the very eschatological orientation to Jesus' death that aids in interpreting this concluding resurrection pericope in the Gospel for Easter. Without this groundwork from the previous Sunday, the lectionary preacher is at a bit of a disadvantage. While there are many Markan texts from the first half of the Gospel during Epiphany, the cumulative effect of Mark's semi-continuous narrative is broken up after Lent 2, when readings from John become the Gospel lections for a few weeks. While the lack of recency of Markan readings is one part of the problem, the theme of the disciples' misunderstanding is developed in particular in sections of Mark's Gospel that are treated only in the season after Pentecost, if at all. The upshot is that without the passion narrative's recapitulation of the disciples' misunderstanding and, ultimately, abandonment of Jesus, that important theme for the resurrection story will not be as easily grasped. One other important element that the Markan passion narrative provides as context has to do with the women and Jesus' anointing for burial—an important driver of the early part of the resurrection story. The Markan passion narrative goes out of its way to mention that Mary Magdelene, Mary the mother of James (the lesser and Joses), and Salome witnessed one or both of Jesus' death and burial in 15:40, 47. They are a crucial link to the action that ensues in 16:1, especially the empty tomb. At the same time, an important element of irony also comes from the passion narrative. In 14:3-9, an unnamed woman pre-anoints Jesus for burial! The reader knows from that text that the work that the women come to do at 16:1 has been already accomplished and that that work was not just funereally gloomy, but a testimony to the gospel itself (14:9), an important theme here reprised toward the end of Mark's narrative. Without this long reading on Palm/Passion Sunday, preachers will want to find some way to place this story in its wider literary context and in connection with Mark's narrative-theological vision.

At the same time, even in light of Mark's overall narrative, the surprising ending of 16:8 has troubled readers for centuries. Even if we are aware of the careful groundwork that Mark has been laying for readers, the question remains: what to do with a Gospel that shows no resurrection appearances, as so much of the rest of the tradition takes pains to show in Matthew, Luke, John, and even in Paul's first letter to the Corinthians (15:5-9)? This may bring us as readers to an unusual conclusion. Mark's Gospel is not satisfied to leave us an ending with closure, but perhaps wishes to offer us one full of *dis-closure*.

LECTION: A SENSE OF AN ENDING
16:1-8; EASTER (ALT.), EASTER VIGIL ABC

The lection begins with good Jewish piety. The women wait until the Sabbath is over to buy spices. Already in 16:1 they announce their intention: to go and anoint the Jesus whose death and burial they had just witnessed. Because they are the last remaining links to those who accompanied Jesus from Galilee to Jerusalem (15:41), they offer the last hope for the narrative's positive conclusion. The disciples fled after the arrest (14:50). Peter, the "rock" of the Twelve, was left at the High Priest's place in tears, having fulfilled Jesus' prediction of a threefold denial (14:72). The only connection left between Jesus and his followers after the awful events of Jerusalem is the presence of these three women who have prepared themselves to anoint him for a proper burial.

The mention of Sunday may play to those Christians for whom the first day of the week is the center of worship. If so, it helps to heighten the irony of the moment for the reader. The women are clearly going to the *tomb* on this Sunday at sunrise. They expect to find a corpse to anoint with aromatic spices according to burial custom. Yet the Jesus whom they go to offer this last bit of solidarity at the tomb is the same one who predicted his suffering and death over three passion predictions (8:31, 9:31, and 10:33), on the journey to Jerusalem, as well as his subsequent resurrection. While their show of solidarity by sticking with Jesus through his death and burial when the disciples had long fled is exemplary, they do seem to have one thing in common with the Twelve: for whatever reason, despite accompanying him all this time (15:41), they do not take into account Jesus' own prediction about his ending on this day. Indeed, in this way, Mark's Gospel also varies from the other accounts. Not only does Mark have no resurrection appearances, but only in Mark do the women leave the scene telling nothing to anyone. They go that Sunday morning expecting to anoint a body. As readers, therefore, we are in a unique position here. We are party to this important information. We witnessed in the passion narrative how many of Jesus' several predictions and promises came to pass: scattering disciples, Peter's threefold denial, rejection by religious leaders, suffering, and death. The mention of Sunday morning in juxtaposition with the women's purpose opens up just a bit of ironic distance with readers as this resurrection narrative begins in 16:1-2.

Despite all of the women's careful funeral planning, however, one thing seems to have escaped their notice until somewhat late. Having witnessed Jesus' burial in the previous chapter, they knew that his tomb would be covered by a substantial stone. The text describes them as saying to one another, "Who will roll away the stone for us . . . ?" From a literary perspective, Mark may just be deepening the irony here by portraying the event as he does. As readers with knowledge of Jesus' predictions, we would have reason to believe already that the women will be surprised by the scene at the tomb. What this does, however, is more deeply ally the narrator and the reader, for whom the language may also have a deeper theological meaning: Who will roll away the stone? Grammatically this is no "divine passive" here, but perhaps the irony points to God, the God to whom Jesus himself pointed as doing the impossible, the ultimate "divine active" of raising the dead. To that end, v. 4 seems to confirm readers' expectations, but with a beautiful economy of language and expression befitting such mysterious apocalyptic events as a resurrection would represent.

Why apocalyptic? We usually think of resurrection in terms of Easter accoutrements: lilies, rousing hymns, butterflies. It all seems, well, so natural. What's so apocalyptic about resurrection? The notion of a resurrection in the tradition, however, comes from an apocalyptic stream. Most language about the dead and the dying in the Hebrew Bible spoke of Sheol as a shadowy realm of the dead. Much of the biblical tradition does not speak of resurrection at all, but muses quite comfortably about death and a kind of half-spent realm of shadows. This changes in part when this more conventional worldview meets up with apocalyptic expectation. Apocalyptic texts often muse about the righteousness of God. If the righteous, however, cannot find justice in this life, and if injustice is becoming so incredibly spectacular in our historical moment, well then God certainly must be intending to raise the dead righteous so they can receive later what they got not at all in this earthly life. Such thinking about death and resurrection begins, in the Bible at least, with Daniel, quite late in the tradition. The injustice of Hellenistic kings like Antiochus IV Epiphanes causes a huge theological problem for those minds intent on reconciling God's good purposes with the awful fate of being a faithful Jew at a time when the ruler demands acts of idolatry and pork consumption. Resurrection is a theological way of sharpening eschatologically the distance between this world and the world that God in God's goodness intends. Between Daniel and Jesus stand numerous apocalyptic writers and figures who take up the challenge (much of the Enoch literature, for example). They generally do not agree in all the specifics. Do the righteous alone rise? Do the unrighteous rise also so they can get their just desserts too? Is resurrection a continuance of bodily life? Is rather bodily life transformed or yield to a disembodied soul? These are not just matters of idle speculation, but speak in deep ways of the connection between the divine promises and human, bodily life now. At any rate, it is this apocalyptic tradition that carries forward notions of resurrection that are key for interpreting Jesus and what happens to him on this Sunday morning after his death. To the reader bathed in such expectations, the rolling back of the stone signals not something natural and continuous, but radically discontinuous taking place. The tomb—death—is being pried open in a way that only God can do.

Therefore, when the women enter the tomb in v. 5, the report begins by using classic apocalyptic features. First, there is the "young man." On the surface, it looks fairly unobtrusive. Mark used the same noun to describe the young man who fled naked in 15:51-52. Here, however this second young man is described in a very particular way. First, he is dressed in a white robe, which sounds like an angelic description. Mark portrays him as "sitting on the right side," a position of authority. Finally, we get the alarmed reaction of the women at the end of v. 5. Together these features are fairly typical of angelophanies in apocalyptic literature, and angels have an important role to play in apocalypses. While Mark is not an apocalypse, Mark seems to be using the apocalyptic mode to make a point about this moment. This resurrection event is accompanied by an angel (recall how such eschatological events are described in 13:27). In apocalypses, angels often serve the function of interpreting, usually because the human recipients involved are at least a little disconcerted and alarmed about what they are seeing (e.g., Dan. 10:2-14; *4 Ezra* 10:27-59).

The young man described as an angel then proceeds by offering an interpretation in v. 6b-7 that is designed to allay their fears and help them understand this surprising event:

> Do not be alarmed; you are looking for Jesus of Nazareth, who was crucified. He has been raised; he is not here. Look, there is the place they laid him. But go, tell his disciples and Peter that he is going ahead of you to Galilee; there you will see him, just as he told you.

He begins by assuring them and speaking of what they already know: they are looking for Jesus, the same one who was crucified. With his next sentence, however, he uses the passive voice to describe Jesus' resurrection (indicating that God is the agent) and thus explain the odd scene that greeted them in the tomb. Because he is resurrected, he is not here. As evidence, the angel points to where he had been laid (of which the women themselves had been witnesses in chapter 15). The proof of Jesus' resurrection here is not a resurrection appearance, but Jesus' *absence.* In light of this, the angel commissions them to go and tell "his disciples and Peter." This is a beautiful commission in that in one fell swoop the message includes the very disciples who had failed Jesus by scattering and denying. The failure here is real, but so is the promise. So the angel goes on to reiterate the promise made in 14:28: that Jesus is going ahead of them to Galilee, where they will meet and see him. In one and a half verses, the angel gives a lot of interpretation and announces the promise in the midst of failure. All that remains is the women's response.

And this is where Mark gets most interesting indeed. Although in the other Gospels, the women fulfill their commission, the Markan narrative gives us no such satisfaction and closure. The women are described as sufficiently terrified and amazed to flee tomb and tell no one. The Gospel then ends with one of the more enigmatic conclusions of all: *ephobounto gar,* for they were afraid. Scholars like to point out that works of literature do not usually end with the little particle *gar*—it's almost akin to ending a sentence with a preposition in English. It's just not done.

So the Gospel that begins with an apocalyptic scene of gospel promise in its prologue does the same at its ending in the epilogue. But what do we make of this disappointing conclusion? Interpreters have tried a variety of approaches. Some argue that the reader should be expecting things to happen outside of the narrative that provide for the proper conclusion. Since we know the gospel got out (at least to us readers), we can trust that eventually the women told the disciples and the disciples carried it forward. Another point of view plays on the reader's role throughout the narrative. Since we readers know what this text is about (unlike the disciples who failed miserably), it is now up to us to carry it forward. Yet both of these works, to my mind, struggle to deal with the true apocalyptic mystery that stands at the heart of this odd Markan ending.

It is important to note that Mark's most famous interpreters, Matthew and Luke, who follow the shape of the Markan narrative through their redactions of this work, end up rehabilitating the disciples and providing resurrection appearances that solve the odd conclusion of 16:8. Perhaps it is best, then, to consider not just the failure of the women, which is narrated here, and the failure of the disciples, which is amply narrated throughout Mark's Gospel but especially in Mark 14, but the nature of the promise itself. Jesus understands the word, as we saw in chapter 4, as a mysterious apocalyptic seed that meets with all sorts of opposition and problems with the hot sun, rocky soil, and even demonic birds. Yet where that seed is planted in good soil, it produces all sorts of harvest on its own. The mystery of the gospel is, for Mark, the mystery of the promise that does its work even in the midst of human failure. And what is mysterious here is also the promise itself. (In my view, a promise is not a guarantee—some automatic thing that works without ambiguity. The promise elicits not sure knowledge, but faith.) To those who hold to it, it is not magic nor some manageable mechanism, but a strange mystery into which we are invited. For those of us who are convinced that life is ambiguous, it bears testimony to a possibility not of closure, but *disclosure*, a word that pries open the too closed realities of empires, death, oppression, and estrangement as well as our own failures and inadequacies and points us forward. As Donald Juel puts it, "God will be put off neither by our failures, or infidelity, nor by our most sophisticated interpretive schemes."[1] An apocalyptic resurrection is not about closure, but a disclosure of a closed reality. Mark asks us to see this as gospel, a gospel related to a hidden suffering Son of the human who is also Son of God/Messiah and his gospel-of-God message of a coming kingdom in which all things are dis-closed in God's good purposes. For this reason, the angel's promise sends readers forth *with* a promise: to meet Jesus in Galilee where it all began, to meet Jesus there where the seeds of promise were first planted. Such a vision requires some ambiguity as its end and invites us out of our closed realities to glimpse something new. People fail, to be sure. But God's promise, even in its ambiguity, "goes ahead."

CONCLUSION

It may seem strange to ask, but what is left after such a promise? Only the tasks of homiletical theology and discipleship. Mark's mysterious apocalyptic Gospel has surprised us and vexed us at every turn—not least of all here at the

---

1. Donald Juel, *A Master of Surprise: Mark Interpreted* (Minneapolis: Fortress Press, 1994), 121.

conclusion. Mark never really lets us off the hook and even at the end asks us to engage. Homiletical theology stands properly at the end of the process of biblical interpretation. Interpreters should rightly let the text speak, as much as possible, on its own terms. Yet the embedding of Mark's Gospel in the lectionary also provides it with a theological overlay. We have noted from time to time how that overlay sometimes offers opportunities and tensions to the contemporary interpreter. It is always better to know what those issues are so we can do our work aright. In the end, however, the homiletical task entails its own theological work. Just as the writers of Mark's alternative endings felt compelled to try to wrest a better ending out of Mark, just as Matthew and Luke sought to try to offer a concluding gospel in a more compelling work, so now we try to engage Mark's Gospel in our own time and place. To be sure, we do so modestly aware that we, too, are theologians of the promise. We are, after all, the recipients of all that Mark, Luke, Matthew and others have sought to narrate the Gospel of a gospel about Jesus and the kingdom he announced. We should receive that gift gladly and with awe. However, this does not free us from the sticky task of taking up Mark's unfinished theology today. The good news, we know, is a promise. And after all these years, the promise must be spoken yet again—not just among people of Jesus' or Mark's days, but among ours. The good news is that we do not have to do so alone. In fact, if we take Mark seriously, we, too, will remind ourselves of the promise that still pulls us forward when we stand up to preach on the first day of the week. "Do not be alarmed . . . he is going ahead of you . . . just as he told you."

Appendix: Further Preaching Resources on Mark's Gospel

Blackwell, John. *The Passion as Story: The Plot of Mark.* Fortress Resources for Preaching. Philadelphia: Fortress Press, 1986.

This book represents a structuralist interpretation for preaching the passion narrative from Mark 14:1–16:8. The structural part is represented in two ways. The individual pericopes are read with a structuralist eye for oppositions: inside/outside, taking/receiving, skulls/thrones, and so on. A more interesting set of structural relationships is found *between* the pericopes of the Markan passion narrative. In an interesting comparison of Jesus' anointing by the woman at the home of Simon the leper and the empty tomb scene, Blackwell finds a unique way of relating these portions of Mark's narrative. Its value is in doing a close reading of the passion narrative with preaching in view.

Blount, Brian and Gary Charles. *Preaching Mark in Two Voices.* Louisville: Westminster John Knox, 2002.

This book reads a little bit like a cross between a commentary and a preaching book. Blount seems to provide most of the introduction (similar to a commentary, although a bit more oriented toward preaching). He also adds commentary for fairly long stretches of material in Mark, from which the preachers select their preaching texts. The differences come through fairly well in the preaching between the two authors. Blount's exegesis clearly tries to take the apocalyptic feel of Mark seriously and this has impacts on his sermons that don't play out in nearly the same way in Charles's sermons. On the other hand, Charles has some great homiletical moments when he seeks to relate Mark to certain pastoral situations: the death of a schizophrenic teenager (text: the Gerasene demoniac) and stewardship (the widow's mite).

Craddock, Fred. *The Gospels.* Nashville: Abingdon, 1981.

Craddock's book is dedicated to interpreting all four of the Gospels, but in the first chapter (pp. 31–64) he focuses on Mark in particular. The introduction is brief but quite helpful. Craddock encapsulates nicely the issues one needs to consider in working with this the first among the Gospels. Along with that,

Craddock provides sample readings of exemplary texts in Mark from chapters 1, 2, 8, and 16.

Fleer, David and Dave Bland, eds. *Preaching Mark's Unsettling Messiah*. St. Louis: Chalice, 2006.

This book is an edited volume of sermons on Mark. It contains sermons by biblical scholars and homileticians like Fred Craddock, Morna Hooker, Richard Ward, and Robert Reid. The material from Craddock and Hooker offers especially helpful tools to preachers on Mark.

Jensen, Richard. *Preaching Mark's Gospel: A Narrative Approach*. Lima, OH: CSS, 1996.

Jensen's book is oriented to preaching as storytelling. He is quite interested in the rising narrative interpretive models in New Testament studies, especially David Rhoads and Mary Ann Tolbert. In a nod toward Tolbert's *Sowing the Word*, Jensen argues that a story in Mark is best interpreted in relation to the whole story of Mark, especially in light of Tolbert's two key parabolic texts: the parable of the Sower and the parable of the Tenants. In addition to this narrative orientation, Jensen joins storytelling to the "living center" of proclamation. We tell stories in such a way that preachers come to a point where they announce the good news in direct "I to you" language. In this way, chiefly through the sermons which make up the bulk of the book, Jensen hopes to exemplify his approach and invite readers to go and do likewise.

Ourisman, David. *From Gospel to Sermon: Preaching Synoptic Texts*. St. Louis: Chalice, 2000.

Ourisman's book is really an apology for considering the synoptic gospels as literary wholes. His second chapter, in which he concentrates on Mark, is good for understanding the Gospel in its final form and appreciating Mark as a unified, literary work or, as Ourisman calls it, a "story-of-the-whole." While there is more general information on Mark, half of the chapter unpacks his reading of Peter's confession in chapter 8 of Mark in view of a sermon.

Reid, Robert. *Preaching Mark*. St. Louis: Chalice, 1999.

Reid's training as a rhetorician serves him well in his careful analysis of Mark's Gospel. He considers, therefore, not only the Gospel's plot, but also its rhetoric—especially through the rhetorical figure of the chiasm. The book features an introduction to Mark, a survey of the various narrative complexes of Mark, and some sample sermons by other preachers on selected Markan texts. If you wish to understand Mark with rhetorical sensibilities, this preaching guide can be quite useful.

Thurston, Bonnie Bowman. *Preaching Mark*. Minneapolis: Fortress Press, 2002.

Thurston's book reads like a brief commentary, but with preachers and teachers in view. The orientation is literary, although she is interested somewhat in the history of the community that Mark is addressing. Because of the literary orientation, she works through fairly large blocks of material. Thurston also includes several preaching, lectionary, and other scriptural helps.

Wilhelm, Dawn Ottoni. *Preaching the Gospel of Mark: Proclaiming the Power of God*. Louisville: Westminster John Knox, 2008.

This book is essentially a preaching commentary on Mark's Gospel. Wilhelm writes with two key perspectives on the Gospel: Mark's kingdom-preaching Jesus is now "on the loose" (Juel) and we are called to join in on God's program. Wilhelm includes several examples and illustrations from a historic peace-church perspective along the way.

Printed in the USA
CPSIA information can be obtained
at www.ICGtesting.com
LVHW021607221123
764277LV00020B/160